KATHARINE AND E.B. WHITE

KATHARINE
AND
E. B. WHITE
An Affectionate Memoir

ISABEL RUSSELL

W. W. NORTON & COMPANY
NEW YORK · LONDON

The text of this book is composed in Avanta, with display type set in Florentine.
Composition and manufacturing by The Haddon Craftsmen, Inc.

Book design by Charlotte Staub.

First Edition

Library of Congress Cataloging-in-Publication Data
Russell, Isabel, 1917–
  Katharine and E.B. White: an affectionate memoir/Isabel Russell.
  p. cm.
  1. White, E. B. (Elwyn Brooks), 1899– —Biography. 2. White, Katharine Sergeant Angell. 3. Russell, Isabel, 1917– —Friends and associates. 4. Authors, American—20th century—Biography. 5. Journalists—United States—Biography. I. Title.
PS3545.H5187Z87 1987
818'.5209—dc 19
[B]   87-20452

ISBN 0-393-02511-X

W. W. Norton & Company, Inc., 500 Fifth Avenue, New York, N.Y. 10110
W. W. Norton & Company Ltd., 37 Great Russell Street, London WC1B 3NU

1 2 3 4 5 6 7 8 9 0

ACKNOWLEDGMENTS

In loving memory of George D. Russell

With special thanks to Ernest H. Nedeau
and with appreciation for the encouragement of
Frances, Fred, and Shirley;
Frank and Betty Nedeau,
Earle and Mary Lund,
and good friend Anna, at Room *4500*

Katharine and E.B. White

·ঙ ONE ৬··

Felicity's on parade again out there, K. She looks like the Raquel Welch of goosedom. And I think the young gander's getting incestuous ideas. What a beautiful spring day!"

"K, I just feel in my bones there isn't going to be one damn goose egg laid around here this spring. Everything seems to be barren—including my mind. For all the writing I'm getting done I might as well be a goose myself."

"A gander, Andy," tartly, from K.

Thus the two sides of EB's character during some of the years of his retirement in North Brooklin, Maine. His mood was up or his mood was down; rarely was he in an average, moderate mood. In all moods, however, low or high, he could find time to speculate on the changing seasons and the well-being of the furred and feathered creatures inhabiting his house and barn.

The number and kinds of these creatures varied greatly over the years; a partial census can be gleaned from EB's own writings but no log was kept, and the bovine and swine occupants of his barn came and went over the years. Their presence or absence was determined almost by whim. In general, cows were apt to be boarders; they belonged to neighbors, who were glad of the chance to turn them out in the lush sections of grass behind the big house and extending down to the shore. There was no pig in residence in the 1970s. I can vouch for this fact because I made discreet inquiries; if there had been one in residence, I would have been hanging around his quarters after work, notebook and pencil in hand, interviewing him. Poultry, chiefly laying hens, and geese occupied most of the barn space.

The pets of the household, the furred creatures (not truly furred at all but, rather, haired) were two terriers: Susy, a small, sweet-tempered West Highland breed, and Jones. Jones was a grim, stubborn, pessimistic Norwich. Both were loved lavishly but they were denied a dog's favorite exercise: chasing cats. There were no felines in house or barn because cat fur induced a severe allergic reaction in EB.

The White's gardener, Henry Allen, shared barn chores with EB. When it came to a choice between vocation and avocation, no secret was made of EB's preference. Grain and watering pans and clean shavings, the hatching of baby chicks and goslings, ways and means of defeating marauding mice— this was the stuff of which real life was made. Most lives, of course, contain obligations of some sort. Pencils, pens, type-writer, and reams of yellow paper were the "other stuff," the appurtenances of less happy hours for the famous writer.

Indoors the baking and brewing, the cleaning and launder-ing and nursing (for Katharine White) also were in competent hands. Edith Candage came from Blue Hill each day to cook. She prepared dinner to be served to the staff in the kitchen and to the Whites in the dining room at mid-day; she left an easy-to-serve supper in the big pantry where one of several young persons in the North Brooklin area could come in at night to serve it. Often Glyneta Andrews from Brooklin would be responsible for the evening meal, and she was called upon to preside in the kitchen for evenings when anything elaborate was needed. EB himself fixed a simple breakfast.

Shirley Cousins, housekeeper, arrived at seven in the morning in order to be available to assist Mrs. White during the interval between the departure of the night nurse and the arrival of her daytime compatriot at 9 A.M. Shirley was reponsible for keeping the house tidy; on Wednesdays Virginia Allen from the nearby town of Sedgwick took over the task, doing heavy cleaning upstairs and down. During orgies of spring-cleaning and on special occasions she was pressed into extra service.

Nurses and nurses aides completed the staff and comprised the largest segment of it, a roster too large for listing here.

In the years of my association with the Whites, eight deeply interesting but often perplexing years, the dominant personality in the household, the leader of the human parade through most of them, was Katharine White. No matter how much a fan admired E. B. White and hoped to gain an audience, no matter how variously he was sought out—asked for on the telephone, addressed in enticing letters, invited to social and cultural functions, rarely was it he who responded. K intervened. She answered the phone, acknowledged letters, talked personally to visiting VIPs and to autograph seekers. However urgent the plea of a letter writer for a personal acknowledgment, she nearly always wrote the reply, standing between her husband and all threat of confrontation by an eager public trying to lionize him. His opinions were his own but K contrived to make them partly hers before releasing them to a clamoring world. He acceded amicably to her fetish of shielding him from unwanted publicity "to free him to do creative writing" but in the four months I was associated with him after the death of his beloved wife, it became obvious that he was capable of managing his literary affairs without someone to run interference for him.

Although the protective shield K held up between him and his avid fans was not essential for him, it was a splendid thing for her, offering great zest for living in the face of innumerable physical handicaps. When her health began to deteriorate in the 1960s and worsened in the seventies, she was cut off from her beloved *New Yorker* editing. Answering EB's mail, conferring with him on present and planned writing and protecting him from the curiosity and demands of an admiring public constituted a reason for living—indeed, an entire way of life for her. Thoughtful as he was of her comfort and pleasure, EB may well have exaggerated his natural tendency to shyness in the hope of strengthening K's conviction of her own worth to herself and to him.

With *The New Yorker* Katharine Angell White had been the right person in the right place at the right time, entering into employment with the magazine in its infancy and growing along with it, even as she helped push it to fame. Eleven years after graduating from Bryn Mawr (in an era when college for women was not as common as it is today) she was acquainted with somebody whose voice was listened to in the *New Yorker* offices and she was hired, despite her youth and inexperience. Subsequent events vindicated the recommendation. She was exactly what *The New Yorker* needed, but just as surely she needed *The New Yorker*. Most of her adult life was centered around it and her persona would have been vastly different without it.

As a fan of E. B. White's for twenty years before I met him, I looked forward eagerly to getting to know him. Of course I wanted to serve them both (realizing at the outset it would be chiefly K) competently and professionally, but I also wanted to get to really know the famous author. It was a slow process; the knowledge was acquired in bits and pieces that required the entire eight years to assemble into the portrait I had supposed could be limned in one. It was literally bits and pieces: more could be learned from the short notes he jotted down as directions to K or from slices of his conversations with her, with the gardener, the plumber, the tree surgeon, or the nurse, than from the writer himself in direct conversation. The first year our encounters were not very direct and they were lamentably few; I was new and untested; he seemed wary. His manner exactly fitted a description given by a number of his local acquaintances: if the dialogue between him and another gave signs of turning into more than a brief greeting, it was as though he backed away, in his mind if not in his body. "Come in," he'd say cordially as you stood timidly on the threshold of his study, but his hand would be held up to ward you off. In the face of that unconscious withdrawal, you could not persist. He had to be accepted on his own terms no matter how long it took.

When I first met the Whites, it was not my intention to write a book about them. If only the idea had surfaced in 1970 instead of in 1977, I would have kept more exact records and treasured every scrap of paper that came my way. If, however, I had come to the book decision sooner and had been more alert in record-keeping, how would the secretarial chores have fared? No matter how fast I worked, K was faster with her demands. She had an insatiable appetite for the printed page and she yearned to see her own words neatly typed, eventually printed, ready to be archived here and there. She had a deep-seated longing to record before she died everything she remembered of the early *New Yorker;* of her own youth; of the youth of ancestors; and a host of other facts unrelated to any of these. There was barely time to jot down in my private shorthand much dialogue that otherwise would have been lost, but much that could have been saved fell by the wayside when I was too hurried and harried by K to find time for extraneous note-taking.

She evinced a deep concern over deaths of celebrities in the performing arts or in the literary world. *New Yorker* contributors, whether writers or those who had done art work for the magazine ("Never, never speak of them as cartoonists; their drawings were on a level far above the mere cartoon!") were supposed to live forever, even if their contributing days were long past. Providence, she felt, ought to have seen them through old age—because who knew when some great inspiration might catapult them back into the mainstream of full production?

When by chance in 1971 I began keeping a journal it was not because of the Whites but rather for the purpose of recording the exquisite sights and sounds of the new home on the coast into which my husband, George Russell, known always as "Russ"; our dear friend Ernest Nedeau; our cat Tuffi; and I had just moved. It was built close to the sea; the walls of windows offered orchestra seats for the endlessly varying, endlessly delightful scene down on the shore and across to nearby islands. I loved it so much that the loving was almost painful. The vivid blue of sea and sky, an autumn moon rising behind Mount Desert, the pure line of a gull's wing when it was leaning into a downdraft made my heart ache. Some premonition warned me when we moved in 1969 to Brooklin that it was almost too perfect to last. It seemed the only way I would have it forever was in memory and so (in case the reality was one day lost to us) I set down my impressions each day. Oddly, though, almost from the beginning of the journal, much of the seascape faded into the background and the Whites took over the foreground, page by inevitable page. When things at their house were unsettling, as happened more often than not, the journal was my therapy. It lessened the brooding over the morning's woes to go through the physical act of converting them to words on journal pages. Once in a while they might even summon laughter; at the very least a chuckle or two.

In the eight years when I worked for them, neighbors (sometimes, after many years of service, alluded to as friends) came in to "do" for the Whites, but those who "did" made it abundantly clear that such service in no way diminished their social status in the town nor did it cause them to feel inferior to their employers. They cooked, they cleaned, they drove the car, they did the laundry—but only the gardener, in the Whites' employ, retained his original title; even that got changed now and then: in K's quaint parlance he became "Henry, our good friend and factotum." Henry Allen was indeed a good friend to them. He passed his twenty-fifth anniversary of service with the Whites shortly after K's death in 1977; he had worn well, he had endured much. He remained faithful and loyal through good times and difficult times; during my term of employment he never once lost his temper in any place where his employers could observe the losing. I wish I could record that I had been able to do as well.

K, struggling hard against a strong recollection of the servant class that had been part of her proper Bostonian childhood, referred to her cook almost apologetically: "Edith, our good friend and neighbor who cooks for us," a phrase she used even to persons who had long known Edith. If K ever had chanced to delve into writings about George Sand and had come across the novelist's delicate euphemism "household personnel" (a surprising usage for the middle of the nineteenth century) she would have been glad, I think, to borrow the innocuous term to describe her own twentieth-century domestic assistants.

I was in the Whites' home for the first time in June 1970 as an applicant for the secretarial position they had listed in a local newspaper. *The Trumpet of the Swan* had been recently published and extra fan mail was anticipated. This was no conceit on the part of K and EB; it was an acceptance of a well-established fact. When the magic name appeared in print, masses of fan mail followed the event, and both Whites were meticulous about acknowledging every communication; meticulous, it sometimes seemed, beyond the bounds of judgment and courtesy. Who else wrote a thank-you for every birthday message received? For gifts, of course, but for *cards?* Even at times when K's health was poor and even though she already had thanked a donor by telephone, she followed up the polite spoken word with the polite written note.

The ad had listed a work schedule of three mornings a week until Labor Day; K therefore, was inundated with applicants from the area who wanted summer work. Their ages ranged from sixteen to seventy-three (thirty of them in all) and I won the coveted spot not so much by virtue of ability as by propinquity. I was the nearest geographically (six miles away); presumably I would be the easiest to summon if extra help was needed in a hurry on my days off; and my age was an important factor: I was well over sixteen (adjudged too young) and well under seventy-three (considered too old.)

The interview was so difficult I nearly backed out of it; I devoutly hoped K would say regretfully, "Good qualifications, my dear, but you simply won't do." As she carried on a monologue about the state of her health and the state of *The New Yorker* magazine, as well as the sad state in which a departing secretary had left her, I was reminded (then, and many times afterward) of Queen Victoria. Having read much about the one, I felt I already knew the other. The longer I was associated with K, the closer I came to understanding the queen. Each time I tried to offer a polite comment or ask a discreet question that morning, K waved me to silence. She learned, I think, nothing about me in that interview while I learned everything about her except what my secretarial duties would entail.

"I have several other persons to see before I decide," she concluded graciously when the clock struck twelve, and she heard her husband's voice in the kitchen. "I'll let you know next week what my decision is. *Andy!*" This last was so sudden, so unexpected, and uttered in such a shrill key that I was caught off balance and jumped up quickly, fearing she was in pain. It evolved that she simply wanted to summon Mr. White to meet me. It did not occur to me then that she had been awaiting his arrival so that he could offer an opinion, but I learned in later association with the two of them how the system worked.

When I shook his hand there came an immediate impression, never fully erased in later years, that E. B. White was a tall man. Statistics say he was a short-to-medium one. I am a tall person myself so his stature could not have been impressive but the illusion indicates how one can imagine greatness of size where there is greatness of intellect and personality. I made a brief complimentary remark about his writing, instinctively stifling the impulse to say something like "Oh, you wonderful, wonderful man! I've loved your books forever! This is the crowning point of my career!" I might just as well have said it. K attached a so-called opinion sheet to my application (her small home-office system was patterned after the immense *New Yorker* one) and tossed it into a folder where a secretary could easily come upon it later. It said "Much the best so far but too jammy about Andy." When I uncovered the notation, I repeated the phrase at home. That was an error of judgment; forever after when I spoke with enthusiasm about a new puppy or a new moonshot, Russ and Ernest said, "She's being jammy about it."

EB escorted me to the car that day, handed me in, in courtly fashion, and uncharacteristically stood there talking about his farm, about K's illness, about my reasons for moving to Brooklin. Confronted by the famous writer, my face only a few inches from his, I was tongue-tied and could only listen and nod. It seemed to me then, and the feeling deepened with the passage of the years, that he was a true gentleman, a gentle, gentle man indeed.

The summons came the following week: "We've decided you'll do," said K crisply on the phone, "and you might as well plan to keep on regularly after Labor Day. I have lots of projects." Indeed she had. Before one was finished the next was begun; when that was halfway worked out, a third surfaced, by which time she had forgotten the first. When reminded of it, she couldn't recall why it had been started and what her plans had been for it, so either it was abandoned in midstream or begun all over again from a different viewpoint.

Many of my working hours were spent in the Whites' big attic, searching for literary or sentimental items that had been packed away in 1939 or 1947 or 1956—"Or just a little while ago," K would say guilelessly, referring to anything sent up post-1960.

Care had to be exercised in the attic where the only place a searcher could stand straight up was along the center walkway. In this large storage room, which was reached by a narrow stairs ascending from the second-floor hallway, much of the storage place lay between the eaves and the peak of the roof. Bumped heads were common in that section—it would have made a fine habitat for the Seven Dwarfs.

The attic was uncomfortably cold in winter and uncomfortably warm in summer; there were no visible bats, though, and very little dust except inside the long-packed cartons. Every search was interesting and profitable—if not profitable to K or EB because I failed to turn up the requested item, at least profitable to me as I ferreted out details of their fascinating past in the process of seeking mementoes of it. Many items that I could not resist laying aside in a special stack labeled "Maybe for use later," turned up years afterward in the book of letters. When I read them there the look of the big attic was superimposed on the leaves of the volume: the sun slanting through small-paned windows, the mortar crumbling from the brick chimney onto the sheet-covered bound volumes of *The New Yorker;* suitcases and boxes of old clothing, meticulously labeled, arranged along one wall; cartons of half a century of literary gleanings, and other cartons of general memorabilia along another; scattered about, old barn and kitchen tools that would have filled an antique dealer's heart with yearning; Joel White's elaborate model trains arranged in precise formation on an enormous table; and the sides of the stairwell about to overflow with empty boxes of varying sizes, many of them bearing labels of New York's finest clothing shops.

When enough attic items had been uncovered, enough of EB's conversations with K and others sorted out in my head, and enough of the old letters read as I copied them for the new book, I finally began to get at as much of the essence of him as ever would be made available and visible to me, and in the crucial four months after K's death, before I left the town of Brooklin forever, I learned the most of all.

K, more than EB, was a note-keeper and saver of photos, mementoes, records, letters, and odd scraps of information, but it was not necessary to resort to them to uncover depths of her character or personality. She hid nothing; she had no secret life and probably few secret thoughts. If she thought it, she spoke or wrote it; only on rare occasions was a written utterance kept secret and then only from her husband because she feared he would forbid the writing of the thought she wanted to express. Hers was as much an outgoing, shared life as his was a withdrawn, reticent one. When I met her she was an invalided but still energetic seventy-six, lacking a few months. At the peak of her physical and mental powers she had been a person to reckon with, been possessed of magnificent gifts and a magnetic personality. Friends of her youth and middle age, career friends (especially writers she had edited at *The New Yorker*) wrote to her and spoke of her to others with admiration, affection, sympathy. Such adulation does not come easy; it never comes free. She earned their respect and devotion. How I longed to have known her in the productive *New Yorker* years, when words probably came easily to her; when she issued directions that were models of clarity; when she assaulted each new day and bent it to her own uses rather than waking to an atmosphere of chronic illness, of having to temper her work to the annoying limitations of her body. All that was left in my time of the vaunted *New Yorker* career was the authority she wielded; that would be part of her aura until the day she died, and when it showed signs of slackening, we on her staff were not relieved—we were worried.

K was the victim of severe dermatitis, a troublesome skin

disease that required daily doses of cortisone to keep it under control and that drug (or perhaps the cortisone in combination with many other prescriptions she was forced to take) inflicted a personality change that was unpleasant. The change varied with the dosage but at times the drug muddled her memory and grasp on reality. One caught glimpses now and then of the younger Katharine, the balanced, competent, cheerful, healthy, and beautiful woman she once had been, and these glimpses made the woman of the 1970s, who was only a frail copy of that earlier person, harder to accept. A reader of this account who knew her intimately in the early years, but only through correspondence in the later ones, may not recognize the Katharine White portrayed here.

It was the image of the young Katharine that stayed in the mind of EB till K's death and afterward. He lived day to day in the later years with the pathetic, stout, quick-tempered, bemused invalid but he never really saw her that way. His kind heart eternally called forth the small, slender, serious bride of his youth.

The two Whites were a study in contrasts during their later years and perhaps also during their earlier ones. The many analyses of EB and his works by dozens of critics and one biographer, and the passing references to the woman and her editing, in books about Ross, Thurber, and others, do not make the second point clear. Instinct says they were opposites from the start and remained so; experience of the two of them in their later years seems to vindicate the instinct. He was all for peace and quiet, for daily living honed to the very skeleton of itself. "Keep it simple!" he intoned a dozen times a day. She yearned for contact with excitement as much as he shunned it. She exaggerated problems out of all proportion to their significance with the sure approach of a dramatist; he dismissed them, orally and on paper, with a waggish nod of the head or pen. Hustle and bustle and general furor accompanied her wherever she happened to be in the house. If an ache or pain kept her confined to bed she summoned nurse, secretary, cook, and housekeeper to her side and issued orders and made copious notes about future projects with a verve and bounce that he loved but were the very antithesis of his yearning for simplicity.

EB's voice was low, his gestures slight, his temper moderate. His presence in any locale was unobtrusive, quiet; K's was volcanic. If, at any given moment, she was not the focus of attention in a room, she was so violently busy with her individual concerns that she could not be ignored for long. It was axiomatic that she would be the center of every gathering. A gathering could be loosely defined as K and EB, K and nurse, K and secretary, K and gardener or cook. K with any two of them at the same time was a catastrophe, as she talked to both at once on different topics.

No matter how steadily EB charted his course, no matter how much he strove for the level-headed, pragmatic approach to every facet of his existence—and enjoined others to do likewise—there was no response from K. Simplicity was just not in her. She peered at a simple problem and at once, in conjunction with her peering or because of it, the problem became complex. No matter how much the staff respected EB's penchant for the soft footfall and moderate voice as they went unobtrusively about their appointed tasks trying to maintain a serene environment for his writing, it was instantly shattered when K catapulted herself into the midst of things. At once all became tumult and clatter; there was much running up and down stairs; doors slammed, and there sounded frequently a loud crying out for someone who was in the attic or basement and unlikely to hear the summons. All tranquility vanished. Peaceful little North Brooklin managed to assume, in a few brief moments, what seemed like the hustle and bustle of a large metropolis.

·ᴥ TWO ᴥ··

For the first two years, I was discouraged by the feeling that I knew less than half of what I needed to know to be as useful to K as she supposed I was. I could neither disabuse her of the supposition nor learn enough of her routine to warrant it. Letter-writing was the only task I fully understood (after I learned to understand that K often dictated one thing while having intended to say something quite different) but letters were only half the story. There were book lists and magazine lists and old catalogue lists and lists of lists and sometimes K was so incoherent about them that they might as well have been written in Russian for anything I could find out. I survived the first six months by sheer stubborn will: it was unbearable to admit defeat after being such a short time in a responsible post that was regarded by friends and relations as the absolutely perfect secretarial slot. Of course these friends and relations were far removed from the scene of action and knew nothing of K, either personally or by reputation. In the town of Brooklin, I learned later, the betting was that the Whites' naïve, defenseless new secretary wouldn't last out the summer. Nobody said anything directly to me—I was "from away"; it was up to me to learn for myself. But I fooled them, and so did K. I discovered that she could be understanding as well as demanding; that although she would countenance no errors in her correspondence and was wonderfully capable of unfiling a meek secretary's employer-proof filing system, she was also a fount of knowledge on matters literary and a generous sharer of anecdotes about famous authors past and present. I nobly suffered her small crotchets and she generously suffered my larger ones. Who can determine now which of us was required to expend the most patience?

The schedule called for Monday, Wednesday, and Friday mornings but the schedule rarely was followed. There was at least one extra morning's assignment each week, with Saturdays especially favored. As surely as I had plans of my own for guests or homemaking over a weekend, K would announce crisply at noon on Friday, "I won't give you your paycheck today because I can use you Saturday." Repeatedly my family urged "Resign," saying that nothing was worth the trauma. Part of me agreed wholeheartedly but another part got me up in the morning and propelled me to North Brooklin armed with pencil, and notebook, and a giant hope that things would improve that day. Success or failure in general depended on the progress or remission of a formidable skin disease titled "corneal pustular dermatitis of Snedden and Wilkinson." Too bad I wasn't cursed with a touch of it myself so that I could have been more sympathetic.

It was EB himself who helped me to survive that first, woeful summer. He was unaware of it, as he pursued a typical routine of fighting an abnormal attack of hay fever, tending his chickens and geese, and answering some of the mountain of correspondence that was the prophesied aftermath of *Trumpet of the Swan* readership—a word he would not have tolerated. The suffix "ship" appended to almost any noun disturbed him as much as did the suffix "wise" appended to anything; a "pseudo-suffix" he termed it. If K's letters sometimes rambled and were sprinkled with clichés, his were gems of clarity, studded with compact sentences and a leavening of wit. He typed them in what he called a rough draft and left them for me to retype; his own first draft usually was so neatly done it needed no copying but it was not for me to point out the fact. If he had used a white sheet instead of yellow paper ("I can't think on white paper; it's an invention of the devil") he could have dispensed with my services. But if he had dispensed with them, there would have been no enduring the period of apprenticeship and the confusion of K's table-desk in the living room, a table piled higher and higher in disarray each morning. When her sometimes jumbled thinking brought me to the edge of despair, only EB's quiet affability and light seasoning of humor kept the ship afloat.

"I am getting to be full of honors but I liked it better the years when I was full of beans," I overheard him say to a friend in his office; then a telephone request came for film animation rights for *The Trumpet* and he replied glibly, "It's too soon to decide since this book is just out of the egg." In acknowledging a telegram of compliments on the popular swan, he inquired of K if it would be proper to say "I seldom have time to read and have not read *The Trumpet* but intend to when things quiet down."

The first few weeks of my inhabitation of the room opposite his study, he came close to ignoring me altogether. His manner was so distant as to indicate suspicion and it was several months before he could bring himself to smile or make a bantering remark. Meditating now and then on the author I had read and admired, I wished I had known him, as well as K, in the early years of his association with *The New Yorker*, the years before the publication of *The Lady is Cold, The Fox of Peapack, One*

Man's Meat, and *Charlotte's Web.* Was it a sudden romantic impulse that had prompted the lively sentiment inscribed in his handwriting on the flyleaf of a worn copy (purchased from an antiquarian bookshop) of *Little Women* he had given to K in 1931? The meaning was clear: it would require four or more other little women to equal his own. The ode "A Compass for Katharine" in *The Points of My Compass* offers incontrovertible evidence that Katharine White was the alpha and omega of E.B. White's world. Reading the inscriptions in other copies of his works that he had presented to K, reading the sentimental anniversary notes, the early letters, one finally learned an indisputable fact: once upon a time K had been young, beautiful, loving, and greatly beloved; and EB's love and admiration never ceased.

EB's birthday July 11, 1970, was celebrated with the usual gifts, jollity, and family dinner that always marked the occasion. Shortly thereafter, however, he had an automobile accident whose physical effects were minor but never again did he drive with the confidence and acumen he formerly had known. He had been taking medication for hay fever; it induced a period of drowsiness followed by a period of alertness and in one of the drowsy times he dozed off and collided with a telephone pole. He suffered only minor bruises except perhaps to his psyche—that was dealt a major blow. K contrived to discover a broken nose, an injured eardrum, and a severe nervous condition, "and I'm afraid the nervous strain of this accident is going to bring on a return of his old ulcer." None of us "household personnel" had the temerity to ask how old it was but we all agreed he was certainly a candidate for one.

In letters that went out afterward, K gradually wrote less of the accident, dwelling instead on John Updike's enthusiastic

review of *The Trumpet* in the *New York Times Book Review,*
emphasizing to me, "John is a good critic and he did an excellent review of each of the three juveniles." In early autumn she
had turned from quoting felicitous phrases of Updike's to dictating her recollections of authors of *New Yorker*-connected
books, as well as of *New Yorker*-connected writers of books.
The division was unclear to me for a year or more, but of course
it had to clear itself up because it was an important distinction
if one were to be knowledgeable about the magazine—and K
was adamant about such knowledge. A good secretary should
have it at her fingertips and no excuse was valid. If you had
been too young to read the magazine in the 1920s and 1930s,
it was your loss, not hers, she insinuated. Start studying.

In talking about titles of books and in writing accompanying
essays about authors for the list destined to go to Bryn Mawr
College Library, K sometimes uttered ambiguities that needed
a lot of unscrambling. The books themselves, assembled in a
particular order (although what the order was supposed to be
I never discovered in six years of assembling) in many rooms
of the house, bore colored gummed stars inside their covers, to
indicate that the books were to be given to K's alma mater after
her death. These books were entered on the list in the order
in which they had arrived in the house. Therefore no alphabetical index identified their position on a certain page. Each book
was entered by title, author, and publishing date and was the
subject of an appraisal of the author and oftentimes of a valuable personal reminiscence. What K wrote rarely satisfied K the
perfectionist, initially; four or more revisions might be required. The digressions often became tiresome for both of us,
but I admired her caring attitude and her persistence.

She was sometimes confused about what had been entered

and what had not; much had been done before I joined her staff and page after page turned out to be a duplication of work finished before my time; sometimes such pages had been typed twice before she could be convinced they had been typed at all. Wolcott Gibbs troubled her most; she began dictating notes on his work and his life, which she modified many, many times and was still attempting to revise in March 1977. It was not Gibbs' literary style or his personality or the great service he rendered to *The New Yorker* that caused the problem. What troubled K was how to describe the events surrounding the suicide of his second wife.

Periodically to Bryn Mawr went a cache of letters, with explanatory notes appended, from authors who had written to K the preceding year. Much of the collection formed itself automatically in the course of the voluminous mail she received. In the case of John Updike, however, she asked him if he could spare any of her letters to him, as well as copies of his to her from the days when she was his editor at *The New Yorker*. He acquiesced with a handsome haul from Harvard's Houghton Library (where his letters are housed), inquiring meanwhile if her husband was going to pursue him in similar fashion. John hoped not because he had only a few EBW gems and wanted to keep them tucked into some of his own books as good-luck charms. But at that time the *Letters* was not even a gleam in the eye of its author, so John was not asked to relinquish a single "rabbit's foot."

When K's health permitted her to work on several projects simultaneously, the confusion was marvelous; she reveled in it, flitting from topic to topic, smoothing out a sentence here, adding an anecdote there, researching lost items in attic, office, and study. The more mixed up the materials and I got, the more she was in her element bringing order out of chaos. "Can you use a dictaphone or a tape recorder?" she demanded one morning at the close of a dictating session.

"Surely, if it would help. Which do you have in mind, Mrs. White?"

"Neither. I just wanted to know. I hate talking to machines so I hoped you'd say no."

"No," I said obligingly, but not the shadow of a smile flitted across the august countenance. It had been a businesslike question; it demanded a reply in kind. No time for frivolity.

The table on which my typewriter lived was so small it held only the machine and my notebook and often small scraps of paper slid to the floor. Then disaster invariably set in, in the shape of Susy, who walked or sat on them when she dropped in to pass the time of day. At times when her master was occupied elsewhere and her mistress too distraught to do more than murmur "Good morning" in an aside, Susy sought out the company of anyone likely to pay a bit of attention. She ambled in and waited patiently for a few kind words and a roughing up of neck and ears. When the work load was heavy, she sympathized; she made it plain that she wanted to assist.

My office had two designations; the second one was "study." This derived from happier days when K was in better health and it was her own work space. In the 1970s she spoke of it in two ways: "You'll find it in the study," or "You'll find it in the office." For the more important workroom in the house there was always a personal label: "It may be in Andy's study," or "I think Mr. White is in his study."

If one entered the house by way of the front door (an unlikely circumstance), EB's study was on the left, with its two front windows giving a view of the lower section of the driveway out to the road and mailbox. In addition to his desk there were floor-to-ceiling bookshelves; on the field/pasture side a window with a cupboard below it and a love seat in front of the cupboard. A grand piano occupied the rest of the space, standing at the right of the door as one looked in from the hall. My office, on the right of the hall exactly opposite his, had two front windows offering a view of the driveway somewhat above EB's range, and a single window on the east wall.

In the front hall, beside the wide stairway that ascended to the second floor, traffic flowed through to the big living room. A person standing in the hall (no door, only a doorway) looked straight ahead into the living room and to the right. That person looked also into an equally large dining room on the left. Both rooms were open to each other at all times. Living-room windows overlooked the driveway on one side and the kitchen entrance on the other. Dining-room windows framed neat lawns, trees, and the distant fields. An enclosed north porch, with glass doors that were kept sealed in harsh weather, opened directly from the dining room on the kitchen end.

The kitchen, pantry, and bathroom quarters were in the ell of the house; here also was a small plant room (where K and EB spent much time in the winter) in a sunny location to the right of the entrance door from the driveway. Beyond the big wood-burning stove in the kitchen, a short set of stairs went down to a shed where trash was stacked for disposal. Once or twice I went into it in a vain search for a mislaid magazine; my impression is that it was a connecting room to a woodshed and barn beyond. To the left, as one came in the entrance door, a so-called "back stairway" gave access to one end of the second-floor hall. This stairway was used chiefly by the staff, and occasionally by EB in a hurry, but never by K because it was considered unsafe for her.

On the second floor a long corridor extended to the left and to the right of the main stairway, forming an exercise avenue for K in the early mornings. Her bedroom with its attached bath was furnished of necessity with appurtenances for an invalid; EB's room, at the end of the hall toward the road, was severely masculine and furnished in the practical way that suited him.

Across the hall from his room was a guest room with elaborate canopy bed, and somewhere a TV room, as well as another bathroom (for EB and guests) completed the second floor. My excursions upstairs were so often conducted at a running pace that the floor plan was unimportant; I opened a door here or there and deposited an armful of something; opened another door to conduct a search. However, I could have made my way blindfolded to K's bedroom.

In his later years EB hated to travel, perhaps because in earlier days, he had rid his system of youth's natural wanderlust by taking a Model-T journey across the country. By 1970 the aversion amounted almost to an obsession. K's invalidism had only one useful corollary: it served as an exemplary excuse when he wished to avoid a long trip. The coming and going by rail (he rarely resorted to planes), the packing, the unpacking in an alien environment, unsettled his physical being and undermined his mental outlook. He liked the regular regime, the uninterrupted normal pattern of his days on the seacoast farm. When his presence was required at the office of THE magazine or at his publishers, he procrastinated as long as possible—he found a dozen plausible reasons why he could not leave home in spring or summer. Failing any sufficient excuse for remaining Maine-bound in the fall, he contrived to get a slight seizure of brief but alarming symptoms. "It seems to be a buzzing in my head, K," or "My heartbeat has stepped up—something's the matter." Reservations were canceled and the trip put off another month. Then Thanksgiving and Christmas holidays loomed. Nobody, surely, would expect a man to embark from his cozy nest during festival preparations? Irrevocably the earth turned in its orbit and winter carpeted New England. Travel schedules were uncertain at that season; whatever it was would have to wait till March.

Somebody outwitted him, though, in October 1970 (it must have taken extraordinary persuasion on New York's part) and he sighed his way to Manhattan for a few days. While assembling his luggage, he appealed for help. He needed an old-fashioned bundle handle to expedite the carrying of a bulky package he had made up. A bundle handle consists of a rounded oblong of wood, about as long as an old-fashioned clothespin, that fastens with two curved metal ends to the heavy cord of a package. It makes for splendid ease of carrying and was a common object in the early decades of the twentieth century, in the innocent days before shopping bags became de rigueur. By fortunate chance I had one of the gadgets at home, on which the long shadow of Boston's original Faneuil Hall Market (and much bundle carrying) had been cast. It was one of a very few of its kind extant in this plastic era and I was proud to be able to fill his request.

Later in the same month, when the petty annoyances of city travel apparently had faded from EB's mind, Jones pushed himself forward, coughing and drooling and complaining. He seemed to be demanding that his versatile master should display some veterinary skills to ease his suffering. At EB's request I held a flashlight while he searched the terrier's throat looking for signs of any swelling or soreness that might be causing the dog's discomfort. Nothing was visible, and Jones cured himself before professional assistance had to be asked. "It may have been psychosomatic," EB told us solemnly. "Jones has traumas now and then. He picks them up from me, I think."

Jones rewarded the nursing assistance nobly: at noon, when I left with an armful of homework, EB was waiting with another armful—an enormous pumpkin he hoped we could use for a jack-o'-lantern. And so we did; when the weirdly grinning mouth and impish eyes had been illuminated by a candle on Hallowe'en Eve, we persuaded our cat Tuffi to pose beside it. EB, when shown the picture, was candid: "I suspected from the start there was a small child lingering in your character."

Nobody would claim that working for K was dull. For a person of slightly calmer temperament than mine, it could have been deemed dramatic. On an average morning, as she passed through the front hall on her way to the scene of action: "I need that letter from Lord & Taylor that came a week ago" and "Somewhere in the living room is that notice Nancy sent me" or "You'd better drop everything and find the permission request from Helen Lane; it must be somewhere on my table." If it took nearly an hour to unearth the wanted item, which might be lying anywhere between a windowsill and the bottom of a wastebasket, it was difficult to conduct a calm and methodical search. I was anxious to begin the important tasks of dictation and typing. She was full and running over with tidbits of literary information that could not be gleaned elsewhere and I was the fortunate vessel into which all that culture was being poured; a little more time with K and I might have earned the equivalent of an advanced degree in English literature.

"Our attic is full of bats and drollery," EB remarked one morning, meeting me on the stairs en route to that cache of biographical bounties to seek some oddments for K. I laughed and he laughed with me, instead of throwing away the line and walking off, as he often did. It was a fine morning for a secretary. Urged on by K—"Isabel had better have her own copy of *The Trumpet* else she won't know what I'm dictating about,"—he had graciously placed a first edition of the book on my desk. It was inscribed, "Isabel Russell, with my best wishes and a loud Ko ho! E. B. White." It was my first gift of a book by the book's author; even the big volume of the *Letters* with my name in the list of acknowledgments, which was to come later, hardly dims the excitement of the 1970 presentation. When we reached the revised edition of *The Elements of Style* in 1972 his attitude was more friendly: he wrote on the flyleaf, "Isabel, a manual for your 'little shelf'—and with thanks." The thanks were in recognition of much manuscript typing, a task so agreeable that the words of appreciation should have been offered instead by me to him.

In an excess of bravery I carried over my own copy of *The Second Tree from the Corner* one day in 1972. He kindly wrote "Isabel—a book of revelations. E. B. White, N. Brooklin." In 1975 I had the good fortune to find *The Fox of Peapack,* long out of print; the price was fifteen dollars. EB professed to be appalled at the cost. K perceptively remarked, "You must bring it over to be autographed," whereat I produced it from my briefcase and handed a pen to the trapped quarry. He wrote, "Isabel—I am touched by your extravagance in buying my books. For $15.00 you could have got the King James version of the Bible. E. B. White, N. Brooklin, May 1975." His dedication on a following page had been "To Katharine." I asked if she would be willing to add her autograph to that page and she graciously acceded, writing under her name, "Who is continually grateful to Isabel Russell." So far and so well had our relationship progressed by 1975, but even then the hardships of 1970 and 1971 lingered in memory and I wished I might have had the comfort of that inscription earlier. In 1976 a new copy of *One Man's Meat*, an anniversary gift from my thoughtful husband, got itself decorated with a fine quip: "Isabel—Whom I admire at a distance—about fifteen feet. E. B. White." That was again a reverse sentiment that should have gone from me to him; surely I had been admiring him much longer than he had been admiring me if, indeed, he did admire me at all. Inscribing books was a chore for him. It couldn't have been easy to have to be ready with the proper words for enthusiastic readers.

Christmas was EB's least favorite holiday of the year. "I'd like to be Jones. I'd crawl under a sofa and not show my face again till New Year's." The entire month of December set his nerve ends to quivering and his migraines to attacking. Each year toward the end of October he recognized the signs and portents that told him the season of torment was about to darken his life; each year he shuddered in the hallways, groaned over the mail; beseeched K to take it easy, not to start too early, and to give checks instead of personal gifts. Each year she nodded and smiled in her beguiling fashion and went her merry way. Taking her cue from stores, where Hallowe'en masks are closely followed, if not replaced, by Christmas decorations, and Thanksgiving gets lost in the shuffle, K wrote early to mail-order houses, requesting all gift items that were necessary to keep relatives, neighbors, friends, associates, and staff happy. Surely no more generous person ever scattered her largesse so indiscriminately across the land, but the scattering took a lot out of her and even more out of her long-suffering husband. The seat of K's operations was a small town in Maine but I was reminded, through a succession of Christmases, of a squire's lady as the mistress of the North Brooklin manor carried her gift-giving to incredible lengths. From nurses and nurses' aides and occasional fill-ins, through household staff, to the White offspring and the offspring of offspring, everyone was remembered lavishly. Gifts went also to shut-ins, to postal employees, to the butcher, the grocer, the milkman, the family doctor; in fact, to anyone who might have done the Whites a good turn during the years past. The number was staggering. EB was responsible for whatever was sent to his own sisters, brothers, nieces and nephews, and for a remembrance to Henry Allen, the gardener, but even there K had her own responsibility as she selected something for Henry's wife.

The problems concomitant with finding the right size, color, material and style of items of clothing for most of the persons on K's list were nearly insurmountable. Inevitably orders sent to emporiums in October got misplaced or lost; our own copies were filed with care when I could pry them loose from K's bench-table but reference to them often was in vain; the department store or specialty shop or catalogue house could not find the first order; there had to be repeated orders and phone calls before merchandise was sent out.

K had one bitter and often-voiced complaint against sales personnel that all of us echoed: they seemed, with the advent of the computer, to have lost their ability to express ideas in writing. Any request for an explanation or description elicited a postcard with checkmarks on it or a phone call to which no reference could be made later.

"Is there no one in your organization who can answer a simple request?" K would fume in a phone call to one of New York's department stores where she had maintained a charge account for nearly fifty years. "I want to find out how many different fabrics are available in this style; also will a medium be long enough to fit a tall girl or do I have to order large? I am a crippled invalid and have to do all my shopping by mail or phone."

Midway of 1970 Christmas preparations, we heard K call from the upstairs landing, "Andy, do you have that Henri Bendel slip? I might as well order the nightgown for your niece when I phone about my other order." As exclusive shops go, Henri Bendel was the most; when I wrote to them for K I used our best stationery and tried for perfect typing.

"Never mind," EB called back, "I've just ordered it."

"Are you very sure? Did you get the size right?"

EB appeared in his study doorway, waving a blank sheet of paper. "Of course. I wrote, 'Dear Bendel: kindly charge and mail to me at the above address one nightgown size 14, color moonglow. I want it for a moonstruck relative of mine. Merry Christmas!' "

K's sigh might have been heard all the way to the kitchen. She wavered a moment, undecided whether to urge "Please don't send it" or to conclude that he was teasing. It was fairly certain to be the latter case, she admitted to the nurse and to me. I didn't dare to laugh loud or long for fear the epithet "jammy" might surface once more. Sadly, for Bendel's clerks, a staid list of an order was typed.

One Christmas gift that came to the Whites in 1970 pleased me as much as it pleased them. I had all the pleasure of typing the note of thanks and then the joy of reading a treasure of a book when they kindly loaned it to me after the holidays. It was Vrest Orton's slim volume, an exquisite paean to a popular New England poet, *Vermont Afternoons with Robert Frost.* EB brought it in from the mail: "I've barely glanced at it, K, but it merits reading through once and reading through again.

One of us should write to Mr. Orton promptly; I'll leave it to you to decide."

There was no period of letdown and relief after the twenty-fifth. We were hard at it on the twenty-sixth with thank-you notes as well as responses to messages on late Christmas cards. Work days during December and January amounted to five mornings and sometimes a sixth but the truly irksome one was New Year's Day. There was no begging off if it fell in the middle of a week and never any recognition of the fact that at our domain the eve was marked by a celebration with friends far into the small hours of the day, so that I was too weary to function alertly at 9 A.M. of the morning after. But K overlooked a dragging pencil; there was a sense of accomplishment for her and that was what mattered.

She and EB seemed to feel troubled when I spoke (rarely) of spending a weekend with relatives in New Hampshire or Boston, even though I volunteered to make up the lost Monday or Friday morning with extra time. A friend assured me that their attitude was a compliment but I knew well that I was expendable when compared to nurse, cook, and gardener, especially when EB's facility with a typewriter was taken into account. He had the filing ability of a tree toad, of course, but why expect that practical skill when, like the toad, he trilled such a winning song?

I dared not voice opposition to any of his directives, hinting at an easier way, but on the topic of filing I ventured an opinion early and often until gradually it became a joke. Like modern forms of travel, he believed that "carbon copies and files and the whole stupid system were invented to complicate a man's life. I'll have no part of it." When a query arose I gave him the best reply I could—often an inadequate one because it was impossible to keep his varied concerns filed in my head—and the discourse usually ended with my heartfelt sigh and the words "If only—". A few times he wore a sheepish expression and prefaced a question himself with the refrain "If only . . .".

K, by contrast, was a veritable microfilm keeper of everything. So meticulous was her system that it was readily possible to discover when she was dictating something she hoped to keep hidden from EB. The clue came in one swift sentence: "No carbon copy of this; destroy the first draft if I ask for a second; can you mail this quietly when you go home?" The last query was supposed to be answered by a nod, never by a shake; one had better contrive to mail it privately if one valued one's position. Top-secret matters could not be relegated to the mailbag because its journey began on the hall table and EB frequently, sometimes almost absentmindedly, fingered the morning's output lying there and often asked K, "What did you write to so-and-so?"

The Whites exchanged notes back and forth between study and living room, as they had been accustomed to do when their respective offices at *The New Yorker* were far apart. His recurring theme, on letters he was turning over to her to answer, was "keep it brief." In vain did he exhort; part of K's charm was that there simply was no brevity in her and much of her correspondence proved she had forgotten his advice as soon as she began dictation. Fortunately for me she never asked for the return of his instructions, so I was able to rescue many of them from destruction.

When a request came from a public library in Cleveland for permission to name a children's reading room the E. B. White room, it was followed by an engraved invitation to the Whites to attend the ceremony. The hero was mildly amused; he gave the invitation to K to acknowledge (regrets) and told her "It's all right, I guess. Or they could just call the room Elmer and not bother inviting us."

A correspondent asked EB his views on love and death. "Think of the enormity of those two subjects!" he protested, baffled, to K. He replied to the letter himself, perhaps fearing that K, in an attempt to explain his precepts, might give away what he chose to keep inviolate. At the door of my office he announced cheerily, "There'll be an easy letter for you in a few minutes. I can do it in two sentences: 'I've always been in love and have liked it very much. Death is the ending of what started by the merest accident.'"

Until I grew accustomed to their preoccupation with physical symptoms and a formal medical terminology for real or fancied diseases, it seemed that the Whites' concern with illness placed them on the fringes of hypochondria. Not recognizing the tendency in themselves or each other, they deeply resented any public comment on it, particularly the one offered by Brendan Gill in an introduction to EB's "The Art of the Essay" that appeared in the fall 1969 issue of *The Paris Review*. That issue was preserved in the household archives and referred to with undisguised bitterness by both Whites. The bitterness was intensified years later when a similar paragraph surfaced in Gill's best-selling book *Here at The New Yorker*. All the while K was unconsciously defending Gill's hypothesis, writing scarcely a single letter that did not begin or end with a reference to the ill-health of herself or her husband. I was forced to learn from dreary experiences in my own family, years later, that both of them (but K especially) deserved more understanding than I and others gave when she fretted about ill-health.

She had a disconcerting habit of spelling out short familiar words when dictating, but leaving me hanging with unfamiliar medical terms or intricate foreign titles that rolled with more ease off her practiced tongue than they did off my unpracticed typewriter keys. Finally it occurred to me to make up my own medical dictionary: a big file card, its edges frayed from much use, listed such unlikely words as diuresis, bronchiectasis, seborrhea, quinidine, arrythmia tachycardia, osteoporosis, Chloromycetin, pylorus, erythromycin, labyrinthitis, macular degeneration of the retina, bronchoscopy, subcorneal pustular dermatitis (the last the actual name for her skin disease). K was concerned when EB had to resort to medical aid for some obscure symptom but the time and money were considered to be well invested if an uncommon diagnosis resulted. Even the matter of a cure took second place to the pleasure of speaking and writing about a new affliction that bore an interesting name. She did not agree with Molière that "Nearly all men die of their remedies, and not of their illnesses." Symptoms and remedies were stimulating not only to her mind; they came in the nature of a windfall to her conversation. "Globus hystericus" was an all-time favorite. Someone in the *New Yorker* office once had been plagued with that mysterious malaise and when EB was not in top form but couldn't be definite about the seat of the trouble, he and K nodded wisely and referred to the *"New Yorker* disease."

In warm weather when a deadline loomed and EB was feeling too much pursued, he fled to his studio down at the boathouse. Because it was unheated it was denied to him in cold weather and he had no choice but to sit down then in the midst of the confusion generated by cook, housekeeper, gardener, nurse, secretary, grocery delivery boy, the telephone, and last—but by no means quietest—K herself, while he tried to block it all out and attend to his writing. Composing tag lines for *New Yorker* "Newsbreaks" went on week after week for more than fifty years and every time we on the household staff read a witty flash line of his concocting, we all marveled that he could summon the right words and the provocative comment every time, no matter how often he was interrupted by the inconsequential. Occasionally he stepped across the hall to seek enlightenment on a word or phrase. It wasn't often that a "Newsbreak" was puzzling to him; even less often, when he was puzzled, could I supply an explanation, but it was flattering to be asked and a matter of private triumph if I could provide a solution. These triumphs ranged from a recitation of the lyrics in the song "I Never Promised You a Rose Garden" to the naming of Peter Rabbit's siblings.

Many candid conversations took place in EB's office/study as K sometimes paused there briefly in the morning when she came downstairs. One of them was occasioned by a question that had come to him in a letter from a child who apparently had a practical and inquiring mind. K informed EB that she had no idea what to write to a youngster who inquired how Stuart Little got into his pants—legs first or tail first?

"You'll have to deal with this one yourself, Andy. I don't even know how men get into their pants so how could I be expected to know about mice?"

"Obviously you never traveled in fashionable circles, K," chided EB. Then, as an afterthought, "Or perhaps well brought up young ladies from Boston looked the other way when men were attiring themselves?"

She refused to be drawn; there was a busy day ahead, much dictation on her schedule. EB capitulated. "All right, just say he puts his left leg in first, then his right leg, then his tail. At least I assume it's left leg before right leg because that's the way I do it."

K murmured her thanks and went down the hall to the living room, his voice following her: "Actually, in regard to Stuart's tail, he can drag it on the ground or tuck it in his pocket for all I care."

A vignette of Stuart's creator that comes often to mind has him sitting at noon in his favorite living-room chair, offering cracker snacks to Jones ("He's a sad neurotic dog, just like his master") and Susy. K might be completing a mass of dictation, and her husband inspired to insert, occasionally, a wickedly sarcastic comment. Her powers of concentration were so great that she rarely heard him, but it took more willpower than I had to shut out his rapier thrusts in favor of the mundane catalogue order.

There came a day when Abercrombie & Fitch in New York was asked to send a sturdy croquet set that would stand up to heavy wear. That time the whole system, from my point of view, broke down. K dictated a paragraph about United Parcel Service; it formed itself readily into little hieroglyphics in my notebook; then, looking at me, she ceased dictating, as sometimes happened, and spoke emphatically, "Now this is very important: you must convince them somehow that we need a set for four or six players with heavy heads and good balls. Surely they must have such a thing." Poor EB choked on his iced coffee; then, in keeping with his "Newsbreak" type of humor, which had the punchline leaning on the less obvious area of the original error, chortled: "Surely, K, some of the players might be light-headed, mightn't they?" Completely unaware of her double entendre, she seemed not to have heard him; she finished off with one brief item and I gathered up pencil and book, preparatory to departure. EB followed me quietly into the office. "I trust you to straighten out that sentence tomorrow, Isabel."

"I plan to insert the words 'croquet set' between the players and the balls," I assured him demurely.

The habit of blue penciling controversial prose out of *New Yorker* manuscripts had remained as natural to K as the snipping of a dead blossom from a flower stalk, and occasionally the habit got the better of her when she meant to write a friendly, complimentary note. A slender volume, *Winter Visitors*, an excerpt from Mary McCarthy's novel due for publication later in the year, arrived at the Whites' as a New Year's gift for 1971 and K went through it with enthusiasm. The novel, *Birds of America*, proved that the author had returned to her proper milieu. "All this reporting she's been doing," K complained to Andy, "just because of this horrid Viet Nam war and the nasty state of the world! She's been wasting her fine talent." In K's letter of response, though, there was a sudden shift of thought as she diverged from high praise of a central character into a discourse on bean pots. The humble bean pot might not be as important in the context of the novel as it had been in her grandmother's day, but K was positive such an item still was available in Castine, where Mary lived—and Castine under a fictitious name presumably was the setting of the novel. Despite Mary's denial in the story, her correspondent was certain bean pots must be available in stores in that small Maine town.

·ঌ THREE ৯··

One of EB's popular "Letters from the East" appeared in *The New Yorker* in March 1971; the section that
generated the most interest was the question of a smelt diet for
gulls. When EB took to his typewriter, flocks of readers were
inspired to take to theirs, offering queries or opinions. The
dietary habits of the seagull had belonged previously in the
domain of biologists or environmentalists but suddenly in
March and April the menu of that seabird became a matter of
great interest on many shorefronts, and our mailbag bulged
with commentary. Somebody in the boondocks asserted that
gulls do not care for turnips. EB accepted that statement as
serenely as though it had carried the authority of the En-
cylopedia Britannica. "Wise birds," he told us, "I won't eat
turnips either."

The situation was handmade for his facility at alliteration,
and the rough notes, attached to correspondence heaped on
my desk for the next few weeks, attested to it. He had observed
that smelts on their way to spawn will be eaten by gulls but
these fish will be passed by on the return trip. "A spent smelt,"
he noted, "is spurned;" also "gulls seek smelts at spillways" and
"gulls gag on spent smelts." Best of all but, I fear, never used,
"Greedy gulls gobble lively smelts but decry dead ones."

A July 1971 "Letter from the East" centered on the tale of an old gander usurping the first hatch of that year's goslings as his very own, while leaving the rightful parent—the young gander—to make do with "leftovers"—eggs that hatched late and often produced inferior goslings. The harried narrator was emerging from the barn as I approached the kitchen door during that interval, and EB stopped to show me the goslings, pointing to the old gander standing guard, and asking cheerily, "Wouldn't you think at his age he'd be fed to the teeth with sex and offspring?"

Someone once said of EB that he had a powerful capacity for reticence and so it seemed many a day when I passed him in the kitchen or a hallway or met him upstairs as I went to K's bedroom or to the attic. A perfunctory "good morning" indicated he knew I was there (or perhaps he knew only that somebody was there and felt it necessary to offer a greeting) but in general his attitude was withdrawn, almost forbidding. The one exception to this rule was the presence of any new life in the barnyard. A hatch of nature meant far more to him than any ideas he hatched in his study and he would talk about and show off goslings, ducklings, and chicks with alacrity to all who evinced interest. But if the season was wrong or Mother Nature betrayed him and he initiated no opening gambit, then it was time to retire quietly behind one's typewriter, wheelbarrow, or pots and pans and make no overtures.

The first brood of goslings I saw were sold later; subsequently, another goose, Liz, hatched eight chicks. The first four got bored waiting for their siblings to crack out; they found their way by themselves from barn cellar (delivery room) into the barnyard where presently they were discovered by Liz's sister Apathy, bereft of her own offspring. Apathy and the young gander took them over; when four more goslings appeared, shepherded by lawful mom Liz, the young gander and Apathy seized them too. EB, who usually left such petty problems to the parties chiefly concerned, was disturbed over the latest larceny, and intervened. He built a little cell under an apple tree and tossed Apathy and the gander into it; then he returned the kidnapped goslings to their rightful parents. Eventually this batch of goslings was sold too. Their disappearance seemed to make no difference to their elders, who paraded up and down the driveway in single file and squawked at onlookers or lolled around the apple tree foraging for fruit and relaxing in the sun.

K's sense of humor suffered when compared to her husband's. He could dredge up just the right phrase to create a laugh for any occasion. Although she could appreciate his whimsies most of the time, she could not match them. Many times, however, she unconsciously precipitated herself into the middle of one of his quiet jokes in a way that underlined the joke's impact. One morning as she carefully descended the stairs while her nurse waited at the bottom with the walker, EB called from his study, "K, Jones has fleas. Just found one in my bed."

"How cheery, is the mail in?" responded K, then looked puzzled when a shout of laughter greeted her query. Aware that her thoughts and statements were sometimes confused by her medication, everyone was careful to erase even the trace of a smile when lapses occurred during periods of excessive medication. However, at the expense of being roundly berated, I was not willing to expose her lapses in letters or reports during the early years when she was not amenable to correction. (K read every version of everything until her vision failed.) Just once when a subtle correction was needed, Fortune smiled on me.

EB emerged from the hallway at the exact moment that K handed over a letter of inquiry from a collector of antique books and said, "Tell him I simply cannot let the Geoffrey Taylor garden books go now, but perhaps I may sell them after I die."

"Do you plan to take pen and paper with you, K?"

"Of course not, Andy; you know I never do when I have my nap. Goodness! Is it nap-time already? We haven't had lunch yet, have we?"

"No, it's only 11:30. I meant, do you plan to take a pen to heaven with you some day?"

"Such nonsense! What brought heaven into this?"

"You said you would sell the books after you die—"

"Isabel, you know what to write; just attend to it and I'll try to straighten Mr. White out."

In the summer of 1971 EB was involved with a revision of *The Elements of Style*. Macmillan wanted an updated edition "and in a weak moment I succumbed," EB remarked to anybody who was privy to the project. K solicited sympathy for him wherever it could be found: "His health is not at all good and he is often in pain." He may have found the work arduous but all was not tedious; many a pithy remark emanated from the sessions he held with K concerning particular usages. I once heard him say, somewhat absent-mindedly, as he looked over a communication from the Macmillan office: "If that isn't ambiguous, I'm a barn swallow and I shall so inform them."

K: If *what* isn't ambiguous?

EB: This neat little tidbit that was on a stuffer the phone company enclosed with our bill. I brought it to your attention at the time. "You can call your mother in London and tell her all about George taking you out to dinner for just sixty cents."

K: Certainly it's ambiguous. Who says it isn't?

EB: Bumby of Mac's College & Professional Division.

K: Perhaps he was the one the phone company consulted when they composed the thing.

EB won out against Bumby; his admonition to "keep related words together" appeared in tandem with the phone company's ambiguous statement in the second edition of *The Elements*.

The movie script for *Charlotte's Web* was the main cause for concern that summer, although EB's share went no further than suggestions and corrections. But he was agitated by a premonition that his children's classic was going to be a cinematic failure; he forecast to K "a long fall and winter of nothing but worry and vexation." Snatches of discussions with her continually drifted into my office, indicating the rise and fall of his barometer. "How would he dare phase Fern out of it? Might as well leave Scarlett out of *Gone with the Wind*." Or, "He seems to be hunting moral implications all the time. Does he have to analyze it? The story's *there*. Let him put himself in a child's place for a moment and just accept it." A little later: "I wonder if I should enlighten them on the facts of life? Bulls don't touch noses lovingly with cows. Everybody knows what they touch. I wish they'd keep Ferdinand [the gentle, flower-sniffing bull in *The Story of Ferdinand*] out of it."

From the time EB gave permission for the movie to be produced until he saw a private screening of it in advance of the release date—and forever after that—he was never wholly easy in his mind about it, as it was too much a part of himself to be loaned to anyone else. No matter how carefully outsiders dealt with his story they could not bring to three-dimensional perfection the inimical world he had conjured up in two. At one point his nervous reaction apparently affected his hearing. "The doctor can say all he likes about labyrinthitis but it's pretty obvious I'm growing deaf." K murmured soothing platitudes but the tirade continued unabated. "It won't be long before I'll be deaf as a haddock and a man who's lost his hearing isn't much good to anybody, including himself. And some day I wish somebody would explain to me why a haddock is supposed to be deafer than any other fish. Did anybody ever prove a cod had good hearing?"

November 12, a windy day, stands out as medal-and-mousetrap day. Shortly after 9 A.M. EB received a sparkling phone call from New York: He had been awarded the National Medal for Literature with its accompanying remuneration of five thousand dollars. It was for no single book but for the corpus or body of his work considered in its entirety. He took the phone call upstairs where K and I were listing books. K remained calm as became the wife of a literary lion but I was intoxicated with excitement. "May I go down and announce it to everybody?" K and EB found this sort of enthusiasm laughable. They were only mildly excited by the news, but for me it was his first award. The Laura Ingalls Wilder Medal, the Gold Medal for Essays and Criticism given by the National Institute of Arts and Letters, and the Presidential Medal of Freedom hadn't been awarded during my tenure. It was unlikely EB would speak to Edith, Shirley, or Henry about his new honor so I begged permission to be the happy messenger, and he assented in the manner of one adult who says to another, "We had better let the child have the puppy or she'll give us no peace."

He paid far more attention to a mousetrap than to the

medal. He had conceived the idea of improving the traditional small wooden spring gadget by nailing it to a larger board and altering the spring's design so that when a mouse was caught, the trap could be turned over and the mouse released, theoretically in fine health. He was not made happy when K questioned the practicality of trapping a rodent and then releasing it unharmed to repeat its mischief in a new area. "It isn't as though it were Stuart Little or a descendant."

In 1970 the addressing system for Christmas cards had been anything but satisfactory. Although I typed all the envelopes and kept track of names of addressees, K and EB continually duplicated each other's efforts; in 1971, making noises like a secretary, I tried to avoid the confusion with a system of card indexes set up in three boxes: one for Maine, one for Florida, and one marked "General." A fourth box, empty except for its alphabetical index, was for the placement of an address card after its use. In theory all cards would be retrieved from box four and returned to their respective places in one of the other three. ".Foolproof" I said proudly to myself. Ridiculous. No system was foolproof when the Whites got their heads together over it. In the most delicate fashion they contrived to mix it up completely with a fine old duplication of card-sending, while at the same time expostulating about the virtues of the new arrangement.

That year K made a brave effort to reduce their card list, protesting that it was all a lot of foolish repetition anyway. EB heartily agreed with her. Oh, how he agreed! As she worked down a list of names (at least two hundred, probably more) produced from my stock, the two of them sifted out nearly seventy that could be omitted. A day or two later K asked for that group—bound with a wide rubber band and left within easy reach because I suspected what was coming—read them all over again to EB and offered a firm reason why each must be reinstated. He bowed to the inevitable and retreated, glowering, to his study.

·❧ FOUR ❧·

The new year of 1972 which fell on Saturday rang itself in to a tiresome beginning. K had phoned on Thursday to say "I think it would be better if you worked New Year's Day instead of Friday, when we'll be having luncheon guests." Caught without sufficient warning to think up an excuse, I fumed privately over having been ordered, rather than asked. Looking back, I have to conclude she was blissfully unaware of acting autocratically. Even if I had been alert enough to murmur apologetically, "Oh, we always go from friend to friend and share the punch bowl, sort of like Dickens's London on New Year's Day," or "We never fail to ride to the hounds on New Year's morning with a hunt breakfast first and a stirrup cup after," there would have been no gainsaying her.

My journal entry for the day says unkindly, "K in a dreary temper; not even appreciative that I wasn't crocked or hungover." Nevertheless there were a few light moments.

"What have you done with my thank-you list?"

"Which one, Mrs. White? The names we still have to do or the ones that are finished?"

"No, no, the other list. The ones who have thanked me. I might want to write back to some of them." I was baffled; it simply had not occurred to me to keep a record of *those* names.

I received a stern reproof—and deserved every word of it. When your employer is an inveterate list-keeper, remember to keep lists.

For more than an hour the only sound was the scratch of K's pen on a legal pad and the cacophony of two typewriters as EB and I unconsciously vied with each other for speed. Then, at the exact moment that he called across the hall, "Do you remember some silly children's riddle about a jonquil or something?", K's voice sounded from the living room: "Where in the Bible is that quotation about hiding your light under a bushel?" There was no question of which answer to supply first.

"It's in Christ's Sermon on the Mount, Gospel of Matthew. Shall I hunt it up for you?"

K looked up long enough to nod her head and went on writing. There were several Bibles in the house, but the only one I had seen was an enormous tome, its covers and spine in lamentable condition, that lived upstairs in the television room. En route to secure it, I paused just long enough to dash off a quatrain and hand it across the hall: "Little Nancy Etticoat/ Has come up to town/ In a green petticoat/ And a yellow gown. Mother Goose rhyme, a riddle about a daffodil."

I read to K from the fifth chapter of Matthew: "Ye are the light of the world. A city that is set on an hill cannot be hid. Neither do men light a candle, and put it under a bushel, but on a candlestick; and it giveth light unto all that are in the house."

"It has a certain beauty, hasn't it?" she remarked.

"Well, yes—doesn't most of the Bible? The King James version, anyway. All the revised versions seem sort of prosaic by comparison."

"I guess I haven't read as much of it as I should have. When we were children we had to memorize the most awful passages;

they didn't seem to make any sense and I'm sure the words and the thought didn't flow along the way this quotation does."

"The really radiant part is the next verse, Mrs. White." I closed the big book carefully as I spoke: "Let your light so shine before men that they may see your good works, and glorify your Father which is in Heaven."

"That *is* beautiful. They gave you better lines to memorize than they gave me."

"No, that wasn't an assignment; I learned it from familiarity. In the Episcopal Church we heard those words every Sunday at the service of Morning Prayer. It was the admonition given to us by the minister just before the offering plates were passed."

"Indeed. Well, how clever of them. It must have helped loosen many a purse string," and she waved a hand to indicate that the discussion was terminated.

In addition to the normal influx of post-holiday mail that year were the telegrams and letters of congratulation on EB's new medal. All of these had to be acknowledged separately from thank-yous for gifts and cards, even though it often meant two letters to one person. When the medal arrived in the mail, K gave it to me to take upstairs and put away in the chest of drawers in her bedroom. Presumably it never came out again, and a measure of EB's interest in the presentation was that he did not attend the New York ceremony in person but wrote an acceptance speech to be read at Lincoln Center by William Maxwell of *The New Yorker.* Laying the box in the drawer assigned to awards, I could not resist taking out the Medal of Freedom from its velvet-lined case. What nearly unbearable memories of poignant circumstances surrounded it. Holding it reverently in my hand, I could again hear my husband's voice on the telephone that long-ago November day: "The president has been shot in Dallas."

"Oh no, oh no!"

"Yes, dear. I'm afraid it's yes."

"But it was just an injury—not anything serious?"

A slight hesitation. "I have to get back to work; I'll let you know the minute I hear anything more."

There was no need for further bulletins. I was not too far from the center of our small New Hampshire town that day to hear the mournful tolling of church bells.

When the Medal of Freedom roster was published in 1963, one might have placed a small wager against EB's appearing at the White House. He was older than JFK; also, he was adept at avoiding the spotlight; but who would have forecast the death of the young ebullient president? The medal was more than a circle of metal in my hands, more than a symbolic gesture of fealty to a common man who was an uncommon writer. It implied something heroic about the giver that transcended its meaning and worth to the recipient; but whatever the implication, it was so bitter a circumstance I could not bear to trace it through.

That winter of 1972 a popular writer was discovered by the curious press to be more addicted to pencil than machine when engaged in his profession. *His* idea of a fine compliment to his wife was to tell her, "You smell like pencil shavings." Trying to amuse K on one of her down mornings, I suggested she might look forward to being informed, "Mmmm, you smell delicious, just like a typewriter ribbon." She tried to repeat the sequence to her husband but lost her way. "Tell Andy what you told me," she commanded. There was the expected outcome: I was neatly outclassed.

Isabel Russell

"K smells like the clean pages of a new book under the Christmas tree," he told us in a throwaway line as he vanished into the hall on his way to the mailbox.

Dog Jones, accidentally struck by a trailer late in March, was nursing bruised bones and wounded feelings all through April. Prior to the incident, and, unfortunately, subsequent to it, he had been wont to stand at the edge of the driveway barking at all passersby, making a great show of protecting his own and his master's turf. Indeed it was this proclivity for fighting off monsters that accounted for the damaging confrontation with the trailer, but Jones learned nothing from it except perhaps that some noisy machine had bitten him and that it was therefore his responsibility to chase all heavy machinery off the highway. "He continues to fight the good fight," said his master on the telephone, "and he resembles me in so many ways it's incredible. He doesn't know enough to give up when he's licked."

It was an estimable character trait; I envied both of them. Somebody else displayed signs of the same trait that month. K received an application for "the summer position" of secretary to the Whites. The applicant, a middle-aged woman with several years secretarial experience, explained that she would be vacationing in the area. She had applied originally in 1970 and was making another attempt for the summer of 1972, in case the position was vacant. I overheard K saying brusquely to EB, "I'm going to keep track of her address; I shall tell her we have no need of her now but it would be well to have someone in reserve in case Isabel happened to fall by the wayside because of illness or accident. . . ." Not being a fatalist I had no fear of falling by the wayside unless some member of the White ménage, especially Jones, gave me an inadvertent shove, but the statement lingered in late night/early morning dreams.

An orgy of spring cleaning—second only to Christmas for unsettling the household in general and EB in particular—began earlier than usual that spring and it started with my office. K's cleaning system consisted of requesting that everything she previously had asked be brought down from the attic should be returned there, even though she had glanced at only a few of those items. Then all file folders taken out of the file drawers for sorting, but still unsorted, were to be replaced in the same drawers. The stack of file folders on the floor under the highboy was to be moved up to the table. Those on the table were to be moved to the sofa. There was, of course, a group of them already on the sofa. Those went, in that system of orderly progression, onto the top of a file cabinet. It seemed wiser not to inquire "What about the ones already on the file?" lest the reply be, "Under the highboy."

EB, engaged meanwhile on some esoteric project about which nobody knew anything, announced that he needed to refer to the verse on their 1970 Christmas card; did I have one filed away somewhere? Of course I hadn't; it had slipped his memory that they had run out of personal greetings before reaching the end of their list and had been forced to supplement it with twenty commercial cards. Luckily our family had saved ours, so I could bring it to him, having first wrapped it in a sheet of heavy brown paper which was labeled ostentatiously in red crayon letters: "Please return intact when finished." Two days later the card, in an enormous carton, was left in my office. A white sheet taped to the top bore the message, in big red-crayon letters: "INTACT here. Transport with care."

One of her husband's ongoing problems was the addenda to K's will; the common specifics of the testament had been assembled for many years and copies of the document were stashed away in a strongbox in EB's study. At intervals, however, he prodded K to complete the additional papers that would assign certain house furnishings and personal possessions to friends and relations. It was a monumental task because K went into lengthy historic detail about each dish, item of silver, or article of furniture in her dictation; it was a chore which she would dutifully begin when there was a lull in correspondence. Equally dutifully she would cut off the project in favor of another more pressing assignment. I worked sporadically on preparing typed sheets from the spring of 1971 until the spring of 1977 without ever achieving coherence or a final draft. Often there was a gap of six or eight months between stabs at the assignment. We felt pushed to get to work on it only if EB made one of three oft-repeated remarks:

"K, we're both going to die some day and nobody is going to know what you want done with all the things in this big house." "K, you've been working on your will for years but I can't see any signs of progress." "K, if you don't do something about your will, it's going to end with an announcement in *The Packet:* 'House and contents to be sold at auction.'"

If he merely inquired in passing how things were going on the will, she gave him a bright smile and said, "Fine." Between sessions it was easy to forget everything that had gone before, and she proceeded to name the same objet d'art more than once, bequeathing it to a different recipient each time while I looked forward anxiously to a day when rough drafts of the will could be copied and repetitions uncovered and brought to her attention. The inventory ranged from such sizeable items as rugs and antique Victorian sofas at the one end to small silver match boxes at the other. We worked a requisite few days on the inventory that spring of 1972, just long enough to quiet

EB's apprehensions; after that, K's attention was diverted to more important lists.

Jones's horoscope for April would seem to indicate he had been born on the dark side of the moon. By sad mischance he contrived to bite local citizen Bill Allen, husband of K's faithful, long-time housecleaning helper, Virginia. Bill died a year later but his demise had nothing to do with the dog bite. He was known as a good man, with all the fine character traits that adjective denotes in coastal parlance, and Jones in no way increased his own popularity rating by having the temerity to select a good man for a target. A pall of impending disaster seemed to hang over the household the following week. "Jones must go," was the edict handed down from EB's headquarters. Jones, wildly psychic, suspected what was afoot and approached his daily routine even more morosely than usual, and that covered a lot of moroseness.

EB remarked that he didn't have time enough to provide all the escorted exercise the dog would need if he was to be kept restrained. He hoped to find a lonely person who would give Jones individual attention while keeping him sequestered, but all of us were aware of the futility of that hope. Jones was a one-man dog; we suspected he would die of grief if parted from the master to whom he offered an abnormal devotion; and it was apparent that EB supported the same fear as he patted the little dog and spoke sorrowfully to him. A large sign, lettered in plain tidy crayon strokes, was attached to the kitchen door for a week: "Please do not let Jones out." K, confined to bed with another painful compression fracture of the spine, dictated a letter to her son Roger Angell in New York. It included a brief dissertation on Jones's misdeeds, ending with a phrase about his being in limbo. "Coventry," I corrected automatically, then chewed my pencil tip in anguish. I hadn't been asked to supply an elusive word; K was so much more learned than I in many areas that a correction indicated a lot of temerity on my part. Besides, she was in pain; it was not the proper time to be engaged in vocabulary disputes. "Of course, 'Coventry'; that's what I meant," she agreed; and kindly paused in her labors to flesh out my meager knowledge on the origin of the "being sent to Coventry" phrase, with its obscure relationship to a county borough in Warwickshire, England.

The bad back improved within a day or two; we could return to the vital business at hand, a project that was worked on sporadically, then put aside in favor of more current enterprises. Favored in April and May was the matter of a box of letters from *New Yorker*-connected authors, personal letters to K that were collected each year and forwarded to the Bryn Mawr College Library. Items were selected from ongoing correspondence with Jean Stafford, Faith McNulty, Christine Weston, Buckner Hollingsworth, Elizabeth Bishop, et al; occasionally a long-ago letter from one of them or from some other literary personage would surface as we looked through ancient files in pursuit of different quarry. Each year the letters were appraised by Seven Gables Bookshop in New York and K fidgeted over all items, sorting and resorting, asking to have them arranged in chronological order and then reverting to a topical listing. Prolific notes, which some day would be invaluable to historians, were attached to the letters, and as in the case of authors on the Bryn Mawr book list, no first effort suited her. Everything had to be scanned anxiously for slip-ups in vocabulary or usage; and the matter of packing—size of box, arrangement of material therein, how it was to be wrapped—was of vast importance. EB, happening upon these weighty preparations now and then, would advise, "Keep it simple, K.

Just put on the cover; get Henry to wrap it and there you are." But he might as well have been advising Jones, and he knew it.

Jones, incidentally, was giving every sign that he was aware he had unwittingly jeopardized his future. If it was possible—and with Jones few things were *im*possible—for him to be acting more dour and cranky than usual, he was so doing. He might have spared himself the effort; only death severed him from his beloved master. Less and less mention of his proposed adoption was made as the days sped by. Finally, the intent to relocate him was accepted as an earnest of the deed; the search for the just-right person was abandoned and Jones settled back once more into comfortable taciturnity.

Despite the literary leanings and backgrounds of both Whites, they seldom engaged in discussions of erudite matters. Their remarks and arguments revolved around questions of suitability, grammar, punctuation, and syntax; brief forays into biographical data and perhaps a minor debate on a specific phrase. Was it extant and accepted or obsolete? The unabridged dictionary, to which we all applied ourselves with vigor, was source book and Supreme Court. Nobody dreamed of appealing.

Once, though, the delving was in deep waters and I was left floundering on the shore. EB's memo to K, attached to a letter from a pedantic correspondent, stated: "I guess he's right about Alexandrine. The English Alexandrine is iambic; whether the French is, I don't know, and the dictionary doesn't say." K began a learned discourse in the number of syllables to a line, the fact of a feminine rhyme being of vast importance to the Alexandrine, and a query about the capitalizing of the initial letter. ("I'm sure you're in error there, Andy.")

Even Jones might have hazarded the same guess I did, that the origin of the word stemmed from the name Alexander the Great and perhaps a particular ode to him; but it wasn't the time for guessing as K spoke to EB about caesuras and he countered with a definition of something so obscure that all I understood was the phrase "Latin prosody." Between them, they came to so inconclusive and unsatisfactory a decision on the Alexandrine that the subject was abandoned and never reopened in my hearing.

K had more important things to worry about, specifically her husband's July birthday, still two months away. She was leafing through several catalogues in search of exactly the type of linen handkerchiefs she wanted to give him when, to her distress, he wandered through the arena and overheard part of the dictation. It meant his birthday gift would not be a surprise. She was chagrined when he said kindly, "Don't go to so much trouble, K. I can make do with a dozen nice cotton squares from Grants' store in Ellsworth; who needs linen and monograms?" She looked so unhappy that it seemed to be the right time to inject a little humor.

"It's not as if it were just *any* nose, Mr. White," I admonished him.

K was instantly diverted and chose to take the light remark seriously. "It certainly isn't. And we're not going to start this late in life making do with cotton handkerchiefs, Andy. So if you'll kindly stop listening in when I'm speaking of surprise gifts, we'll get on with this order." Pretending to be much abashed, he bowed himself out.

On the same day a copy of Louise Bogan's *A Poet's Alphabet* arrived in the mail. K gave it to me to star and add to the list of Bryn Mawr books but it looked so familiar I was certain it was already listed. "Well, if it is, just look through the shelves and find it," K ordered, but I disobeyed, reaching instead for our copy of the Bryn Mawr list and hunting for the book in the later pages. Luck was sitting on page 70; a notation indicated that the Bogan opus had been a recent Christmas gift to K from EB, who, had he been approached, could have answered our question immediately. Pondering on the list as an accurate source for the answer to many questions, an idea occurred to me. Why not compile an index of the list alphabetically by authors' names, with the page numbers on which their titles could be found? It would save an incalculable number of hours of book search. Hesitating, I broached the matter to K. She could see the wisdom of time saved and was in hearty accord although perhaps not exactly shaken to her foundations.

Going home that day I detoured through the small plant room off the kitchen to speak to Henry Allen. A large sign in EB's familiar lettering was tacked over a section of the plant bench. It warned all to "Beware the mantises." There was a group of baby praying mantises on the window, recently hatched from a tiny nest on a large twig fastened to a post. I recalled that three such nests had arrived via United Parcel Service a month previously and that when I encountered EB carrying them to the cellar I had wondered what their purpose was. Now I knew—or at least a few days later I did. EB was discovered on his knees tending them in the tulip border, and he called me over to admire them. There appeared to be thousands hatching all at once, far too many for one border, so I asked, "Shall you keep them all here?"

"Yes, all but the ones I send to Sunday school."

The publication of Roger Angell's book on baseball, *The Summer Game,* was a blissful one for his mother. There was a splendid Tuesday in June when the Sunday *New York Times* arrived in the mail. K, as was her custom, checked the obits first; then turned to literary events in the *Times Book Review.* "Roger's first!" she called triumphantly to EB.

"Impossible!" he rejoined, coming into the living room to check her statement. I didn't blame her for looking highly indignant; it appeared that he was lacking in his usual tact but it turned out to be a mutual misunderstanding. He supposed she meant first on the best-seller list, but he knew the book to be too recently published to have attained that status. She supposed he was aware that she was reading the prestigious leading page of the *Book Review.* It was exactly the right time to interject and tell her I had purchased the book for my husband. "Bring it over in July when Roger comes," she instructed me. "He will autograph it." So I did and he did; he seemed not to find autographing the burden that his stepfather found it.

Presently, there not being anything particular to worry about, K began to fear thieves who might break in during the night and steal her inscribed first editions of EB's works. "In your spare time get them all together and wrap them in that tight paper that's like Scotch tape only bigger," she directed, "and put them all on the bed in the canopy bedroom where they'll be safe." Predictably I got called away from that assignment before it was completed and it was a long time before the books reached the bedroom sanctuary, such a long time in fact that the most valuable book in the collection got separated from its fellows and was presumed lost—or stolen—in the interim.

Initial work on EB's proposed book of letters, which was eventually published in the autumn of 1976, got under way in the summer of 1972, with the selection of his goddaughter, Dorothy Lobrano Guth, as editor. Mrs. Guth's father, Gus Lobrano, had once been fiction editor and later, managing editor of *The New Yoker* and a close friend of both Whites. They called her "Dottie" (sometimes spelled "Dotty").

Some mornings—but not many—the Whites were relaxed and comfortable, with EB busy at his typewriter but pausing to offer a brief witticism about something he was asking me to copy for the *Letters* manuscript; and K content to dictate a plausible number of items and to discuss alertly some future duties. Then came the day when she decided abruptly that the box of authors' correspondence for Bryn Mawr must go immediately in the mail. The immediacy was so immediate that when I had wrapped the package I must drop everything else and dash to the North Brooklin post office with it. "Mark it 'manuscript.' Send it registered return receipt, first class, special handling." It took a bit of time to persuade the post office that all K's orders simply must be incorporated in one mailing; when I returned—the errand having consumed half an hour at my speediest—she was chagrined to find much of the morning gone. An hour beyond my usual departure of noon, and half an hour past her own lunch period, K was still dictating. In vain I glanced at the clock; in vain Edith beamed anxious signals to K. Finally EB came to our rescue with the mild remark that surely the rest of K's dictation could be postponed until the next morning.

"I'll have twice as much ready by then," K told him plaintively. "I plan to make notes all evening." It was evident she had no idea what time it was.

"Then let Isabel work in the afternoon while you're napping."

"Certainly not. When would she have time for her own nap?"

Surprisingly, one July morning, there was no left-over dictation in notebook and no stack of handwritten letters awaiting copying. No interrogations, no requests; EB was nowhere in sight, nor was K visible. Her closed bedroom door indicated the nurse already had begun the morning routine so there was to be no secretarial conference. On the office table, very much in my way, were the plastic-wrapped books representing K's personal collection of her husband's writings. Idly turning the pages of *The Fox of Peapack* and then *The Lady Is Cold,* I was struck anew by the beauty and ingenuity of the inscriptions EBW had prepared for KSW. Maybe somebody some day would like to have a record of those inscriptions? The two alma maters, Cornell and Bryn Mawr, were the most likely contenders—after me—so, in a list-making fervor akin to K's own, I inserted the requisite number of sheets (two pieces of white paper, one sheet of yellow paper, and two carbons) in the typewriter and set to work.

I was in the midst of typing the ode "A Compass for Katharine" from *The Points of My Compass* when K sent down an urgent request for me to bring to her bedroom a list of reminders she had left "somewhere" in the living room. Remembering that she liked to be kept informed of all developments, I handed over all but one of the inscription lists, asking to have the sheets returned to be completed. She was pleased and gratified with the inspiration that had brought forth the copies ("They can have much wider circulation this way in different archives; thank you, my dear.") but I never was able to separate her from the lists again, despite many requests over the years. Later, she checked carefully to see that everything matched, but the order never came to take the books out of the crowded office. It had been part of the original direction, of course, but was later amended to "Don't carry them upstairs until I've checked every one." When I pleaded one last time to effect the transfer, explaining that I needed more space, the answer was the same:

"Not till I check to see if the list is complete."

"We checked several days ago." (Me, meekly.)

"We'll check again." (She, sharply.)

Incredibly but assuredly one book, *The Lady Is Cold*, was missing. "I told you so!" said K triumphantly and set me to work hunting for it.

"This is unbelievable, Mrs. White. I know it was in that stack of wrapped books because I copied the inscription from the flyleaf. See, here it is. I couldn't have invented that."

"Of course not," she agreed amiably. "I know the book was there—I've been reading it."

Did she think I had taken it? Propinquity was the issue here and who had easier access to treasured volumes than the secretary who handled them every day? A careful search of sofa, bench, bookshelves, her bedside table, revealed nothing. The Lady, wherever she was, was securely hidden. Even the tried and true system—if I were a book, where would I be?—yielded no result. Likely K would forget the matter in a day or two; unfortunately I would not. A lot of Sherlocking went on after hours that summer.

Beginning in August with one six-page letter about a fire that burned the barn at the nearby Joel White home, K was engrossed with the fire for many weeks to come. Her attention might have been directed to it for a longer period except that a new interest suddenly usurped its place, as she disparaged the biography of Anne Carroll Moore (superintendent of the children's division at the New York Public Library) written by Frances Clarke Sayers. K had no quarrel with Sayers; it was simply the mention of Moore's name that brought back to mind an old grudge that K. was pleased to dust off and trot out into the sunlight again. In an exchange of letters and in an article published back in the dark ages before Charlotte spun her immortal web, librarian Moore had ventured to criticize EB for his first classic for children, *Stuart Little*. She had, in sober fact, tried to persuade him not to have it published, lest it damage his image.

"I wish I could have pinned her down as to what kind of "image" I was supposed to have had. If I had any, I never recognized it," said EB ruefully.

K had neither forgiven nor forgotten the incident. My journal stated mildly, "She gets very overwrought on the subject." How overwrought she was about to get I did not suspect in early August but I was to find out in succeeding weeks as the Moore biography remained in the forefront of her mind, and her strictures against book and woman filled up page after page of correspondence, until finally EB, sufficiently disturbed by the tirades, ordered a moratorium on the subject. And so it would ever go until the next book or the next fire came along to direct her wrath or her attention elsewhere.

During K's later years, a few young fans of EB's inevitably received acknowledgments that contained misinterpretations but they continued to write to him, and occasionally a polite note came back to K herself, bearing an expression of sympathy for her illness. A little girl named Diana did not receive a message intended for her long ago in 1972. I have recalled the circumstances often and wished there were some way to let her know she was not intentionally overlooked. An envelope directed to her was duly returned to North Brooklin from a post office in another state; it was stamped "insufficient address" but of course it contained all the address poor K had been able to provide. Who was to know whether it was Diana's address on the envelope or the address of someone else that had got mixed up with her name? K's letter itself was perfectly lucid, having to do with an episode and a word in *Stuart Little* about which Diana (or someone else?) had inquired. It offered a simple description of a soft drink known as sarsaparilla, popular in the days when the Whites were young. When the letter was returned, all K's lucidity vanished. "I think perhaps the child who asked about sarsaparilla was a boy, and if Diana's letter went to him, [the letter to the boy] will come back also and we can rewrite the two letters and envelopes." Mercifully, in the press of other literary events, she forgot Diana and the unnamed lad, and at the end of a year I felt safe in destroying the returned letter in the kitchen stove when the fire was burning briskly. Wherever Diana is, if once she lived in Glen Ellyn, Illinois, and wrote to E. B. White, this account will assure her that her letter to him was opened, read, and answered. If she didn't ask anything about sarsaparilla, maybe it's just as well she didn't receive the 1972 communication. The name of the boy who may or may not have been the one to raise the matter of the soft drink is shrouded in mystery; there is little hope that he might recognize the episode in these pages.

K was especially upset that August. She was much worried over EB's incarceration in the Blue Hill Hospital with severe neck and shoulder pain. Her staff rallied around, offering comfort in the way of working different shifts or extra hours, delivering mail and messages and even some special dishes to tempt the invalid's appetite at the hospital, but K's woe was deep-seated.

Jones was inconsolable, too, as always when his master was more than a house- or a lawn's-length away from him. He wouldn't eat, and he wandered sorrowfully from room to room, up the front stairs and down the back ones, seeking the familiar figure, listening for the familiar voice. If Jones was missing his master to such an extent, was it not probable that his master was missing him? When Jones and I had agreed on the possibility, it seemed logical to assist him in composing a bulletin of his own to amuse his bedridden god. We worked around a well-known paragraph from *The Elements of Style* in which the reader is cautioned about the use of "wise" as a pseudo-suffix. In the book there were a few ludicrous examples: marriagewise, prosewise, salt-water taffywise. Jones felt capable of contriving some additional ones.

"Dear Master—Sorry you're feeling down and out but that's how life goes, age-wise. I'm beginning to feel the pinch myself. (Neckwise, nosewise, paw-wise, tailwise, and salt-water taffy-wise.) Things at home are about as gloomy as they can get—at least that's how it appears from my end of the bone. I keep listening for your foot-steps but all I hear is the heavy tread of your domestic minions on their appointed rounds. Everybody means well, I'm sure, but nobody sees the world from a dog's eye viewpoint, so nobody understands my special needs. My appetite has fallen way off. Please do come home before my hair begins to follow it. Lugubriously yrs, Jones."

When the patient returned, Jones was the first to be thanked. EB had felt much pleased to know he was missed, "companionshipwise." With her spouse safely established in his study again, K could concentrate most days on important matters but there were times when I suspected her of urging me into the attic on a fictitious or, at the very least, an unnecessary search. (If there's nothing to occupy the youngster, send her up attic to hunt through the button box.) The amount of paper stacked up on her desk-bench and a certain tone in her voice (the amount of paper negligible and the tone fretful) was a clear index of the load. There wasn't quite enough to do and secretly she hoped it would take me a long time to locate something in the upper regions. On one of those assignments I came across a fragment of EB's history that I had not seen in print before and have not seen since. It was identified as the menu for the golden wedding-anniversary dinner for his parents, Samuel Tilly White and Jessie Wallace Hart White, held April 27, 1930, in Mount Vernon, New York: Bouillon, Little Rolls, Celery, Olives, Salted Almonds, Mushroom Patty, Green Peas, Roast Capon, Mashed Potatoes, Asparagus, Fruit Salad—Cream Dressing, Bride's Cake, Wedding Forms, Biscuit Tortoni, Mints, Bonbons, Demi-Tasse, White Rock, White Grape Juice Fruit Punch.

A family photo was taken on the day the celebrants were assembled and EB looked surprisingly like the EB of the present, despite the passage of so many years. K's likeness was enchanting; it gave a glimpse once again of the young K, the bride of less than a year, the ephemeral figure that dwelt in EB's memory.

It was a rare occasion when a secretary would have the temerity to set up her inadequate opinions against EB's learned ones, but it was a different matter with K because sometimes it was essential to argue gently in order to avoid a repetitive mistake. If an instruction could be carried out by fulfilling her intention rather than her command, all went well; other times she forged ahead on her own and when something was botched it was too late to interfere, but at least an attempt could be made to soothe her and try to patch up the split seam. On one occasion EB walked into the living room in time to hear me ask, "Ought we to write this, Mrs. White? Won't it be inconsistent with what we told him before?"

"I always say consistency is the mother of contention," EB told us with more than his usual gravity.

"And abstemiousness is the mother of boredom," retorted K. Obviously he was delighted at her quick reply, which was in direct opposition to the air of abstraction she often wore when his discourse ran on outside her sphere of concentration. He continued the exchange: "Verbosity is the mother of absurdity."

I ventured a modest contribution: "Enticement is the mother of immorality."

K returned to her papers with a slight wave of the hand to indicate that if others were in the mood for games they must play them without her. EB, in high good humour, offered: "Punishment is the mother of recompense."

I responded, "Forebearance is the mother of excess."

He ended the series: "Fatalism is the mother of catastrophe."

Presently K ceased general operations to inquire how it had been when I attended an historical building open-house day in the town of Castine. In one of the open homes I had met her good friend, author Mary McCarthy. I suppose I waxed over-enthusiastic (jammy?) about the experience; meetings with authors inevitably bring out the worst in me, enthusiasmwise, and it provided the ideal opportunity for a neat riposte. "So, at last, Isabel, you were able to meet a real live author," dead-panned EB.

On a cold windy October morning K was determined to supervise Henry's planting of daffodil and tulip bulbs. Nothing said by her husband or household staff could dissuade her, and she sallied forth wrapped like a mummy in her scarf, trench coat, gloves, and rubber boots, staunch in her belief that only she could direct the job properly, and happy in her conviction that she had shown herself to be stronger than the forces opposing her. From our various posts in house or garden we all shuddered through the half-hour session while she triumphed over us then, and later. Two of us came down with colds but she suffered no adverse reaction from the exposure.

Then came a bonus day when a request in the mail opened K's memory to a flash of reminiscence that set her to chatting for half an hour about her childhood, her ancestors, and her career at *The New Yorker*. The memories were motivated by a request from the University of Nebraska for photos of K's sister, Elizabeth Shepley Sergeant. Elizabeth had written a book about Willa Cather; in recognition of the approaching one-hundredth anniversary of Cather's birth, personal material relating to her life was being garnered, and the contribution of K's deceased sister to the Cather legend was considered to be a significant segment. Down from the attic came a box of old photos and we spread them on tables, chairs, mantel, and finally on the floor, while K sought the appropriate ones. Various gems of memorabilia were found among the pictures; everything was handled carefully, described in rich detail, and set aside in case it might some day be a worthwhile memento for a child or grandchild of the Sergeant branch of the White family. It was all greatly admired by us both, and we became so involved in this sentimental journey that it was well past lunchtime before a hasty note and a package of photos was ready to be dispatched to Nebraska. The hurried, last-minute note was quite unlike K's usual meticulous efforts but we had been so engrossed in these souvenirs that it was difficult to bring ourselves back to the present in order to give the university's request the attention it merited.

Sometimes it seemed that EB's mail could be categorized under a mere two headings: praise from fans and requests for more writing from him that would result in more praise from still more fans. When *Redbook* asked for an article that would offer advice to children in their own selection of books, the magazine received a typical turndown. The editors were informed brusquely that EB never had known what to tell children about anything and that at one time he had written an article about not knowing what to tell them. K and I, probably in common with *Redbook*'s editors, felt there was much irony in such an excuse from a man who had been royally entertaining children with the written word for three decades. By the 1970s, many adults who had been thrilled by *Stuart Little* and *Charlotte's Web* in their youth were grown up, married, and beginning to introduce EB's books to their offspring.

It was exceedingly pleasant to be at work typing copies of his letters for a proposed book, rather than to be engaged in K's correspondence on the days that her outlook was pessimistic. EB was not above mentioning his health in his correspondence but only when it was relevant to the circumstances. One of his favorite expressions was "I have a fierce attack of the Uncommon Cold." Even when spoken, the two words sounded capitalized. Once, when down and out with an Uncommon Cold, he apologized for writing a rambling letter and explained that it was difficult for him to write short, rational sentences when "in extremis."

In the days when he was a full-time staff writer for *The New Yorker*, EB formed the habit of jotting down ideas and catch phrases on menus in New York restaurants or on concert and theater program notes, and sometimes in the margins of museum and book catalogues. K spoke of these from time to time and produced one or two of them from her archives, but a whole treasure of them must have gone into New York (or *New Yorker*) wastebaskets, never to be retrieved—although, ironically, EB retrieved the immensely valuable doodlings of James Thurber in the early days of the magazine. When the Whites retired to Maine and seclusion, there were no longer any theater programs or restaurant menus at hand for note-making purposes. EB did most of his creating at the typewriter, in his study in cold weather and at the boathouse when the temperature was mild.

When his thoughts or spirits were ruffled and his creative process stymied, he would sometimes discuss ideas with K, frequently interrupting her dictation. At such times I was the supreme beneficiary of the disruption. There was every justification for sitting tight and waiting for K to continue dictating; no justification (according to K herself) for leaving the room. Thus, when EB was working on a *New Yorker* piece to be titled "The Browning Off of Pelham Manor," he wrote in fits and starts and talked over several versions of the opening paragraph with K while I waited.

"Shall I say 'I achieved unconsciousness before I was aware of it'? Or 'before I knew anything was up'? Or isn't that a good beginning? What is there to say about a womb, anyway? What single thing is there about a womb that's funny, K?"

"Absolutely nothing," she told him grimly, having experienced some woes of her own in that regard. She was good-natured when we both laughed; then she suggested that perhaps he had found being in the womb a tight fit when he inhabited one. That inspired him to concoct, "It was badly designed and ill-ventilated."

His typewriter keys could be heard operating briskly for several minutes, and K had completed dictating two letters before he returned to ask, "If I say I failed to relate to my mother, would it be humorous to go on, 'Hers was just like all the rest of them [we assumed he meant her womb]—no character of its own unless you include me in it'?"

K altered it to "unless you want to count me,"; he seemed undecided but her suggestion was incorporated in the final version.

I had been with the Whites for three of their wedding anniversaries when on the morning of their forty-third K was in a reminiscent mood, so I put aside notebook and pencil and listened with concentrated attention to her account of the important ceremony. Naïvely I assumed I would recall every detail when I sat down to write in my journal. Alas, all I remembered was that her Bryn Mawr class ring was used in lieu of the traditional wedding band, and that the minister apologized for the mussed-up condition of the church, where there had just been a funeral service. "All this on Friday the thirteenth!" emphasized K. (At a later date when EB and I were talking about the wedding, he told me that they were married on a Wednesday, but that often "of late years poor K gets confused in her memory of that day and I never correct her.") The obliging clergyman assembled enough witnesses to make the marriage legal, and his dog and their dog Daisy (a canine the Whites shared and unaccountably brought along for the ceremony) began to fight and had to be restrained in separate rooms.

"Our honeymoon consisted of a dinner celebration at some restaurant—I don't recall the name—and there we encountered some *New Yorker* writer—I don't remember who—and she was standing around fuming because her escort hadn't arrived."

By the end of November plans were afoot for EB to go to New York on business that would include a private screening of the *Charlotte's Web* film. K was suffering from a physical disorder that continued for several days; it began to seem probable that the New York trip, already postponed several times, would be postponed again, it being unlikely that EB would desert K when she was ill, but to the general surprise of all, he did go. On November 27 I worked for her at night (from 6:30 to 9), writing letters and doubling as attendant until the night nurse came on duty at 9 P.M. Her correspondence contained typical complaints about Andy's being far away and the difficulty she had carrying on without him, with no mention of the staff waiting, ready to serve her at a moment's notice.

When EB returned he was besieged on all sides by the "Big Question." Many letters typed for him during that year had contained fearful references to "it," which in those days usually meant the spider movie. We hoped the fears were groundless and the worry unjustified. He said, "Well, frankly, it was just about what I expected. Not really good but perhaps not as bad as I had anticipated." How can one help but smile at that assessment in consideration of all the happiness the film version of *Charlotte* has since brought to countless viewers?

On December 13 there was a poster-size sign with the words

"Bike Post" sprawled across it, and a request from our bicycling author that I desist from other duties and fill in the message so that the sign would be visible to anyone on the road. He planned to attach it to his bike when he delivered a piece of mail from Brooklin to North Brooklin, as part of a publicity stunt dreamed up by James Russell Wiggins, publisher of the weekly newspaper, *The Ellsworth American.* His ride was designed to draw attention to the way mail delivery between towns had been slowed when central sorting was moved from nearby Ellsworth to faraway Bangor under a new, more "efficient" postal system. EB, no letterer at best, had pretty much spoiled the sign, but I fattened it out as best I could to hold up our honor in view of the publicity that bike and rider were likely to get from the local press. They got more than anticipated, more than EB would have let himself in for had he known about it in advance. It was too late to back out when the CBS News television cameras zeroed in on him on the road near his house. He, Mr. Wiggins, and Henry Allen were all to be seen on Walter Cronkite's news broadcast that night. We were sure EB was being truthful when he protested he had known nothing of the plan for national television exposure; we all were certain he would have been found cowering behind his bicycle in the barn cellar—if he hadn't just gotten on his bike and disappeared—had any hint of the extra publicity reached him in advance.

Christmas preparations followed the pattern of preceding years: a melee of lost orders to be traced; wrong colors and wrong sizes to be returned; wrong tags on many boxes, necessitating an ungift-wrapping and a great waste of paper, ribbons, and tape. The UPS deliveryman was as ubiquitous as the mailman; wastebaskets bulged with discarded brown-paper wrappings; the beribboned parcels in the canopy bedroom grew and grew; the telephone jangled insistently whenever all were busy and hating to be interrupted; neighbors appeared with home-made wreaths and children dropped in with small delightful offerings. If I failed to keep track of a direction I had never received, K was not to be appeased. It was difficult to be patient but I failed to recognize what I now understand only too well: she was growing old, her health was failing, she was not in-defatigable. For all I know, while I was sighing over small problems, she looked at me on a bad day and saw pointed ears and horns.

·⦿ FIVE ⦿·

After having been pushed into working on two New Year's Days, I was able to beg off in 1973. There would be no mail in or out and there was nothing so pressing it couldn't wait one more day, I hinted; and K sighed but agreed. On the second, when I had expected to be inundated with letters, I was assigned instead to be Henry's assistant in untrimming the Christmas tree. It had taken three Christmases to convince the Whites that this important task could be delegated safely to anyone but Henry and themselves. Tucked away somewhere there must have been a list of qualifications, and I had managed to come out on top in the categories of "tidy" and "trustworthy" and whatever the opposite of "butterfingered" would be.

"I feel like Longfellow," announced EB, coming in to ask for some sharp pencils just as the last Christmas ornament box had been deposited in the attic. It was hard to deduce why the New England poet would be on his mind. "That nasty poem of his that children used to be tortured with, something about 'Learn to labor and to wait.' Christmas always makes me think of it," he added.

" 'Tell me not, in mournful numbers,' " I quoted, and he shuddered.

"I had to commit it to memory in fifth grade," he explained, "and I think that's where I picked up my life-long phobia about platforms and public speaking. It was around this season of the year and we had to recite for our parents and visiting dignitaries. I hated the poem anyway—we weren't permitted to make our own selections—and I nearly choked on 'Life is real—life is earnest— /And the grave is not its goal', but I struggled through to 'Lives of great men all remind us / We can make *our* lives sublime, / And, departing, leave behind us / Footprints on the sands of time.' Somehow my tongue got twisted on that last lilting lyric and it came out 'the tands of sime.' Probably if I'd gone right on, nobody would have noticed but I imagined I heard somebody tittering, and I got so rattled I forgot the next seven lines."

He paused and stared out the window at the winter landscape, at drifts of snow blanketing K's barren flower borders, stepping-stones of ice glazing parts of the driveway, and Susy and Jones cavorting under the old apple tree at the side of the house. For the moment he was miles and years away, locked in that segment of time when he and the century were young and hopeful.

"What happened? Didn't anyone rescue you?"

"Oh, the teacher kept trying to prompt me with the next line but I was beyond help. All I wanted to do was to get off that stage and hide, so I shouted the last line, 'Learn to labor and to wait' and fled."

In previous months of January he had little chance to avail himself of secretarial services as the maelstrom of K's thank-you notes whirled around my desk. Each year the number of thank-yous seemed unaccountably to outweigh the number of gifts, but who would dare to mention it? Despite my five mornings of work each week and several afternoons given over to typing at home, EB's needs got short shrift. With a typing speed of 65 words a minute, I wasn't exactly a slouch but K could accumulate faster than I could disperse and her spouse made none but absolutely essential demands, being well aware of the work load. I heard his droll tone from the doorway shortly after the Longfellow exchange:

"Must be fun to come to work and just lounge around, the way you do, Isabel."

Sadly, K's vision was worsening. She had slow-growing cataracts, about which doctors could do little, and she had difficulty reading with any speed; she often misread even when proceeding slowly. Her ear was still quick to discover oddities of phrasing, however, and we laughed together when a portion of dictation for the post-holiday mail referred to Dartmouth College's new policy of admitting women students: "They will take in a hundred females each year until the sexes are fifty-fifty," avowed K cheerily. "We'll have to straighten that out," she added, with scarcely a comma's worth of pause.

January brought *Time* magazine's cover story on what the three of us considered an infamous movie, *Last Tango in Paris.* EB and K could accept the *Time* account with equanimity because they could be held in no way responsible for the peccadilloes of the *Time-Life* chain, but they felt personally wounded by *New Yorker* movie critic Pauline Kael's enthusiastic review of the movie. *The New Yorker* was permitted to do no wrong; if it slipped on a rare occasion, no matter how far removed the error of judgment or good taste was from the Whites' jurisdiction, they felt somehow to blame. So vehement were K's and my discussions on *Tango* that EB was moved to remark in mild surprise, "I didn't suspect either of you had such violent tempers."

On January 29 EB was forced to admit himself twice for sojourns of several days each at Blue Hill Hospital; the first time because of what he termed vertigo, from inner ear imbalance, and the second for treatment of a violent onslaught of the "Uncommon Cold." Nancy Angell Stableford came by plane from her Pennsylvania home to keep her mother company when the second ailment was diagnosed as bronchitis and it seemed EB might be absent for some time. Nancy, with her finely honed sense of humor, was a good antidote to K's desolation; she was a source of entertainment, as well as of assistance, to her mother. When EB at last was at home and convalescing, I, having taken over his virus, was so sick that I missed nearly a week of work for the only time in the years I was employed by the Whites. K assured me with some asperity that anyone who didn't take flu shots was asking for trouble; and in that household, it had to be admitted, they certainly were. (I have taken a shot dutifully every year since, latterly with the feeling that K's kind ghost was sequestered in the doctor's waiting room, urging me on.) Her advice was delivered in a sharp tone but the accompanying action was gentle and typical: the gift of the beautifully bound little book *Winter Visitors* by Mary McCarthy, to lighten the boredom of my banishment. I was touched and pleased to read her inscription: "To Isabel with love and gratitude from Katharine S. White."

March 19 brought the announcement from husbandman White of the first goose egg of the season; K nodded, to indicate she had heard but her attention was engaged elsewhere. She dictated a six-page, typed letter to an author friend on the subject of James Thurber's book *The Years with Ross*, over which she had been fulminating from the time of its publication in the late 1950s. "I won't go into the details of what is wrong with it because it would take too long; my working day is only six hours." That morning, by the time she got around to writing an irate letter to *The Bangor Daily News*, which had taken an editorial stand that displeased her, EB was wandering restlessly around the dining room, having been turned out of his study while it was undergoing its annual spring-cleaning. K pursued her dictation hesitantly and finally broke it off to tell him she couldn't concentrate on her subject while he listened. He grinned widely and vanished into the kitchen.

"I didn't fool him, of course. He knows I wanted to get rid of him. If he had stayed he'd have made me shorten it and change it all around."

Shortly thereafter EB was off for the forty-mile drive to Brewer to fetch home a broody hen he planned to use for the hatching of eight wood-duck eggs, the gift of a nature-loving friend from New York. Rhapsodizing over the beauty of the male wood duck, EB inquired if I had ever seen one. I hadn't the heart to admit that I knew them feather perfect, having plucked and feasted on many of the birds in New Hampshire days when friends went duck hunting in the fall and presented their trophies to my husband and me.

A journal entry for April 23 was inscribed in red ink: "Oh frabjous day! After this long time K finally unearthed her copy of *The Lady Is Cold*. It was right where it had been left, in the TV room, in a carton of EB's material for his *Letters* book. The carton was marked 'Don't Touch' and natch I obeyed orders during the search."

Assuredly it was the spring of EB's discontent. He caught one cold after another; in the middle of May he was confined to his bed with a severe one. K asked him whether because of his indisposition she should phone and tell me not to come, but he said, "No, she'll have to come today because I have a package that must be wrapped." When I reached K's sanctum to await her orders and her pleasure, this conversation was relayed to me not as anything odd or surprising, but rather as the basis for her first request of the morning. It may have been a routine situation to both of them but it gave me pause. In younger days I had been a teacher accredited by fiat in two states; I had also served two secretarial stints in New York, one at Lord & Taylor, the other in the office of the vice-chancellor of New York University, before opting for country living. What was this that I had come to? I was needed at the Whites' to wrap a package. On sober reflection, though, it was comforting to find that my package-wrapping talents had passed muster. Both K and EB were stern critics of the sloppily wrapped affair. A garment arriving in the mail from Saks Fifth Avenue might be contained in a firm box securely sealed with brown paper-tape, but when it had to be exchanged for a different size, the Saks package was not good enough—the box could not be retaped and returned. Lots of extra tissue paper, twice as much tape, plus a cord, insured the safety of its interior. Heavy brown paper, more tape, and thick twine were adjudged essential to keep its exterior inviolate.

I was well aware that Henry could wrap a better package than I could, but often he was engaged elsewhere so it was important for me to be a good stand-in, package-wrappingwise. Nevertheless it was ironic that, with six persons present in the house that morning, a seventh had to be summoned to wrap a package. At any rate I had come a long way since World War II, when my father took charge of all packages being mailed from our home to servicemen, and particularly chided me for my ineptness with knots.

By the middle of the month EB was so far behind on "Newsbreaks" that he indoctrinated me into the mysteries of selecting and pasting them. Another "first," another break-through, even if not on a very high level. I settled down happily to my cutting and pasting, envisioning the way the finished product would look on *The New Yorker*'s pages, with EB's pithy comment appended. I hadn't the slightest doubt that all my own paste-ups would be instantly recognizable by me and all my friends and relations.

Late in May EB was full of minor discomforts, just major enough to make bed seem more inviting than desk. K and I were in the bedrooms, rummaging through an interminable number of boxes to find one that would fit a Sergeant family heirloom she was going to send to daughter-in-law Carol Angell for her birthday. "Do you need Isabel for anything?" she called to the invalid down the hall, "because if not, she'll be wrapping that silver tea caddy."

"What silver tea caddy?"

"That heirloom one from my side of the family—you remember, Andy. It's for Carol."

"No, I don't remember. I feel like an old family heirloom myself." The tone was grumbling; he was the bored spectator at a monotonous parade. While I fetched the caddy to his bedside for him to admire, K assembled gift wrap and ribbon in the guest bedroom, opposite his room. He joined in the conversation: "Carol won't like it. Who serves tea these days?"

"Lots of persons do. It might be a nice change here from the cocktail hour, Andy."

Consternation was writ large on the usually benign countenance. "For God's sake, K, when a man is down, don't try to put him out. I was just lying here wondering if anyone would be able to mix a passable martini for me this noon or if I'd have to struggle down and do it myself."

Late in June I was set to the delightful task of copying complete in manuscript form EB's small book *Here Is New York*. Never having read it—although by a trick of good fortune I was soon to own a copy—I doubly enjoyed this assignment, which indicated EB was still vacillating on a decision about a publication date for the *Letters*. Was *it* to be the first volume in the uniform edition of his works or should the *Essays* precede it? *Here Is New York* was going to appear in its entirety in the *Essays;* momentarily that manuscript seemed to be taking precedence over the *Letters*.

During the summer he was thinking, speaking, and often worrying to his New York agent, Jap Gude, over a phone call from Hollywood about the making of a movie version of *The Trumpet of the Swan*. The call came from the producers Hanna-Barbera, who had been responsible for the "near fiasco" of *Charlotte's Web*. EB did not use that phrase about the immensely popular film on any occasion except when "chatty Joe Barbera" was attempting to get his hands on Louis the swan. "He is all full of sweetness and light with the film in the can but he was remote as a goat when I offered suggestions on the screenplay."

"You had better tone that down a bit before you write to Mr. Barbera," advised K mildly.

"I'm not going to write to him. Let Jap take care of it."

"Have you written to Jap yet?" K wanted to know.

"No, but I know what I'm going to say. It's going to be a one-liner: 'I don't want to hand Joe Barbera *The Trumpet* to blow.' " He got no appreciative smile for his pains. K had learned early and remembered late that "A pun is the lowest form of wit," and she served up a reminder frequently.

The expected letter to Jap Gude did not materialize that morning but some more old letters, to be copied as manuscript,

did. One of them spoke of Mrs. Freethy and her thirty artesians. It was an odd phrase and I inquired about it. "Nobody
has that many wells," I told EB, trying to excuse my curiosity.
He was obliging; he explained that Mrs. Freethy had been their
cook in Maine in the 1950s, a time when the name of Queen
Elizabeth II was a headliner. Mrs. Freethy had remarked to
him that "a gown was being made for her [the queen] by thirty
artesians." As a malapropism it was charming but for lack of
space it was edited out of the *Letters*, as was many another
cheerful anecdote.

Summer was punctuated by another hospital trip for EB and
a strict diet to be adhered to on his return; by a visit from
Walter Cronkite one afternoon when he was vacationing and
visiting in the area; and by some confused business letters K
and I had become involved in. We had difficulty straightening
them out because she seemed to be writing to granddaughter
Sarah and a Boston jeweler (with an order for a porringer for
Sarah's new baby) at the same time. Unable to summon the
word to mind, she had referred to the porringer variously as "a
kind of cereal dish with handles" and a "silver baby's bowl for
porridge." EB did not help matters, listening in, sipping iced
coffee, and playing with Susy.

"Who has a silver baby, if you don't mind the inquiry?"

She did mind and he was ignored, but her lapses sometimes
were contagious and the porringer episode induced another
one, partly my fault. Writing once more to a friend about a
choice of college for Martha White, her 19-year-old granddaughter, K said, "New-fangled, boys and girls all mixed up
together." Then she added, "No, that's not the way to express
it. What's the term I want?" All that came into my head was
"bisexual." Fully aware it was wrong, I risked saying it nevertheless and the three of us were overcome with mirth. Like-

wise, the elusive word came to all of us at approximately the same time. "Coed" we announced to each other proudly.

By Labor Day K managed to have half a dozen important tasks that had to be attended to on the holiday, and EB finally looked and sounded better after a dreary July and August. He showed me a single praying mantis living in the plant room. "I've decided to call it Reggie. It has an insatiable appetite so save all your flies for it." Feeling a bit ridiculous but anxious to be helpful, I toted along a packet of six flies on Wednesday. Reggie was decidedly a long and lean type and my flies were on the corpulent side but he managed to adjust himself to the entrée.

Off and on all that summer, while copying material for the *Essays*, I had dreamed ahead to the publication day, full of impatience to be through with telephone consultations, exchanges of letters about format, book jacket, price; signing of contracts; proofreading. When could one hope for the book itself? In the winter? In spring? Surely before another summer. What a blow fell in September, the day EB placed the manuscript in the mail! The covering letter that I copied from his rough draft had him suggesting they retain the manuscript in their files for a year or more, publishing his *Letters* first. My own selfish reaction was that I longed to see in print the material I had hovered over so conscientiously; I was convinced the essays would have a wider, more eager audience than the letters. I was never so wrong as on that conviction; neither did I suspect how much copying lay ahead on the *Letters*, nor how eagerly I would be awaiting *its* publication. The *Essays*, as it turned out, arrived in the mail one day in the autumn of 1977 when we were unaware—and scarcely cared—that publication had taken place. The household had changed to an extent no one could have visualized in 1973, and the appearance of a carton of new books (ordinarily a circumstance for rejoicing) was relegated at that point to the category of minor happenings.

Every October for more than fifty years I have whispered to myself, "O, World, I cannot get thee close enough," the opening line of Edna St. Vincent Millay's poem, "God's World." So it was exciting to find that some of K's correspondence that month was about the poet. Nancy Milford, who was preparing a biography of Millay, wanted anecdotes or impressions from K, since Millay had had a brief *New Yorker* connection during K's early years there. The biographer wanted also to drop in at the Whites' on her way from New York to do research in Camden, Maine, but K refused, justifying the refusal with a plea of ill health.

She might just as readily have excused herself by leaning on the full mailbag. It was brimming over with messages from children who probably had made the acquaintance of spider, pig, mouse, or swan during summer vacations. Once in a while when an address or a teacher's comment eluded her and a frenzied search ensued, even EB's office was not held sacred. It was neatly ransacked as bookmarks were shaken out of books; the wastebasket explored; even the sheet music on the seldom-played piano sifted through. If, as happened occasionally, the missing items were not found, the upheaval rarely was in vain. Nearly always we uncovered some lost possession that had been overlooked before, and K's joy in the recovery of buried treasure mitigated her dismay over the letters that could not be acknowledged. Mothers who had read *Charlotte* in their own childhood and were now reading it to their offspring often confided the fact to the author. "Makes a man feel old," complained EB after one search, as he settled somewhat stiffly down to a noontime break. "Another twenty years and I'll be hearing about their grandchildren. I hope I'm not around for that."

"Well," commented K, imperturbable that morning about future discord, "it's only you who has changed. Isn't it nice that Stuart and Charlotte and Louis never age?"

"I suppose so. If I believed in reincarnation, I might like to return as Wilbur, although I suppose Stuart had more fun."

The autumn leaves had not yet fallen when, in October, requests began going out to K's favorite New York shops. EB's hair seemed appreciably more gray and the lines in his forehead deeper.

"K, for God's sake, it's not even Hallowe'en yet! Can't we postpone Christmas plans till November?"

We couldn't and didn't. The season was such a busy one that there was scant time to record some of K's innocent but hilarious utterances. One of them, however, connected with New York's Brooks Brothers, has stayed carbon-copied in memory. I was told to ask Andy what they had done about his order for a red man's bathrobe. How I longed to append an irreverent "Pocahontas" at the end of my note to him.

K, however, had many moments of inspired writing and speaking. A journal entry recalls the coherent and compelling note she struck when Solzhenitsyn's Nobel "Lecture on Literature" came into her hands: ". . . I have just read it through and was moved by its sorrowful beginning and elevated by its inspiring last chapters." Her summing up of Harold Ross's special genius, in a remark worthy of EB himself, was made more than once to friends or relations who happened to initiate a literary conversation: "The art of starting a magazine from scratch was to see potential talent in small beginnings and Ross was great at that."

Isabel Russell

The Watergate scandal blotted out many other all-encompassing issues. "We are living through history, my dear. What a pity. Disgraceful, utterly reprehensible history. I feel almost personally responsible to coming generations who will be reading about Nixon's perfidy."

I carefully hid from her the taint of Republicanism that had flowed through the veins of my ancestors for generations; I understood only too well her feeling of personal responsibility. If she, as an Independent, felt that way, how much more was I to blame for the President's misdoings, in view of my heavy labors for the Republican party in past years? A journal entry for October 24: "K leaning on the sorry state to which the presidency has been brought 'by that archfiend in the White House.' Was roundly scolded because I said I simply couldn't bear to listen to Nixon's apologetic explanations on TV tomorrow night, re the dismissing of Archibald Cox. She said I must listen if I wanted to be well informed on current events. To insure it, she would question me at work on Friday. Grrrrrr. Sometimes she makes me feel like a third-grader cursed with a severe teacher. Later, the proposed speech got changed to a press conference; then even that was postponed. Coward. [Nixon, presumably.] But it got me off the hook."

Usually when I arrived at work at 9 A.M. there were staff members—cook in the kitchen, housekeeper in living room or office—to talk to about the weather and the temper of the household; but now and then would come a morning when K and Edith Candage would be in conference in the bedroom and Shirley Cousins would be at work upstairs. If Henry was not in the plant room or EB was not hovering over the wood-burning stove in the kitchen, there was no lingering at the back of the house; I went directly through the front hall to my office. On one such morning in November it became obvious immediately that Jones had lost his biscuits on the front hall floor at the foot of the stairway. I fetched paper towels, a basin of detergent and water, and a rag and went down on my knees to clean it up. K, coming along the upstairs hall on her walker, leaned over the bannister to watch and to ask, "Isabel, have you enough to do if I spend some time with Henry on bulbs when I first come down?"

I waved my free hand at her, "Yes, plenty to do," and away she went taking her morning exercise stroll up and down, up and down the upstairs hall, while I continued to exercise myself, in more ways than one, over the rug. Perhaps her distance vision was failing to such an extent that she was unable to focus from upstairs hall to downstairs. If so, the slow-growing cataracts were maturing more swiftly than the doctors had predicted.

I was urged up to the attic early in November to seek out a group of postcards that had been mailed to K from Europe by her sister Elizabeth. By happy coincidence in the carton that held the box of postcards was a copy of an anniversary ode composed by EB thirty years before. It bore the date, November 13, 1943, at the top of the sheet, then the title, "Wedding Day in the Rockies." I scanned it hurriedly and was enormously impressed by a poet who could find a rhyme for "Wyoming" when composing a beautifully orchestrated sonnet. I carried it down to K and was rewarded with an absentminded smile and the comment, "It's difficult to remember so far back but I think I was pleased with it." She returned it to me with an air of "It really doesn't matter much now," and that, of course, was too much for a sentimental handmaiden to bear. EB was in his lair talking to Jones, so I handed over the sheet with an urgent request: "Please, please file it somewhere readily available and let it be printed some day for your readers to enjoy." Naturally he gave no pledge, and it was eight long years before he decided to share it with the world.

On November 16 he met Dorothy Guth at Bangor Airport. She was to spend a few days at the Whites' home going over the basics of her editing chores for the *Letters;* there was much tedious groundwork to be covered in the way of collecting correspondence before any other aspects of editing and publication could be considered. The daily grind proceeded at an uneven tenor during Mrs. Guth's visit. I did extra typing, much of it at home, and saw her only briefly during my tour of duty. She was mild-mannered and accommodating, and managed to proceed competently with her assignment, unruffled by K's interruptions and comments. During her stay the dining-room table and many of the chairs were littered with notebooks, papers, folders, and other paraphernalia; there was much diligent searching out of material from shelves in the bedrooms, study, office, and attic. EB asked, each time I came within his line of vision, "Do you recall—?" Sometimes I did, but more often than not I didn't. He was preoccupied and nervous and it was not the time to speak smugly of carbon copies that should have been kept. It was one of the infrequent occasions when his occupation, rather than K's, came to the fore and caused some disturbance in the household. Nobody minded; certainly it was his turn. K and I were by no means comatose, though; Christmas, after all, was just around the corner, even though Thanksgiving turkeys were still strutting and gobbling in total innocence of what lay ahead.

I made out a running list for K to indicate to whom thank-you notes had been written as soon as gifts began arriving in early December. She had opened several of them and written her appreciations promptly, so one Monday morning I tried to get a list of persons she might have contacted in my absence over the weekend. "There were two," she said, handing me a memo with one name on it.

"What was the other name, please?"

"Oh, that was for the big red tin box of pretzels; whoever unwrapped it threw away the brown paper and there was no gift card inside so I don't know who sent it."

"Oh. Then you wrote only one thank-you."

"No," firmly, "*two*, I said."

"Then please may I have the name of the second one?" She was exasperated. "I just told you: it went to the person who sent the pretzel gift. I didn't have any name because they threw away the outer wrapping." With that I had to be content, until about five minutes later, when she called from the living room, "Just say pretzels on the list." Fully three weeks elapsed before I learned that she had not, as I foolishly feared, dispatched a thank-you to "the little man who wasn't there." She had instead followed the sensible procedure of writing a note of inquiry to the gift shop whose imprint was attached to the box cover.

On Thursday, December 13, I invited a friend for lunch and a pre-Christmas shopping expedition to Camden; she had just accepted when K phoned to ask me to pick up an item at the village store on my way to work. Nothing had been said on Wednesday about my being expected the following day. I called my friend, apologized, and requested a postponement; then I made haste to do K's errand. Coming downstairs at 10 A.M., she gazed at me thoughtfully. "Well, my goodness, here you are. How does this happen? Is it Friday?"

"No, it's Thursday. You asked me to bring along cream from the store, Mrs. White, for your luncheon guests."

"Oh. Oh yes, of course. They must be coming today, then. Are they?"

I stifled a hysterical giggle. "I don't know, Mrs. White. I don't even know their names."

"Well, somebody had better know their names if they're coming today. Andy! ANDY! Is anybody coming today?"

He was an oasis of calm in the turbulence. "Nobody today, K. Those two young persons from Bangor will be here tomorrow."

"Well, of course. I suppose the cream will keep—but you're a day early with it," she said, leveling an accusing look at me. "It's fortunate you decided to come today, though, because I won't be able to work tomorrow, but I can use you Saturday." With uncanny prescience she had contrived to pull the rug out from under my weekend entertaining, too. Sometimes I felt pilloried.

On the following Wednesday she was in bed with what she termed "another aggravating back crunch." On top of the stack of papers and cards, proliferating in wild disarray on bed and bedside table, was a card addressed to Merrill Leach, the associate of the Merrill Hinckley store in Blue Hill where much of the household shopping was done. The envelope contained a check, a gift which was supposed to have been mailed early in the month. I recalled handing it to her at least two weeks previously for her signature. I remembered also that she had asked for it a week ago—"It's lost; what did you do with it? It must be found,"—and I had located it again that day and placed it atop the cards to be signed. Apparently it had slipped notice. I picked it up and tried to persuade K to sign it while I stood by; then it could go safely downstairs with the out-going mail, but she waved me away impatiently. There were a dozen items to attend to—the check could wait. Get Carroll Reed Ski

Shop on the phone; leave Bonwit's number available for a call she would make. Put these on Andy's desk for him to read; bring down two large cartons from the attic. Wrap four books in gift wrap, two with ribbon to go under the tree, the others plain with cord to go in book bags; mark the titles on the outside. Phone Allene [son Joel's wife] and ask what size skirt she wears; ask Edith if the turkey came. Call Maison Glass in New York and find out where that plum pudding and caviar is. Pretty soon it will be too late.

EB had a few packages of his own that needed "fluffy stuff or something." Was I awfully busy? Of course not; besides, I'd rather do fluffy stuff than anything else I could think of. At noontime my desk was still snowed under. I popped into K's bedroom and snatched her good-bye line away from her. "I hope your back will feel better tomorrow; I'd better come to work again or we won't be caught up by Christmas Day."

"Certainly. I can use you every day until the holiday."

Next morning, before I had had a chance to inquire about her health, she cried: "I've managed to mislay Merrill Leach. Or perhaps we never did write a card for him? I vaguely remember something about it last week, don't I? Did I make out a check? Can you find him?" I began to laugh and went on and on helplessly, unable to stop or to explain.

"Nice to find you so pleased with life this morning," commented EB, stepping into the bedroom to give a magazine to his wife.

"All I did was say 'Merrill Leach' and somehow it set her off," responded K.

"Maybe you've said his name once too often this season," EB told her, ingeniously putting his finger on the problem with the first try. When I had conquered my laughter, I became, once again, the exuberant beagle bugling after its quarry, and managed to run it to the ground in a brief time. Merrill Leach was being used as a bookmark in the volume K had been reading in bed; he was all properly signed, with the check folded inside, so I gladly sealed him up and ran downstairs to consign him to the mailbag before he could be sidetracked once more.

On the day after Christmas EB was deeply depressed by news of the death of his oldest friend, Howard Cushman. For half a century they had kept in touch; when visiting was not possible, they relied on telephone and correspondence. It was a severe loss: Cushman had been an important chum in EB's youth, especially as his companion in the vigorous cross-country journey celebrated in *Farewell to Model T.* I knew little of Cushman beyond the chatty letters that came across my desk with the draft of a reply clipped thereto. The Model T book added slightly to the saga, and some of the old letters I was typing for the *Letters* enlarged the picture, but there were many other persons entwined in the life of the Whites who were more familiar to me than Cushman was. About many of them I could have said something that had admiring overtones, in an effort to extend comfort, but not this time. It didn't seem to matter; when death struck, EB's reactions were not merely those of a writer; they were similar to reactions of the computer expert, the postman, the athlete. He was touched, but then carried on. All he needed for a short time was someone to listen, someone to look sympathetic, someone to respond with empathy to his own desolate expression. He sat on the Victorian couch in my office, swinging one leg, toying with K's sterling-silver cigarette box on the coffee table, while reminiscing about college escapades he and Cushman had shared. Then he walked back and forth between fireplace and table, picking up odd trinkets, holding them up to the sunlight, and replacing them, pontificating meanwhile on the woes of growing old and living long enough to bury one's contemporaries, for whom one cared deeply. Abruptly coming to a halt beside my desk and observing the heap of papers piled upon it, he apologized. "I just wanted a wailing wall," he explained, turning away.

·ও SIX ঙ·

Pardon me just a minute, K. I have a request for Isabel."

"Well—well, I don't know. This *has* to go in today's—"

"It won't take more than a minute. Isabel, do you remember if I wrote to the Library of Congress last week? Or any time this month?"

"It doesn't sound familiar so I don't think so, but of course, maybe—Oh dear—"

He broke in. "Don't say 'If only.' I'm afraid it would break me up."

There was one way to aid the recall. "Do you remember," I asked him, "whether you were answering a communication from them? Or did you initiate the correspondence?"

"That's easy. They didn't write to me; I had a request for them."

"Well, then," triumphantly, "you didn't write, because if you had written, I would have been trying to pin down the exact address and zip code and I would remember the effort."

"Good thinking, and it just proves what I've said all along— we don't need carbon copies. Now I want to get this right out so if you can just hold off on your things until next time, K?"

"Certainly not." She was tapping her foot in frustration by

then. "This letter I'm doing is all for your benefit. I'm trying to order your comforter."

It was exactly the line he wanted. A boyish grin erupted. "That can wait, K. You're all the comforter I need. Anything more would be sheer indulgence."

Early in March I came to work at exactly the right moment to view a goose-and-gander parade that EB was watching from the window of my office. Five geese and two ganders were strolling single file across the yard and along the driveway in dignified procession, so serious in their objective of getting from wherever they'd been to wherever they were going that one could almost imagine they were toting placards for the support of some great fowl cause. They were being led by the patriarch of the clan, who had fathered most of the brood, followed closely by Felicity, who had laid most of the eggs and hatched most of the goslings. Status and consequence must have been discussed before the trek began, EB remarked, because Apathy was trailing meekly along after Felicity. (Apathy was a non-entity in the barnyard hierarchy, having shown a regrettable tendency to lay soft-shelled eggs.) A couple of nondescripts, unidentifiable, formed the rear guard.

Dotty Guth was expected to arrive late in the month for another conference and more work on the *Letters* manuscript, and by the middle of March K was in a frenzy about the annual spring-cleaning, far in advance of the yearly rite in April. She had faced Dotty's previous visit with equanimity, and this time, it seemed to her staff, she had less reason to be disturbed because Dotty, her husband, and two children were going to occupy a rented cottage in South Blue Hill.

My office, formerly K's study, was the focal point of spring-cleaning schemes. The big airy room contained several choice examples of Victorian furniture, and a fireplace that EB thoughtfully lighted on cold days. A magnificent cherry high-boy, storing office supplies, shared one wall with an antique mahogany table—the table so heaped with garden catalogues that they would have threatened the stability of a less well-made piece of furniture. A comfortable easy chair (in which no one found time to take any ease), a sofa, and lamp table occupied the opposite wall. There were floor-to-ceiling bookshelves, three filing cabinets, and a dictionary stand, as well as my typewriter table and a Governor Winthrop desk. A closet door opened on one side of the fireplace; a connecting door to the living room was on the other. This small pass-through had space for a telephone and a few miscellaneous objects. In general the office was so crowded with miscellany that I formed the habit of carrying an attaché case to work, in order to have a spot for the safekeeping of pencils, notebook, carbon paper and other sundries; and I sometimes wondered, especially when we were enduring a period of a mislaid manuscript or valuable book, if K harbored vague suspicions of its having been carried off in the briefcase.

Periodically she would announce, "We simply must do something about your crowded office." The implication seemed to be that I was crowding it unduly by my mere physical presence, and perhaps I was, being a tall, long-limbed person. On March 15, K, leaning heavily on her walker, bustled in, full of energy and inspiration and plans to uncrowd my office.

"We shall have to put away all the file folders," and she seized four of them and tried vainly to push them into a full file drawer.

"I'm afraid there's no room," I apologized, but she continued to crush them. "You'll just have to make some room," and she abandoned the half-open drawer and approached the table. "What are all these catalogues and magazines doing here? We shall have to sort them out and throw away the old ones. Bring them into the living room; while I'm sorting, see what else you can clean up."

Almost instantly she became so engrossed in an article on water lilies in one of the magazines taken to the living room, that it was plain to see she would be submerged half an hour or more, so it was the right time to execute a plan I had long had in mind: investigating the fireplace closet to see if there would be space in it for the untidy cartons sitting under the highboy.

The pried-open door revealed a conglomeration of skates and rubbers. Arranged along a clothes-rod were several old raincoats and a jacket. It all looked like just the sort of thing to donate to a yard sale. The closet was very deep and dark; unfortunately, therefore, nothing was visible beyond the coats. More unfortunately I was not curious enough to move them. I scooped up the junk on the floor and pushed it into a corner of the office, ready to show to K. Then I dragged three of the obnoxious cartons into the closet to fill the space where the junk had been. It made such a splendid beginning that I was inspired to greater accomplishments. I had no further designs on the closet, at least until K had been consulted, but I did have high hopes that she might be persuaded to part with some of the older files in the cabinets, thereby freeing space for the ones that were littering chairs and tables. I removed an armful of folders not looked at in years from one of the file cabinets, and, operating under the assumption (later proved erroneous) that she would agree to store them in the attic, I squeezed all the other folders into their places. If she proved not too obdurate about discarding issues 1968 through 1973 of catalogues from Saks, Lord & Taylor, Omaha Steaks International, et al., there would be a chance to make the whole room tidy.

When a propitious moment came, I interrupted her magazine scanning: "I wonder if we could look over some of the boots and skates and clothes in the small closet and see if any of them are suitable for a rummage sale? Then I'd have room to put all the cartons out of sight there." Valor could go just so far; discretion kept me from admitting that some cartons had already been moved.

K was baffled. "What small closet?"

"The one in my office."

"I don't know what you're talking about. Let me see the things." She examined with care an armful of boots and skates. "Well, I can't imagine—well, well. None of these things have been used for years; I thought they were discarded long ago. Put everything over there; we'll pack it for a charity event."

Aware from past experience how likely she was to change her mind between lunch and dinner, I longed to get everything out of the living room into a box labeled "Sale" but didn't dare insist. If, however, I had ceased speaking of the closet right then, part of the operation might have been successful. However, flushed with my small victory, I brought out an armful of clothing into the living room. K gave one horrified look: "These are our good raincoats, we wear them all the time. Where did you get them?"

I was meek and embarrassed. "From the office closet."

"There isn't any closet in the office. These came from the clothes closet. Right there." She pointed behind my chair to a door on the right of the living room fireplace. I had opened it just once when requested to copy a label from a certain Brooks Brothers raincoat. I opened it again, mystified. In back of the coat rack, barely visible through the remaining garments, were three obnoxious cartons on the floor. An open door beyond them let in a bar of light from my office. It was scarcely the time to laugh but neither would it have helped to cry, so I took the cheerful route and in all justice to K, it has to be recorded that she joined in, generously conceding that she had forgotten the closet's double doors. Back went the raincoats; back, after considered second thoughts, went boots and skates. Back also (unobtrusively) went the cartons to their original home under the highboy. Out of eighty or so nursery catalogues only six were discarded; back went the rest onto the crowded table. She could see no reason for transferring unused folders to the attic so back they went to the file, and out came the others to be once again disposed gracefully on coffee table and couch. An abortive expedition all round and it served me right—what else but disaster could be expected from the Ides of March? Presently we settled down to dealing with fan mail from children and the entire clean-the-office episode was shelved haphazardly. "What an exhausting morning!" K observed to EB at noon, "we've cleaned out the entire office— and such an accumulation as there was!"

"Good job!" approved EB, whose own quarters were always shipshape and inviting, "I'll have a look." He disappeared through the small passageway and was back almost immediately. "Admirable," he complimented, and briefly raised his martini glass to each of us. "I don't know how you girls manage to accomplish so much in so little time."

K's guest preparations approached their zenith as she began stocking the Guth cottage with groceries, bedding, and small niceties. Presently it became too much of an effort for her, so one chore, food shopping, was delegated to EB and he was baffled by a few of the "fast-food" items on the list. What, he wanted to know, was cranapple juice? How much frozen orange juice should be purchased at one time in reasonable expectation of its holding over for a week, and how did you prepare it? Was there any such thing as a good brand of instant coffee?, he inquired, voice dripping with sarcasm. The way he pronounced the word "instant," as though it were a loathsome adjective unfit to be paired with an honest noun like "coffee," conjured up a vision of his own early-morning brew perking away in an old-fashioned enameled coffee pot on the wood stove. Had the instant version been prepared from beans ground in an old-time coffee grinder? I felt called upon to defend absent, innocent Dotty, who had supplied the list. "Instant coffee is a perfectly good substitute for the real thing when you're in a hurry," I assured him, "and Dotty will be busy working with you when she's in Maine and won't have time to linger over breakfast. Probably at home she has regular coffee, just as you do." Food topics were often intertwined with more lofty subjects when I was saying noontime farewells to the Whites; fortunately for our family's reputation, I could vouch for all our rice being wild, all our bread being mixed and kneaded by hand, and our coffee beans ground in an electric grinder.

Dotty and her godfather were unobtrusively busy in the dining room when next I reported for work; papers were spread out on the big table and they sorted and discussed, murmuring in low tones. Although EB interrupted K's dictation now and then to pose a question or to request that a sheet be copied, K bravely carried on, dictating five pages to the *New Yorker*'s William Maxwell in regards to Helen Thurber's laments about the Bernstein biography of Jim Thurber. A generous allotment of the letter was given over to K's own distress about the way the description of her divorce had been handled in the book, and at that juncture in the dictation she carefully moved the session to my office, ostensibly to insure that she didn't disturb the literary laborers nearby. Later in the week she gave up temporarily on her own projects so that when I appeared at work it was merely to collect typing assignments from EB or Dotty to take home.

During one day of the Guth visit all members of that family were invited to dine at noon at the Whites', in celebration of the small daughter's birthday. It had been a long time since K had entertained exuberant children; with the exception of John Henry Angell, all her grandchildren were in their teens or older, and greatgrands were still babies. The party so exhausted her that she was unable to come downstairs for the evening meal. After the four Guths had departed homeward, she spoke in a letter to a friend of how she had entertained Dotty, her husband, and their three children at a birthday fete. "Probably it seemed like three but there were only two," EB corrected, overhearing, and K managed a feeble smile at her own expense.

The months of May and June were unusually hot in 1974; EB's allergy to various weeds and grasses nearly overpowered him and K's vitality was notably diminished. On the first cool day, therefore, she was her most impetuous self when it came to sifting over moldy matters. The first of these that caught her eye was a letter from Mollie Panter-Downes in England. It hadn't been acknowledged and it was, horrors, six months old. Right under it was a Medicare pronouncement she was sure had not been read by Andy. "Take it to him immediately and ask what he thinks." [He thinks Dammit, I don't want to be interrupted.] There was a batch of children's fan letters from a school in Hawaii. They appeared to have come direct rather than to have been processed in advance by Harper and Row, and such letters demanded prompt replies because the student writers had not received the general Harper acknowledgment and folder (with a' bio and catalogue of EB's books) that preceded the more personal North Brooklin touch. "We have left undone those things which we ought to have done," K quoted gloomily from the Book of Common Prayer. I had just time to scribble a reminder about an envelope of keepsakes for Cornell; then we were launched on the usual long stint of dictation and six months went by before the Cornell envelope received its initial contribution.

Came a letter to K from a friend who was convalescing from a long illness; a nurse had been delegated to write the letter for her. It revealed a few facts, unwittingly, about the nurse herself: doubtless she was willing and obliging, and she wrote a neat, legible hand, but as events transpired she was wandering in unfamiliar territory when the topic of best-selling books arose. Midway through a discussion of books K's friend had been reading, the letter diverged into a query about the Washington scene—or so we assumed, when there was a reference to Watergate Dam. "Very odd," K commented, "because she never has cared a fig about politics. Twice when I mentioned Nixon in my own letters she never bothered to comment."

I glanced where she pointed; the writing was clear; the nurse had referred to Watergate Dam. Because the word Watergate and its related subject, Nixon's involvement, was one of the items uppermost in the minds of informed persons at that time, K felt justified in mounting her favorite hobby-horse and galloping off at a great pace. Hoping that this time her words might have some effect, she castigated the president thoroughly in abrasive language, and in a long summation, forecast his ultimate downfall.

Finally she paused to light a cigarette from the stub of a

relinquished one. "Do you think it will do any good to harangue her?"

"Well, if she's not at all politics-oriented, I fear she'll just skim over it. It's odd, though, that she would veer to Watergate when she was in the middle of a sentence about bestsellers."

"There isn't any title that sounds like Watergate Dam, is there?"

Of course there was. "Do you suppose she meant Richard Adams' book *Watership Down* and the nurse sort of blocked it out in her mind because she wasn't familiar with the Adams opus?"

"Well. Well now, certainly, that's exactly what happened. Oh, that careless nurse!" and forthwith my notes were scratched, and the dictation begun again, with K leaning heavily on rabbits where previously she had leaned on the White House.

July 11 was a milestone in misery for EB, the beleaguered writer. His physical condition was fair but his mental attitude was not. He could experience no euphoria when there was so much work to be done on the *Letters* manuscript and other projects; when the stack of unanswered fan mail on his desk spilled over onto the typewriter table; and when the occasion of his seventh-fifth birthday inspired more than the usual number of persons to hound him with excessive, expensive congratulations on having achieved the three-quarter-century mark. Reminded that he would have to take a road test for driving before the end of the year, he growled, "The only rule I know is 'Never hit anybody or anything.' The rest of the rules are just so much raggle-taggle."

Many a well-wisher saluted him in verse of sorts. Hoping not to be outdone, I whisked up one of my own and was pleased to learn I had achieved the blue ribbon for brevity:

Isabel Russell

To E.B. White on the
Solemn Occasion of His 75th
Hardly a person is now alive
Who really looks forward to seventy-five.

A nine-year-old boy, in a brief letter, went directly to the heart
of the matter: "Happy birthday. Write and tell me all about
what's going on there."

Charlotte's creator had been invited by *The New Yorker* to
write a piece in honor of his special birthday. On the day of
the magazine's deadline he could be heard dictating it by
telephone to New York. Later he said smoothly to K: "I would
have liked to show it to you first but I knew you'd want me to
rewrite it and there just wasn't time." She had been discussing
an entirely unrelated matter with him: how much could they
afford to contribute to two local fund drives, one for Blue Hill
Memorial Hospital, one for the Brooklin cemetery? It was a
simple decision: "Give the most to the cemetery, K; we'll be
there longer."

A birthday-gift book, James Lipton's *An Exaltation of Larks*,
engendered a brief discussion on the medieval terms of venery.
For the first and only time in our association, EB and I were
on relatively equal terms of literary acumen. We confessed to
each other that we had not known a group of larks constituted
an "exaltation." "A pride of lions" was as far as his or my
vocabulary extended in connection with the so-called beasts of
venery, referred to in modern parlance as collective nouns.
Lipton had researched with painstaking care; then he had
added some original terms of venery to the old ones. We
couldn't resist inventing a few of our own. In one of those rapid
exchanges of phrasing that came so readily to EB, but not so

easily to me, we compiled a small list. He led it off and I followed slowly:

"A fervency of preachers."

"A soaring of seagulls."

"A resignation of spinsters."

"A modesty of maidens."

"A humility of religious."

"An exaggeration of advertisers."

"A torrent of terriers," as Jones and Susy came tearing down the hall, into the study, up onto the small sofa, and back through the hall, in an excess of high spirits.

"An isolation of hermits."

EB had the last word, enlarging on one of his favorite aphorisms: "There is nothing new under the sun, especially when it comes to arranging words in the English language. Within a month or two somebody else will be given credit for what you and I have just spent a painful few minutes composing." There were more important matters occupying his mind that day, but he poked his head into my office late in the morning to offer "A discrepancy of computers," and after that the subject was closed.

Early in December K began dictating a series of long letters, alternated with short notes, to friends and relatives, the gist of the message being "we aren't going to send Christmas cards this year because postage rates are climbing so." The futility of spending postage to save postage did not occur to her, but finally EB remarked on the idiosyncracy. She brushed his objections aside. "I know, I know; it's a pity to run up the postage bill but people will expect to receive cards from us so this is an absolutely necessary expenditure." On the eighteenth, with a week still to go, she began to fear the holiday was creeping up too fast and she might be found wanting. "I must give you your Christmas gift before you leave, so be sure to remind me," she admonished. "You might get sick and not be here Friday or Monday." I reassured her that I planned to stay healthy and to hang right in there helping her until the last minute, but it was as though I hadn't spoken. "In fact, I doubt you'll like it. It's ugly."

EB, emerging from the coat closet with his jacket in hand, said, *sotto voce* and sad-eyed, "We make a practice of giving ugly gifts to the unsuspecting." The present K referred to was offered in addition to the regular *New Yorker* subscription and a basket of Florida citrus fruit. It was *The New Yorker* full-page diary for 1975 and the selection of drawings ["Do not refer to them as cartoons"] was, as always, incredibly funny. The gift cards had progressed to "Much love from Katharine and Andy White," with a postscript of profuse thanks for assistance rendered above and beyond the call of duty.

Another year (1975): new calendars, the new date to remember on letters and checks, new projects hanging around about to be added to the old. Would we ever get to the assembling and packing of the garden books? Indeed we did, on a Saturday when I had (foolishly) scheduled a cookfest at home.

Cartons and newspapers were stacked in big heaps upstairs, downstairs, in the dining room, north porch, and hallway by the time I arrived.

K: We'll wrap in the office.

ME: How can we? There's no table or desk space.

K: On the floor, of course.

ME (kindly but firmly): Really, Mrs. White, neither your back nor mine can take the strain of wrapping books on the floor.

"Well," thoughtfully, "the north porch then." Splendid decision. The north porch, with its big, sturdy (empty) table was where we always had wrapped items before.

"Where's my pencil? Where are my glasses? Where are the Sierra Club books? [She had presented them to the local library.] Where are the lists?" Rereading my journal account and recalling the day, I think of the bugbear of those lists: it took five of them, three for me and two for her, and it entailed much scurrying to duplicate packing-lists five times for each carton while checking them with the larger lists in hand, especially since K's two lists rarely *were* in hand: they were laid down under books or newspapers or wrapped inside other books that she was packaging while I was checking.

As far as was possible in my relationship with the Whites I refrained from mentioning to them any matters of ill-health or other family problems, being well aware how many difficulties of their own they had to surmount, and recognizing how easily they became disturbed over even minor crises. Early in February, however, the rule was broken because I had to explain why I was late for work, having had to transport the dear friend who lived with us to the hospital that morning after he had suffered a violent nosebleed. K dwelt with sympathetic animation on all the gory details and called EB in, when he was passing her bedroom, to share them with him. "Nosebleed?" said he in a reminiscent tone. "Who had one at the office?" K started to reply but he went right on, "Ah, yes, it was McKelway— remember, K? He died young. It was liver, of course, but along the way he had lots of nosebleeds. They never could decide whether there was a connection."

With that piece of good cheer to fortify me, I repaired to my typewriter where I was engaged chiefly in copying a rough draft of a "Letter from the East" that EB was preparing for the fiftieth anniversary edition of *The New Yorker.* My friend, I am happy to report, survived the nosebleed and several others, developed no liver problems, and did not die young.

Brendan Gill's *Here at The New Yorker* was published that winter; a copy naturally reached the Whites, and it caused K some anguish because her memory and Gill's were sometimes at odds on events of the early years. When her concern reached the stage where it was unsettling her physically, her favorite writer came as near as he ever did to scolding her. "I will not let any book affect your health, K, my dear. If you wish to continue annotating that book, you must keep calm; if not, I'm going to hide our copy."

Mindful of the terrible threat, she began concentrating on an error she thought she detected when Gill had been recounting an anecdote that was precious to her. She referred to it as "The tale of Thurber's seal's whiskers" and managed to relate the story to me one day in most entertaining fashion. It was not a piece of dictation intended for the Bryn Mawr—or any other—list; it was merely a pleasant conversational interlude. It was interesting and amusing; I should have been alert enough to set it down in shorthand immediately, exactly as she told it, because there might come a time when she decided to preserve it for future generations. Only two days later I was chagrined to have my afterthought realized; she dictated the seal story, but it differed widely from the spoken version of two days before. There was no time in the day's crowded schedule to attend to the seal. When I next reported for work she had forgotten the previous dictation; a third version of the seal episode had been written in longhand and left for copying into a smooth draft. It made peculiar reading and little sense.

Worse, there was no humor in it, as there had been in the oral recitation.

Mustering all the strength that could be mustered, I approached her to say tentatively, "I think we're a bit mixed up on the seal's whiskers. You know, Mrs. White, you are probably one of the very few persons who can tell the story accurately. Please, don't dictate it. Just tell it to me in your own words, as you did the other day."

For a moment I was certain the seal and I would drown. Her expression indicated faint outrage and perhaps it was justified. Was I setting myself up as an editor of an editor's work? Turning it over in her mind, however, she seemed to see the wisdom of it; it was likely she had struggled a long time over the written version and was not fully satisfied with it; an oral account could prove to be the easy solution. So she began once more and recited the incident lucidly and without hesitation, and we both laughed again at the conclusion. With some difficulty I got away from her to type out the tale before it eluded memory; her strident tones followed me across the passageway and into the office: "Remember, I have three important letters that must go today." When the seal's whiskers were returned to her, she had a pencil ready and twice started to cross out a line or add a word, but each time she thought better of it. The habit of editing was so ingrained, she scarcely could have read the Preamble to the Constitution or the Gettysburg Address without blue-penciling them. Finally she nodded and handed the sheet back to me. "Put this in the Gill folder. You've finally got it right."

EB was engaged in simpler matters. He showed us a fan letter, containing a snapshot taken in the Philadelphia area, of a sign near the lake that was part of the city zoo. The lakeside sign announced that the two famous swans, Louis and Serena, from *The Trumpet of the Swan*, had courted there. That small honor accorded his book by zoo officials pleased EB tremendously, far more than had many a prestigious award that had come his way. It was typical of him; little things meant most. He had been wearing a long face for several mornings prior to receiving the zoo bulletin and I had been on a sharp lookout for anything that would lighten the somber mood. The zoo sign looked to be the precursor of more cheery occasions to come, and so it proved. When I had a question about a superficial error in a letter left for copying, his rejoinder was upbeat:

"As long as I don't have a bat in my hat."

"Or a rat in your vat," I offered. Surprised to receive a reply, he stopped to think a minute about a rejoinder: "Or a cat on my mat."

I couldn't contrive additional rhymes on the same sound so I changed to "Or a mink in your sink."

He was as ready as though rehearsed: "Or a fox in my box."

"Or an ox in your lox—but I'm afraid that's rather heavy-handed," I apologized.

"Heavy-hoofed, you mean. How about a mole in the coal?"

"Or a skunk in your bunk?"

"Ugh! I'd rather have a jay in the hay or a bear in my chair."

There was no end to the possibilities and he was wearing a broad smile, so I contributed one more, "A lark in your park," as I inserted a sheet in the typewriter.

"And a bee in your ghee," he concluded, taking the letter to be corrected into his study. I went back to K's assignments while waiting; when he brought in the new version of the correspondence there was a lightly penciled note at the top: "A finch in your winch," it said. That was, supposedly, the final word on the rhyming but I had been saving the best for the last and I appended it on a pink slip to the finished letter: "A gnu in your canoe." He was in the living room when I stopped at noon to make some arrangements with K. "A goat in your moat," was his acknowledgment of my polite good-bye.

Late in April EB went to Ellsworth to take a test for his license renewal—his seventy-five-year-old driving test, according to K. He was absent during most of the morning, and I was solicitous about his state of mind, wondering if he had been nervous about the exam when he left home. "Perfectly calm," stated K soberly, "except he forgot Henry."

"Henry?"

"Yes, he arranged yesterday with Henry about the length of time he'd be away and asked him to go along for moral support. This morning, though, he drove off without him."

When I stepped into the living room at noon to hand correspondence to K, there was the newly tested hero stretched out in his favorite chair, letting off steam. "I passed easily," he boasted, "but it was solely because of the Mercedes. The inspecting officer was much enamored of it."

Something I had read in my childhood about a much-revered Catholic saint popped into my head. "I knew you'd be successful," I told him, "I prayed to Saint Jude."

"Saint Who?"

"Saint Jude. The saint of the impossible."

K saved him from the necessity of a response by informing us that this was National Secretary Week and that all employers were encouraged to write a letter of appreciation to their secretaries. "But of course I didn't do it because it would only have made more work for you, so I will simply say that we greatly appreciate our secretary," she stated graciously. I said "Thank you," but was truthful with my opinion: that the recognition was unnecessary and made not much more sense than a National Pickle Week, which ran a weak second to Groundhog Day.

Presently an invitation arrived in the mail requesting the pleasure of the Whites' company at a social gathering on the following Saturday. "Come for Derby Day. Juleps. Time: 4:30. Bring your money." K was mystified. What sort of invitation was that? Had I ever seen a similar one? What did they plan to do with her money? I explained that it was a betting party. "If you take along a small sum of money and your horse wins and you parlay it into a big sum, just think: you'll have a fine contribution to make to the retirement gift for Martha Tyler when she leaves the Brooklin Library!" K rarely laughed heartily about anything but something about that sort of party appealed to her sense of humor and she went off into such a paroxysm that it brought on a fit of violent coughing, and I began to regret my light-hearted comment.

In Bangor on May 17 my family and I watched an appealing and satisfactory performance of *Charlotte's Web* under the title *Wilbur and the Web*. It was produced by a group known as The Theatre of the Enchanted Forest and director and performers offered a thoroughly professional presentation. They had applied through official channels for permission to create their revised version of the classic, and were blithely unaware of many another scenario that had been enacted offstage with a curt "No" prior to the day they were told "Yes." There had been voluminous correspondence exchanged in advance between EB and his New York agent, as well as with his attorney, before the favorable decision was reached. Nowhere in the country had similar groups been given any encouragement to proceed; anyone—and there were many—brash enough to go ahead without first obtaining official sanction was quickly disabused of the idea that any part of *Charlotte,* including her name, could be used for any purpose whatsoever. The Bangor group achieved its purpose by way of native status. EB was a pushover when it came to doing favors for residents of his adopted state.

Among the sentimental cameo portraits of EB that flash now and then through memory is one of him as he appeared on a balmy, fragrant day late in May. As I walked through the gate and under the big apple tree to the kitchen entrance, there he was, perched on the back steps, baby-sitting a couple of goslings who had been permitted to wander freely on the grass. Susy sat close beside him; his arm was around her and she clung with enthusiasm and muddy paws to his jacket, peering up at him with an expression of ecstasy. "Spring and Susy have me in their clutches," he averred.

Another cameo is totally different. He is sitting at the dining room table surrounded by manuscript pages, card indexes, notebook, scissors, and paste. His aspect is woebegone and he is clutching his head in both hands. The three years it took to assemble and edit the *Letters of E. B. White* were not altogether idyllic for the book's author. The manuscript was a persistent and unwelcome ghost, haunting his waking and sleeping hours, and he was more than half certain it would prove to be the worst of all possible specters at the bookshops— a turkey. The fact that my opinion was totally opposite (as the days went by and more and more interesting and wildly funny material appeared in my domain for retyping) did nothing to dislodge his pessimism. "You say things like that just to cheer me. You're not being strictly truthful." "You knew I was within hearing distance; that's why you began laughing so hard over those corny jokes." "I might as well be prepared for the worst right now; the letdown won't be so bad later."

Copying part of an introductory section one day, I noted that a doctor who had been summering in Bar Harbor was referred to as a "high irrigationist." "Whatever *that* is," I remarked, pointing to the phrase when EB came into the office with more notes. There must have been a series of light moments in connection with health—or the lack of it—that long-past summer, because a delighted grin spread over the patient's face.

"That doctor was a very fashionable one, so of course his specialty had to have a fancy name. But what his work actually amounted to was giving enemas."

"Oh," innocently, "I was guessing it meant a defect of character."

"Perhaps I had better pull you off this assignment; you are trying to beat me at my own game."

EB had a special talent for the role of grandparent and it was put to good use that summer with toddler John Henry Angell, whose parents spent the month of July in a shore cottage in a section of Brooklin known as The Haven. They brought along a baby-sitter, but sometimes when Roger and Carol were on a short sailing cruise or engaged in other pursuits that might have been wearisome to the youngster, he was heartily welcomed at the big house for a few games of croquet or various mundane farm diversions. He was fortunate to be there on the day the sage of Allen Cove announced he was tired of working over that year's crop of potential goslings and was about to give up on them. He departed for the barn to clear the nest of remaining eggs when suddenly he discovered a cracked shell and heard a gosling peep.

Shades of James Herriot! With John Henry standing by, delighted, Grandfather managed to separate the tiny prisoner from its cell; then he established a temporary home for it in a carton that was placed at the coolest edge of the kitchen stove. There the undersized fellow grew and prospered and before John Henry returned to New York, the bird was released to join its flock of elders and betters strutting around the barnyard—a sight that grandfather and grandson could view with immense satisfaction from the citadel of my office windows.

Late in August EB and K had received an engraved invitation to a September 23 reception at Vice-President Rockefeller's Washington, D.C., residence. The affair was a housewarming, and the United States Congress was to be honored. "Informal long gowns" were the order of the day for the female contingent, and the invitation had been addressed in the full name that was EB's pet hate: Mr. and Mrs. Elwyn B. White. On the morning of the big day, I by chance uncovered the invitation under a stack of old mail; clipped to it was one of EB's jovial messages: "K. Here's a clambake we mustn't miss. Wear a long nightdress." It had to be presumed K had written formal regrets by hand on her own engraved stationery. If not, it was too late to worry about it.

K's birthday (September 17) found her dispirited; she hoped for a long life span so that she could achieve many things, even though her already heavy burden of ill health increased each year. She was now in her eighties, and her eighties filled her with dread. One source of temporary comfort was the calculating of friends' ages; if they were even one year older—and still active—it helped. I spoke to her of my own friend, Adelaide Irving, an energetic lady of eighty-eight. K's attention was captured at once. "Eighty-eight years old! Imagine! Is she in a nursing home?"

"No, quite the opposite. She's touring Spain on her own—
by which I mean a sort of guided tour but not one of those
senior citizen groups."

"All alone? Has she no family to stop her from taking such
a risk?"

"Yes, she has children and grandchildren, and they protested that it wasn't safe at her age, so she found a companion."

"Well, I should think so! Even so, she has great courage.
Who went with her?"

"Her cousin Helen, age ninety."

There was a long pause while she considered whether I
might be exaggerating. Then she saw that I was holding Adelaide's last letter in my hand for proof, so she accepted the
incredible statement with more ease than I had accepted it
when the news came to me. It brought a whole new dimension
to her attitude about being an octogenarian, and a few times
thereafter she prefaced a complaint with the observation, "But
I ought to be able to manage; just think of that dear old lady
in Spain!" In the back of K's mind Adelaide was still in Spain,
months and even years later, journeying round and round while
time obligingly stood still and held her there.

September and October were the busiest months of the year
at my home for two- and three-day visitors; those same months
found K full and running over with authors' correspondence to
be annotated for the Bryn Mawr collection. More often than
not she "could use me Saturday" and many a Saturday morning
I felt ill-used indeed. Occasionally, though, the labor was light-
ened by a happy literary spoof. We had been sorting out letters
to and from several writers for several weeks when K said
unexpectedly one Saturday: "This will interest you as a cat
lover, Isabel. She says she began naming the first kittens after
George Eliot characters but with the cat being increasingly

prolific she's going to have a problem. She's given away a Maggie, a Tom, an Adam Bede, and a Silas Marner, and she plans to keep at least one from the next litter, but all that's left for a name is *Scenes of Clerical Life.*" Who was the ingenious "she" of the letter? Mary McCarthy? Jean Stafford? Rebecca West? The English novelist Elizabeth Taylor? Proper credit cannot be given; all I know is that some best-selling author friend of K's had memorialized the works of George Eliot in a fine furry gesture.

On November 13, the Whites' forty-sixth wedding anniversary, K was able to take two sips of a fine old champagne while EB and I, if memory serves, easily downed two glasses apiece. I was roundly berated for tactlessly looking forward four years to a golden celebration. I should have known better: they were superstitious in matters connected, even if remotely, to health. K had underlined the connection in this case by having returned recently from the local hospital. Her congestive heart failure had engendered much worry and flurry, with the fire truck bringing oxygen, the ambulance being summoned, and everybody wondering if she had the necessary reserve of strength to overcome the seizure. She had, of course, and she would prove it again to the anxious bystanders the following year.

Three fan letters from children were segregated from a score of others in December and left on the desk of the addressee to await his pleasure. A little girl from the Midwest was forthright:

"I want to be an author too. What advise do you give out? I'm ten years old but you'd be serprised what I know." "I'll bet I would," agreed EB mildly, laying her question aside for future cogitation.

A boy from the Bronx was not seeking advice, he was offering it: "If I was you I'd be writing alot abowt Stewart Little that mowse."

Another New York boy wondered if "you played with spiders ever? My mother read me Charlottes Web but when I got a big spider she yeled and ran."

"I shall inform him that women give lip service to Liberation but underneath they are fundamentally fragile," promised EB.

Christmas was unusual that year only because of the restraints placed on its chief celebrator. The hectic bustle of the preceding weeks was perhaps ten percent less hectic than in other years. I was enjoined twice, in severe tones that EB rarely used, to keep close watch on K, which meant, among other things, that I could help trim the tree the day before Christmas. Full of the spirit of the season, she had set aside her walker and was hurrying here and there selecting her favorite ornaments for the branches of the perfectly shaped fir balsam Henry had cut, and holding up trinkets for our admiration while she discoursed on trees that had graced her childhood home. At such times, when she was pursuing a task with enthusiasm, her eagerness outweighed her judgment and she was likely to take the maximum risks with only the vaguest consideration for her own safety. EB admired her vitality but feared her distraction.

·ᴈ SEVEN ɞ··

Early in January 1976 EB began to act more like K than like himself, pulling open file drawers and closet doors, sorting through old packets in pigeonholes, and riffling the contents of assorted cartons brought down from the attic, after they had been dusted assiduously by Shirley. The object of the search was an old Christmas card, destined to be an illustration for the *Letters*, and the search commenced on a weekend so I missed much of the urgency of it. "Have you seen anything of a short poem and a long dog, a dachshund, descending a stairway?" he called across before I had taken off coat and mittens. I had indeed; the poem was in the lowest drawer of my desk among other old photographs. He sighed when I handed it over.

"Why didn't I think to phone you yesterday instead of wasting all that time?"

I stretched the truth by a few hairs: "I couldn't have helped; we were away all day. I should have been able to read your mind and leave it on your desk before this."

The remainder of January divided itself neatly into two segments of unequal importance, but in the midst of them EB spent a short time at the hospital where his doctor treated an irregular heart rhythm.

The essence of segment one was a renunciation, as the grand piano in EB's study was taken away one afternoon on the first leg of its journey to Roger and Carol's apartment in New York City. A mailbagful of correspondence preceded the flitting, as K secured estimates from movers here and movers there; consulted experts about the hazards of moving the instrument in winter weather; fretted about tuning, then about insurance, and spoke more frequently to her busy husband about the piano than about any other topic. He wore the resigned air of a man who discovers there is no furor like a piano-moving furor, especially with a perfectionist like K at the keyboard.

In segment two, which came to be labeled "The Xerox Affair," EB was submerged to the exclusion of nearly everything else. The sponsored-writer system and its concomitant, [in his words] "the erosion of the free press in America," touched on theories that were at the core of his writing philosophy, and this time K could achieve nothing in the way of pacifying him and to direct his attention to less controversial news. However, when she realized that his forthright statements were being widely circulated in the press and were bringing him commendation from the top echelons of publishing, her attitude shifted abruptly and she began abetting him with wifely enthusiasm as he sharpened his lance and continued to tilt at the Xerox windmill.

EB had been deeply disturbed for several weeks by an account he read in *The New York Times* about an article that was scheduled for the February issue of *Esquire*. The article, an innocuous piece about traveling through America, had been written by Harrison Salisbury, a former associate editor of the *Times*. Salisbury was to receive no payment from *Esquire;* instead, Xerox Corporation would offer a generous remuneration of $40,000 for the piece and $15,000 for expenses. *Esquire* had assured the public that Xerox was not going to tamper with Salisbury's material; they were not going to attempt to influence the writer. They might, however, run a full-page ad preceding the article and another at the end of it. *Esquire*, of course, would take in a generous sum for such advertising. EB decried the commercialism of the arrangement.

Electricity was in short supply one stormy day but that was no deterrent, as EB moved his typewriter to the dining-room table and continued to expostulate about the Salisbury-Xerox-Esquire connection by the flickering glow of two tall white candles in the antique silver candlesticks that were among K's choice possessions. It would require an announcement of more than passing significance to divert his attention, and it was to be a sad winter for him and for K when the announcement came, and they learned that their dear friend Frank Sullivan had died. A frequent contributor to *The New Yorker*, Frank had been a friend of EB's since college; he befriended K at *The New Yorker*. A reporter from Saratoga Springs, telephoning to secure some personal and professional recollections of Sullivan, was fortunate in her timing; K was at her lucid best and could contribute several pertinent anecdotes to be used in an article.

Spring brought news of a more jubilant kind when a letter reached EB from Xerox Corporation, informing him that they were not going to subsidize any more magazine articles, and that two pieces already planned were going to be aborted. Although he expressed his satisfaction in only a few letters, K saw to it that the triumph was widely broadcast; her communiqués on other matters were shorter than usual as she hurried to circulate the last act of the Xerox drama.

"Other matters" naturally piled up on her table, awaiting her attention. While I was on my knees in front of the table one morning, trying to pry her address book out of the heap, EB emerged from the telephone closet (a passageway between my office and the living room) and reached over me to pick up *The New York Times* from the sofa. He miscalculated by an inch or two, and a foot-high stack of papers and magazines slid off the bench-style table, part of them landing on me, part on the floor. There were several sheets of personal correspondence among them as well as one permission sheet (always of prime importance; it should have been signed and returned promptly) and his quick glance took them in. "Isabel, how does K manage? How do you keep up? How can you stand this confusion?" His tone blended equal amounts of denunciation and sympathy.

"I can't stand it. That's why you come upon me so often sitting down."

"I'm glad you can joke about it but it must be discouraging when you're hunting for things."

"It is—my left eye never knows where my right eye's looking and I am growing just a smidgeon cross-eyed, but Mrs. White is very patient with me." He joined in my laughter, but not heartily, and his parting admonition left little doubt where he stood on the matter: "I'm afraid you are too patient sometimes." It was a remark meant to be pacifying, of course. His own devotion and his own patience so far exceeded mine that it was like the classic comparison of the elephant and the ant.

May 25 was a Tuesday, an extra-work morning for me. On Monday K had been unable to maintain her regular pace, or much of any pace; although she offered no complaint, I suspected she felt unwell. Her parting remark: "I must do better than this tomorrow; you'll come tomorrow of course?" gave me a sense of unease that propelled me to work fifteen minutes early, although there was no certainty of any assignment being ready in the office.

It was like walking through a scene in a play previously rehearsed; I was familiar with the script but hated to deliver my lines. Housekeeper Shirley Cousins stood outside the kitchen entrance, calling and waving urgently, just as she had called and gestured another Tuesday the previous November. I took the shortcut past the chicken yard and under the apple tree. The tree had been bare and sleeping then; now the sap was stirring in its limbs and there was a hint of the fragrant blossoms that soon would envelop it. The ground had been dull and frozen before; now it was a carpet of green and there were spring flowers in the border. How many more springtimes would there be for K? Two attacks of congestive heart failure, only six months apart, demanded more than routine concern. Although this time she did not lose consciousness, the burden of responsibility fell more heavily on Edith, Shirley, and Henry than it had in November, because EB was not at home, he was taking the Mercedes to a Bangor garage for a tuneup.

K's recovery at the hospital proceeded at the same relatively swift pace that it had before. Her vital signs were encouraging by Wednesday morning; she was vastly improved on Thursday; on Friday they spoke of releasing her next day.

EB occupied some of his time that week inventing a series of quips for the written tags he attached to fan letters he was turning over to K for reply. He pursued two alternate courses when she was feeling under the weather: either he held back all fan mail in order to lighten her load or, if she insisted on working anyway, he went to extra lengths to make her laugh. She rarely succumbed but I laughed enough for two, finding the contrast between his witticisms and her proper prose inordinately funny.

"K, thank him for the book, which I will be ready to read in about seventy-five years from now when I get caught up." "Tread lightly on this one's toes—not enough to cause him to cry." "Tell her I hate all animals. The only pet I have is a 6 ft. alligator that shares my bathtub." "This one's out of his mind. Maybe you'd better not answer it. On 2d thought, you better had. For all I know, I may be out of mine too." "Say I don't read any manuscripts except my own. That's about as much boredom as I can take."

That summer, despite poor health, K forged ahead with a task to which she had committed herself voluntarily, the preparation for the Cornell Library Rare Books Department of a list of foreign translations of her husband's books, chiefly children's books. Almost immediately the list began to transform itself into a series of irrelevant remarks, repeats of the same title, and/or a search for vaguely recollected creations that were not in existence. Somehow they had entangled themselves in K's mind with other editions and other titles that had not been translated; and sometimes K's confusion of the Bryn Mawr list with the Cornell list caused her to add reminiscences about the contents of a book as soon as the foreign title had been copied. Gradually the List of Foreign Translations began to expand itself into a sort of minor annotation and thesis.

Although foreign language titles of EB's juveniles were similar to the Department of Agriculture's cabbage catalogue in that they could not be classified as exciting reading, there is a certain wistful appeal in some of them, such as the Berlin edition of *Charlotte's Web: Schweinchen Wilbur and Seine Freunde,* and the French one (a translation that exasperated K) *Les Aventures de Narcisse.*

In addition to copying from each book the tongue-twisting, eye-twitching letters of its title, we had to deal with publisher and city; thus, a Viennese edition of *Stuart Little* incorporated a long line: *Rikki Die Abenteuerliche Geschichte,* Einer Kleiner Maws, Verlag Carl Ueberreuter, Heidelberg (no date); and a Scandinavian edition of *Charlotte's Web,* engagingly known as *Fantasiska Wilbur* was full of traps for the unwary. "Norwegian edition," it read, "Oslo, 1973; A/S Nationaltry keriet & Forlagsbokbinderiet."

When we reached Indian-language editions of *Charlotte,* the titles were unpronounceable; we simply had to know our book as we labored over publisher and place: "G. P. Parchure Prakashan Mandir, Bombay, 1963; language—Marathi." In Finland the title of *Charlotte* was simple—*Lotta Ystavani*— but the rest was intricate indeed: "Werner Soderstrom Osa-keyhtio; Finnish edition, Helsinki, 1954."

K was no slouch when it came to foreign languages; she could read off French, German, Italian, and Scandinavian titles with an accent that was a joy to hearken to. In her enthusiasm she might snatch a book from shelf or carton, recite title and publisher with impeccable pronunciation and remarkable speed and return it to its place while her lagging secretary was still floundering under the impact of the unfamiliar spelling. Inevitably EB, writing tag lines for "Newsbreaks," would inject a question from across the hall; one noontime it was "Is there a special wild card in playing poker?" Fancy, I said to myself, his never having heard the expression "deuces are wild." And did I look like a poker-playing type?

In connection with the foreign-titles project, a sort of attic clearinghouse endeavor fell to my lot. I was sent to find a group of Charlotte's Web books to go to Cornell. "Bring down all the editions of Charlotte that aren't on the Cornell list," ordered

K. It was a logical request in that I had made many trips to the attic over past weeks to retrieve all the *Charlottes* that *were* to go on the Cornell list. At no time did I discover why I was bringing down the second group but after a while, probably early in 1977, the matter ceased to be puzzling because more relevant puzzles superceded it.

A change of habit that had to do with K's well-being, with her tenacious grip on life, had been nagging for weeks at my subconscious and finally a day came when the change brought itself out into the open, and all of us on the staff were able to recognize it for what it was. "It" was a pattern of inaction that had been growing slowly: she was clinging to the comfort of her bed and the quiet sanctuary of her bedroom longer and longer each morning. Instead of arriving downstairs promptly at ten o'clock or a few minutes earlier, as had been her longtime custom, she had been gradually pushing her work schedule further and further into the morning. Her nurses, who were uneasy spectators and reluctant listeners as K invented ruses to serve as delaying tactics, were quick to verify our suspicion that she was postponing active participation in her day as long as possible. The pace she had set for herself and had followed faithfully and to a remarkable degree for so many years was becoming a burden; she could no longer cope with a schedule that she had established. The changed schedule, though, did not directly affect my own work; there would always be enough assignments from EB to take up the slack.

Early in the summer when we belatedly got around to one day's demands, K began dictating a letter to Nancy Milford, who had posed some questions about Elizabeth Sergeant's association with Willa Cather. "You'll know how to phrase it," K began as a prelude to her dictation. "Mention several of the books my sister wrote and lean on the Cather connection." A minute later EB interrupted the session by tossing a copy of his bicentennial-of-our-country column for *The New Yorker* onto K's table. When there was a new composition to be read, it could not wait. "Go in and begin typing Nancy," K directed, "I must read this at once."

EB disappeared upstairs but K was unaware of his going. Her eyes were glued to the typed pages he had given to her; when she was engaged by any piece of printed matter, her concentration was absolute. She was so oblivious to anything around her, including entrances and exits, that it was disconcerting. If you had departed, she might instigate an exchange of ideas as though you were still there beside her. If you entered the room unsummoned, she failed to see you, and if you didn't interrupt her, it could mean an agonizing wait. From my office, after a time lapse, I could hear her begin to discuss the piece aloud; it was several minutes before she realized the room was empty. Then, apparently theorizing that EB was in his study, and quite forgetting that he couldn't hear her from that distance, she raised her voice.

I popped in to say "He's upstairs, Mrs. White," but it didn't seem to register. "Shall I bring my book for more dictation?" I inquired, hoping to divert her.

At that moment EB, having heard echoes from his resting place in the upper hall, came down as far as the landing. At the same moment K trotted out with her walker, determined to get a reply from him.

"Oh, there you are. Well, it's beautiful," she told him. "Clever. Funny. One of the best you've ever done."

"No, it's not all that good. Not the best, but I know one thing: it's absolutely the last."

"Well, you've said that before and then written another piece; I hope there'll be more—where's Isabel?"

Isabel Russell

"I'm in here, Mrs. White, typing the letter to Nan—"
"No, you certainly can't read it now. I can't spare you. You'll
have to wait till it comes out in the magazine. We'll get that
dictation finished."

I came to the doorway, pad and pencil in hand and stared
at her, at a loss how to reply. Above me on the stairway, EB
raised his hand in an almost imperceptible gesture and shook
his head ever so slightly. It was appalling; twice in one morning
a sure indication that K was not hearing or, worse, not understanding what was being said to her. It was of no use to dwell
on it and I was convinced it was not up to me to initiate any
discussion of it with her husband. If any initiative was taken
it had to be he who took it—so I said, "Yes, Mrs. White," and
followed after her as meekly as any ewe lamb. As it happened,
there was an opportunity to read the piece anyway because EB
decided he needed a fresh copy.

A bicentennial project for the state of Maine produced a
request that resulted in a chuckle from the recipient and a brief
letter of refusal. "They want me to run in a bicentennial parade
and carry a torch," he called across the hallway. I did not join
in the laughter because that would have been tantamount to
admitting there was something ridiculous in the request being
made of a man his age. Doubtless the initiators of the event
at Kittery readily understood that he was physically unable to
run even a short distance and pass a torch from one runner to
another.

Some incidents, some mistakes, some ambivalent attitudes,
some eccentricities of the written or spoken word, can be
looked back upon with sighs or smiles; but early in July 1976
my journal records an episode that evokes neither sigh nor
smile in recollection; instead, a lingering sense of shame. We
were compiling another list. Whenever a time lapse occurred

between the original notations and the mailing of them, K grew troubled about her purpose in ordering a specific record. The result often was the same: begin again and try to achieve a compilation that was slightly dissimilar. Well after 12 P.M. one day she dispatched me to EB's study on a futile errand: she wanted a particular Penguin edition of one of his books—a copy he did not have, according to his own record of foreign editions that I had consulted twice previously. A memo attached to the list in hand established that fact. To pacify her, I made one more search and then reported, "I'm sorry, Mrs. White, but we have no Penguin edition here. You may recall we hunted before and couldn't find one, and Harper and Row told us there wasn't any."

"I don't believe it," she said sharply, without looking up from a sheet she had in her lap. It was the wrong tone, the wrong phrase, at the wrong time on the wrong day. For the first time in more than six years, and with perhaps less provocation than on a few other occasions, I lost my temper.

"If you don't believe it, you will simply have to search for yourself, Mrs. White. It's long after twelve o'clock; I have guests coming for the weekend; I'm going home."

The instant I began to speak, she began to reply, having immediately grasped from my angry tone that trouble was brewing. Ordinarily I would have stopped talking the minute she interrupted, but this time I contined to speak. I doubt she even heard what I said, but that I was tense and annoyed came through to her loud and clear. She was attempting to cover up my voice [If I don't actually hear this angry voice, maybe it will go away] and she continued to comment as I gathered my briefcase and purse and walked back through living room and dining room. "I wasn't speaking to *you* about not believing it; I was reading from the Harper notes and I meant *them.*" Her voice followed me as far as the kitchen; it didn't matter to her that others of the staff were nearby and could hear our altercation. I paused briefly to pat Susy and to say good-bye to the nurse, because both of them were obstructing my exit route, and I heard her say, "Oh dear, Andy, I had a terrible misunderstanding with Isabel and she is angry."

Next morning it was obvious from his attitude that he was concerned and sorry, trying to be conciliating without at the same time seeming to be disloyal to K. I felt distressed, not only about my own impatience the preceding day but that I had been the unwitting cause of a loss of dignity, however slight, for him. Transparent as a child, he came out of his study to say "Good morning, Isabel; it's not very pleasant to be working in this hot weather," before I had a chance to speak. Other mornings I was nearly always the one to initiate a greeting and in answering it, he rarely used my name, just flung a quick "good morning" at me or at anyone else who had spoken, as though he resented having to say it at all and already was anticipating with dislike the demands a new day was going to make upon him. After the pleasant greeting, he began a discussion of *Time* magazine's treatment of the Xerox affair. It was possible that neither he nor K had expected me to appear that morning, and if so, his loquaciousness may have been caused partly by relief.

Later in the morning K offered a handsome apology for the difficulty which was still, in her mind, a misunderstanding. I must remember that I was "a friend, not merely an employee, and very important" to her. Far less of an apology—in fact, none at all—would have sufficed. I accepted it instantly and added that part of the blame was mine because I had been too quick to take offense.

A few days later EB called across from his desk, "Does *TV*

Guide make a practice of sending along a jar of jam when it requests a writer to do a column?" Not being a writer fortunate enough to have received any solicitation from that magazine, I couldn't advise. I could inform him, though, that many conservative publications had been doing odd things lately to direct attention to themselves; maybe *TV Guide* had joined them. For many weeks a folder advertising that magazine had reached my house via a carton of eggs delivered by the local dairy. It seemed an unusual partnership and nowhere had the *Guide* or dairy bothered to explain the unnatural coming together of the two unrelated products; but I was sure an explanation for the gift of jam must be somewhere in EB's letter, although he assured me there was not. He handed over a brief reply to be copied. Predictably it was a summary refusal of their request.

"Want the jam?" he asked, so I took it and thanked him. Under no circumstances would he have eaten it himself or permitted K to touch it. He was exceedingly wary of food that had been prepared by anyone other than his domestic staff, a member of his family, or a near and trusted neighbor. "Probably full of hemlock," he added on his way upstairs. I removed the jar from the package; at the bottom of the box was a small crushed envelope and inside was a typed note bearing the salutation "Dear Mr. White." In seeing that much, I had seen also the opening sentence, which said the sender had made the jam himself. "Don't write that letter to *TV Guide*," EB instructed when I took the message to him, "I'll have to wait a while and then make sounds like a contented author full of homemade jam." It was sometime in August before he got around to sending a polite thank you to the assistant managing editor of the *Guide*. To Mr. William A. Marsano, wherever you are, I hasten to say your jam was the finest we ever ate at our house, without a trace of hemlock or any other foreign flavor in it. We gave it the treatment it deserved: spread it thickly on homemade white bread and permitted some privileged guests to share it.

Jill Krementz, the noted photographer, spent a couple of days in North Brooklin late in August pursuing EB with her camera—around the house, the barn, the grounds, the boathouse. A camera, like a microphone, brought out the worst in the man. He froze when the lens was aimed in his direction; it made him nervous just to look at her photographic paraphernalia spread around the living room. When the visitation was over and Jill had departed, I asked him how it had gone. He had a picturesque phrase for the ordeal he had been through: "It was absolutely impossible. When those proofs come, you're going to find me looking like an old gray muffin."

The folio of proofs contained a generous gift to the Whites from Jill: an album of selected prints—big, beautiful, expensive, the cover lettered in gold "North Brooklin" with the date. Anyone who has read the *Letters of E. B. White* or the *Essays of E. B. White* has seen examples of her work. One photo with particular charm illustrated an article in the fall 1976 issue of the *Columbia Journalism Review*. Susy occupied a prominent spot in that one, and many who saw it agreed on one point: Susy was the star of the show, the Miss America of dogdom. Only one other print impressed family and staff as much. It was rarely seen outside the Whites' home (until it appeared on the program of the memorial service for him): a fine photo of EB in the barn, swinging on the rope swing he had put up for the grandchildren.

It was exciting to peer through Jill's lens at her vision of him and to discover that her vision was our vision. An unwilling subject cannot be coaxed into a flattering position; he will not pause and offer the best angle. How she must have struggled to outwit him when he refused, as undoubtedly he did, to offer a winning aspect to the camera. She had to have been quick-witted and doubly quick-fingered to create so many striking, lively studies of him.

But K could scarcely stop to enjoy the artistic merits of the collection. Her mind was on Christmas gifts. Which prints to order for whom, and how many? Before Christmas came Roger's birthday (well before, in September, in fact); before anything else came the necessity of selecting from amongst Jill's photos publicity shots for the *Letters* book; what to do, where to begin? First things first, in logical sequence, never had been part of K's credo. The Christmas gift selection would be an arduous task, she proclaimed, we must get on with it. Most days EB would have put down a firm foot on such an out-of-season suggestion but for once K was let off easily.

"Don't hurry the holidays, K, there's plenty of time," he said mildly, and settled down comfortably with the album in hand. His reaction apparently was two parts gratitude to one of amazement that Jill could have found him out so cleverly. The backgrounds were stripped of artifice; he seemed to melt into them or to be just emerging from them, and in every case the look she captured was exactly the one he thought he wore when at his best. There was nothing of the old gray muffin about it.

Very much against his inclination but with the dogged air of a person who recognizes that his publishers have some rights, EB let himself be persuaded to sign fifteen hundred autographs on single sheets that would be inserted in a special limited edition of the *Letters.* September 7 saw them on their way to Corona Machemer, an editor at Harper and Row—after a few weeks of signing, a pause for writer's cramp, a resuming of signing, more pauses in which to rub his aching wrist. I pitied him all through the operation. It was no fun signing one's name even 150 times, never mind times ten. I helped him arrange the sheets and wrap the package. What a whimsical joke for Corona when she opened it! On sheet 1501, laid carefully on top of the required number, he had written in bold script, "Henry James."

EB needed research assistance in a letter going out on September 16; his own library having proved inadequate, he had to resort to the Brooklin Town Library. It was a rare occasion when we couldn't uncover an esoteric fact in the Whites' extensive collection of reference books, but many of them were not of recent vintage, and EB was seeking a current biography. All he wanted to know was whether the president of Bates College possessed a doctoral degree. It was an insignificant statistic that would be used in a letter of minor importance, but in EB's code of manners one never wrote "Mr." if the addressee had achieved his doctorate and styled himself by it professionally. The Bates president was not going to be delighted with the letter, no matter how his title appeared. Once again EB was about to refuse a proffered honorary degree.

Setting about the library errand, he had a kind thought for the local children who patronized the building in swarms, during school hours and afterward. He took along a large papier-mâché sculpture of Louis the swan, with trumpet—a gift to him from another group of children.

"How I wish I could have *The Weekly Packet* photographer come and take a picture of Mr. White with this display," said librarian Nancy Hitchcock wistfully as she got out a copy of *The Trumpet* to place beside the sculpture, "but I know from what you say that he'd hate the publicity." Imbued with a protective instinct toward both my employers I held my tongue, but I wanted to say, "He's a pushover for your type of young woman, Nancy; go ahead and ask him." He was, in fact, far more likely to put himself out for the small hometown organization than for sophisticated TV network reporters or big universities. Nancy was folksy, cheerful, and overflowing with the particular virtue her position required—endless patience. As both Whites frequently remarked to visitors, the hamlet of Brooklin had been immensely fortunate in its librarians. Besides Nancy's predecessor, Martha Tyler, who had nurtured the Library through unimpressive early stages to a surprising vitality in later years, there was assistant librarian June Eaton, who was noted, K emphasized, "for going far beyond the call of duty when it came to matching the right books to certain fussy readers, and trying to locate sources when researchers were stumped."

In October there was a struggle between the Whites and their secretary over the spelling of one word appearing in a manuscript too late for inclusion in the *Letters,* so I assumed that it had to be part of the forthcoming *Essays.* The struggle had begun when the original piece, a "Letter from The East," was being "processed" for *The New Yorker.* A section of land along our coast, a strip jutting into Blue Hill Bay, was set down by EB in his draft as "Herriman's Point." I had seen the name printed on two different maps as "Harriman's Point," and so informed EB, but he was adamant and produced an older map to prove his point. The second time 'round I was more troubled. "The official sign on the main road directs tourists to 'Harriman's Point'," I reminded him.

"That's no proof. It's probably a modern spelling or, more likely, a modern error."

"It's a very *Harrow*ing situation for a typist," I insisted, "and you are harassing me. How would you like it if I wrote that I was being heressed?" I was certain I had him boxed in, but it was not so.

"When you eat those tiny fish they catch off Herriman's Point, surely you don't refer to them as harring?"

In due time the piece appeared in the *Essays* with Herriman's spelled to suit EB. My husband said sharply, "You made a typo in copying 'Harriman's Point' or else you didn't proofread with your usual care."

In a domestic situation that month in which K, the chatelaine, might have been excused for speaking in vehement imperatives, she instead remained calm and unflurried. We all admired her patience when Jones suddenly realized that the loveseat in his master's study, on which both dogs frequently reposed, had been newly redecorated with a light, patterned silk. With his uncanny penchant for pleasing everybody at every turn, Jones managed to roll around in a foul-smelling substance he found outdoors, then very promptly to come indoors and transfer most of it to the sofa and the light-green rug. A bath was in order; he took it as a personal affront and glowered and barked en route to the bath, in the bath, and at intervals afterward when anyone came near him. K had selected a beautiful fabric for her decoration, one not likely to withstand the ravages of canines, but she held her tongue and offered no reproof. The staff was unanimous in its opinion, delivered discreetly behind closed doors: either an old blanket should be placed on the new sofa cover or Jones should be drowned in the bathtub.

The visit of Kathy Hall, from Cornell University Library, early in November, required some attic research. The quest had been carried on during my days off but subsequently I became the happy beneficiary of part of it. Among the extraneous material heaped up in EB's study was a large photograph of himself. It was one of Fabian Bachrach's best—a fine studio portrait, taken I guess, when EB was in his early fifties. He was impeccably attired in a light suit and patterned tie, and the photographer's sensitive film had penetrated the naturally serious expression and imposed on it the faintly wistful air that EB always wore in repose. I absolutely disbelieved his dour statement that he was trying to find enough courage to toss the photo into the heap of trash he was accumulating to send to the dump. It seemed to me he was hoping to be dissuaded from destroying it. No better dissuader than I for miles around—and it ended on top of my briefcase. "Please autograph it, Mr. White; otherwise somebody might think I stole it." With great goodwill he signed it, "To Isabel with love from young E. B. White."

The foraging in the attic had, of course, brought on one of his dust-allergy attacks. K, coming downstairs a day later, paused at the door of his study to inquire, "Did you call Dr. Britt for an appointment?"

"No," morosely, "I'm too sick to go to a doctor."

The Reader's Digest that autumn produced a "Best of 200 Years" list of books for children. It was purportedly compiled by the Children's Literature Association, an international organization of teachers, librarians, authors, and publishers. *Charlotte's Web* led all the rest; when the matter was brought to his attention, EB was vastly amused to learn that his unassuming spider outranked *Tom Sawyer* and *Little Women*. The usual number of fans, secure in their belief that he would be ignorant of the honor, sent the requisite number of letters telling him about it, and K struggled valiantly to acknowledge each communication in a season when she was naturally very much occupied with December holiday concerns.

At the end of a five-day work week, when confusion had been piled upon confusion and K was sounding irrational (to state the case mildly), I came to an abrupt but positive decision that I would not try to pacify her—after this year—through another Christmas. The announcement was greeted with disbelief at home. Russ and Ernest, fearing I would melt like a sundae in the hot sun when the time came to implement the decision, prepared a formal document and obliged me to sign it. The inserted cut-off date was October 1977 because that was approximately when K began attending exclusively to Christmas preparations. I was willing (pleased, in fact) to sign. It was the awareness of that paper secreted away in a small safe at home that sustained me through the fretful days of November and December 1976. At least these would be the last of them, I consoled myself.

Not being gifted with any prophetic faculties, I couldn't foresee that this would be K's last Christmas, and that my own troubled state of mind would carry me no further than the following spring in the Whites' service. An addiction to astrology might have proved useful in those crucial days but I was too busy charting K's improbable passage toward the holiday to give any attention to my own horoscope. Probably Scorpios were being advised all through December 1976 and January, February, and March 1977 to hold their tongues, mind their manners, and approach all business decisions cautiously, lest they make mistakes they would regret later. If I had possessed second sight, no sharp retort of K's would have seemed offensive; her muddled directions would have had only minor impact. However, without the essential extra perception, I began to feel sadly that I was accomplishing little of value for her and was, myself, growing daily more nervous and ill-tempered. Was her disposition (for which there was much justification) gradually turning into a communicable disease like measles or chickenpox? If so, it was time and past time for the connection to be severed.

The frenetic pace of holiday living and giving pushed K into another physical trauma in November. On one day there had to be respirator treatments administered at home; later, a trip to the hospital with fire department and ambulance again summoned, and the situation was more complicated than formerly by the patient's determination that she would be all right at home—there was no need for hospitalization. Scarcely an hour after her departure the nurse who had been on house duty phoned us to dictate a list of items to be brought to K, who was issuing directives from under an oxygen tent in the intensive-care unit.

The first copy of the *Letters* book off the press, kindly addressed to the Whites by Corona Machemer, arrived in the mailbag while K was still absent. Although EB had stated positively that he was going to keep it from her until her return home, he relented a few days later and sent it along to the hospital. "I hope it may quiet her; she keeps asking if it came."

When she was home again, exemplifying in fine style Dickens's ghosts of Christmas Past and Christmas Present, there appeared an item in my own mailbox that dwarfed in importance anything in hers. It was my copy of *The New York Times Book Review*, which always arrived several days ahead of the publication date. This review would accompany the *Times* Sunday issue dated November 21, 1976, and the Whites would receive their book review, enclosed with the rest of the newspaper, in the mail on Tuesday, November 23. (As my husband had stated in regard to the phenomenon of our own *Book Review*, "It's incredible service; it comes in the mail before it's been printed.")

In the coveted front-page position, exactly as I had envisioned seeing it, was Wilfrid Sheed's review of the *Letters of E. B. White*. Shaking with excitement, and trying to read and eat at the same time—because if the review was favorable I wanted to phone the good news to K and EB before hurrying off to an afternoon secretarial mission—I slopped a dab of cottage cheese on one corner of the page. It left a sodden spot when tissued away and the spot still remains, a testament to haste and excitement, these many years afterward. In view of all the skepticism and pessimism at the Whites', the review impressed members of our household as eminently complimentary and satisfactory. When I had spoken once, hesitantly, to K about anticipating a front-page spot in the *Times Book Review*, she had been derisive: "We're not stupid enough to be thinking in those terms. Nobody's book of letters is that important. We'll be lucky if it rates a paragraph or two anywhere in the *Book Review*."

The only negative note we could uncover was a sidewise swipe or two at *The New Yorker*'s style, but even that stereotype was judiciously fair to EB. Mr. Sheed had seemed to be implying that the young *New Yorker* was the product of EB's style and that the young *New Yorker* was best.

Even in that hasty first scanning, I was at fault for failing to remember that *The New Yorker* was not supposed to be criticized at any time, by anybody, for any reason or purpose. Sober reflection might have brought the warning to mind but that noontime there was no interlude for reflection of any sort, so I phoned K in a reflex action to relay the news about the superior review. Catching the note of exuberance flowing over the wire, K could not conceal her impatience to read the review, and EB was promptly dispatched to borrow the paper overnight. That left no opportunity for a second, more in-depth perusal—though I doubt it would have changed my mind much—so the words K was using on the phone when I stepped into her bedroom next morning came as a distinct shock.

The call, one of several she made that morning, was to Dotty Guth, and EB was listening in on the guest-room extension and interpolating a few comments of his own. Clearly the subject of the conversation was Wilfrid Sheed, and K was nearly screaming in her exasperation and denunciation. A terrible, terrible review; why had they chosen that man, of all reviewers, to do it? Everybody knew he held a deep-seated prejudice against "the" magazine. (If "everybody" did know that, "everybody" certainly had kept mum about it for several decades.) He surely had it in for Andy but how did he dare to be so obvious about it?

Somehow it was as though she and her husband were reading a different review from the one I had read, from the one I was glancing through again as I picked it up from where she had flung it at the foot of her bed. As far as I, and others, have been able to determine, Sheed's credentials were impeccable; he has advanced to the stage of being a bona fide critic's critic, and his own writings find warm and receptive audiences. In a few letters on the topic of Sheed that went out from North Brooklin that week, K employed an odd phrase, "Of course Andy and I are immune to criticism," that might have made me smile quietly to myself on a different occasion. There was no humor to be derived from Sheed's review. Nothing went right that morning for K and, by extension, for any of us. Sheed was behind it all, she implied, and I ran a close second in iniquity because I hadn't been able to read between the lines of his review and detect the betrayal. When, therefore, a check that was supposed to be sealed with an order blank got mislaid, K was indignant. She was sure I had dropped it on the stairs; if not, then did I put it in an envelope going to somebody else? The reply was "No" to both questions but she refused to be pacified that morning. The nurse was sent downstairs to repeat both accusations and to assist me in the search. Neither of us was capable of conducting a sober, careful turnover of magazines; like restive teenagers we had to stifle a desire to giggle. The check surfaced at last in K's checkbook on her bed. Although I hadn't seen EB anywhere while the hunt was in progress, he must have heard some of K's imperious directions to nurse and secretary. He called me into his study to repeat a caution he had voiced previously: "I'm afraid this senility thing with Katharine makes her get upset over little items. We must try to bear with her."

The mood of the day did not improve when EB returned from a medical appointment in Blue Hill. Doctor Britt chose that morning to inflict, all unknowing, a great unkindness on one of his favorite patients. He reported that a recent cardiogram indicated EB's heart was in good condition. It was a sobering moment for the victim of the upbeat report. Off and on, when he felt weary or discouraged or just not quite up to par, he had been pleased to think he could hold his heart responsible. At infrequent intervals its mechanism had hinted at a need for repair; he had got into the habit of being a little jocular about it: "My heart is trying to find a pace of its own." Now modern medical technology had closed the door on worry, on sympathy, on jocularity. It was an unsettling state of affairs for a person who had for many years kept a careful record of his body's most vital organ, had monitored every palpitation, and consulted with his physician when there was the slightest variation from the norm.

Before I left for the day, he pulled himself together to issue an edict with regard to the Sheed review: no more correspondence, either pro or con, should be written. Leave it alone; forget about it. Ignoring the ban, K wrote promptly to Herb Mitgang. Then, having second thoughts, she dictated a disavowal, directing him to destroy the first letter. The second message, like the first, was supposed to be mailed secretly by me, but, because this was to be accomplished on a Saturday, it would not be so easy. On Saturdays the post office closed at noon; ergo, at 11 A.M., EB or Henry carried the morning's output to Brooklin or North Brooklin (Henry)—and sometimes Brooklin—(EB). That morning Henry left at eleven and nothing was said about mail so K presumed she was safe, but she was too sanguine. EB crossed her up: "I'm going out with a package, K. You might as well give me the mail."

Flustered, she replied quickly, "I haven't any," instead of covering up with "I'm not quite finished; Isabel will take it." When he had departed, she was worried. "I do hope he goes to North Brooklin today of all days."

"I'm sure he will, Mrs. White. He doesn't often go to Brooklin."

"But if he does happen to, he'll catch me in a lie. What are you going to say if you meet him?"

"I'll say, 'I have to buy a roll of stamps, Mr. White. Do you need any?' "

"Good girl; I wouldn't have thought of that."

Luckily for her peace of mind she never did learn that her spouse elected the Brooklin post office for that morning's business. He was stepping back into his car as I emerged from mine. "Need any stamps?" I called across, trying to look and sound like the efficient employee with nothing but her employer's office needs on her mind.

"No, thanks. I don't like the artwork on the current issue so

I'm not using any," and he waved and drove off, with Jones perched beside him, wearing the smug expression of a dog who might recently have been consulted about the artistic merits of a specific postage stamp.

In the usual whirling snowdrift of ribbons, paper, catalogues, and gift lists that encased the Christmas tidings of that year was a new, although old, addition: a group of original Audubon prints, discovered in an antique trunk in the attic. Predictably some of them were wrapped, tagged, and made ready for mailing when, as they were intended as gifts to friends in the Brooklin-Blue Hill area, they should have been set aside to go under the tree. It was not surprising K had trouble with the Audubon prints: younger minds than hers might have quivered at the obligations she shouldered each December. But I was frightened by her reaction to a mixed-up list: "I can't find one of the prints and nobody has seen it. Somebody must have taken it. They're trying to make me think I'm losing my mind." The remark was part of a mounting cluster of evidence that she had the beginnings of a persecution complex. I knew little of the science of geriatrics and wished I knew less.

Another day K and her bed were adrift in shirts; lists from six department stores were required to settle the question of which shirt was intended for which person. Meanwhile her nurse stood by hopefully, waiting for an interruption that would remind K of her presence and of the time, as they were already half an hour late with her daily bath-and-ointment routine.

"We'll have to order something for Nancy from Edinburgh House. I wonder if it will get up here from Florida on time? Don't forget to get a lot of cartons out of the attic and cut them up for cardboard backing when we mail the pictures. We haven't mailed the pictures yet, have we?"

That was a mystifying one, the first time that pictures, as differentiated from prints and paintings or drawings, had been mentioned. "No, I haven't seen any pictures. You don't mean the prints we sent to the Bryn Mawr Library?"

"Of course not! I mean pictures. Photos. To the family, all the ones Jill Krementz did for publicity. One to everybody. Write down all my family and show me the list and I'll choose which ones. Andy will have to help me. Call him. Wait a minute—where's the mittens list? I need a big box for Sarah, it will have two pairs of mittens in it. What else is it supposed to have? Have you wrapped all her things? Don't forget to put in *The New Yorker* subscription card. I looked for those cards everywhere yesterday—why don't you leave them where I can find them?"

As I picked them up from a trayful of holiday items on her bedside table, the phone rang. Mercifully, it sounded like a long, involved conversation; by the time she hung up the receiver she would be ready for the nurse and a secretary would be forgotten.

I made my way downstairs with an armload of "stuff." Peace settled down like a mantle. It was snowing heavily; the dead grass and mottled brown leaves were being masked with a soft immaculate whiteness that muted the sound of passing traffic. Jones was snoring in the study and Susy dozed at my feet. Mingled with the staccato click of typewriter keys were comforting kitchen sounds: the oven door being slammed, the gurgle of water running. Over all was the aroma of Edith's Christmas cookies, wafting their spicy flavor through the house. There were a dozen letters to do for EB, each with a cryptic note of directions clipped to it, at least half of which were literary gems themselves:

"This is a long one but don't try for perfect typing; just x out errors. He's for guts, not for tidy."

"I think this one indulges in 3 martini lunches with a sandwich, but he forgot to eat the sandwich. Take your choice on addresses; note he gives 2 with no preference."

"I think she's raw Women's Lib. Don't give her any comfort by putting 'Ms.' anywhere; call her 'Miss.' "

"I can't make out the name; if you can't either, try a reasonable facsimile and then we'll both sit back and laugh at the P.O."

By the time I was ready to leave, he called me into his study to look at a brochure of exquisite handcrafted silver jewelry from a shop on Deer Isle, about 15 miles south of Brooklin. He planned to journey there with Doris Wolfers, a friend who knew the designer and who would help him to select Christmas gifts ["I've always thought Doris had excellent taste"] for his "dear, helpful girls." I knew already who they were, but he enumerated them, "Harriet [*New Yorker* secretary], Dotty [goddaughter and *Letters* coeditor], and Corona" [an editor at Harper and Row]. Had I ever shopped at the silver place, he wanted to know, and which of the designs would I select if the choice were mine? He was operating on the solid theory that three opinions were better than two, and I was pleased to oblige but I assured him, without embarrassment, that I did not shop for jewelry, no matter how beautiful, in the price range of seventy-five to one hundred dollars and more. The only fine gem in my modest collection is my diamond engagement ring. Handcrafted silver was something to be admired in catalogues and in the windows of boutiques but it never had found its way to my jewelry drawer. No matter; it was the "youthful viewpoint" that he needed.

The following Tuesday he displayed the silver gifts and entered a request for "three of your most extravagant wrappings and ribbons." The necklaces for Dotty Guth and Harriet Walden were of simple modern design and the total effect was graceful understatement. These necklaces would look equally well when worn with cashmere sweaters or formal gowns. For Corona Machemer there was a silver neckpiece with matching bracelet, an interesting design, quietly decorative. The gifts seemed to be tremendously important to EB; he hovered over the cushioning with tissue paper and cotton in the individual boxes, then left me to my own devices on gift wrap but returned to supervise the outside packaging. There was no possibility of employing heavy brown paper directly around the gift wrap, he decided. The bows were so elaborate, his directions having been followed meticulously, that they needed the added protection of a second box before the brown-paper stage. Henry was summoned to take over the final layers because K was anxious to get on with the last of her greeting notes. She was traveling a familiar circuit of Christmas gift-giving. John Henry had been uppermost in her thoughts and on her order blanks during the first of the month. Grandson Jon Stableford's wife Cindy preempted the next segment. Had I sent one of the cookbooks to her? What about the children's mittens and Jon's *New Yorker* subscription gift card? In two days she made the same inquiry four times—and why not, given the length of her list?

Unfortunately for everybody, her appointment for routine eye examination was scheduled before Christmas, and there was dreary news from the opthalmologist. The diagnosis was a worsening of her cataracts. We all felt it keenly but K was the stoic of the group. She would accept no commiseration; her attitude was impassive and the terms she used in speaking of the deteriorating vision were not exaggerated. However, as she dictated a letter to Roger, there was a tremor in her voice that betrayed her fears. A partial loss of sight was proving to be a nearly insuperable handicap; a complete loss was unthinkable; still she downplayed her own troubles to mention to friends that Andy was miserable with sinus congestion, but also with nerves over the confused bustle of Christmas. She concluded that something would have to be done about it another year.

Christmas 1976 at the Whites' was different from former ones. There was the same tumult and bustle, the running around on twice and thrice-repeated errands, the plenitude of gifts, the incomparable decorations, a delicious underlying fragrance of balsam, and an air of expectancy that had been part of it other years, but over and above it all loomed "The Book." Everywhere one glanced one saw a copy of it—in some places several copies. They were grouped together in EB's study awaiting mailing bags to distant places; they were settled on the sofa in the upstairs hallway, ready for family and nearby friends; they were to be found decoratively wrapped among more mundane offerings of the season. K had a copy on her living-room bench and another on her bedside table for ready reference. I had one, for the same purpose, in my office. When there was a knock at the kitchen door, the caller invariably was a neighbor carrying the book and requesting an autograph. The whole ambience of the household that season was the *Letters.*

When I left work for the day, I often toted some of the ambience home with me: there were letters to be typed and inevitably they contained a reference to the book or to a review of it. At home also there was my own precious copy much in evidence—in kitchen, living room, or a bedroom, depending on who had been dipping into it. My name was in the index and that occasioned some pride. None of us ever had been indexed before. "Don't hang up your stocking this year," instructed my husband, "there's nothing Santa Claus can leave that will compare with what you've already received." My copy was pragmatically inscribed: "Isabel: You had a lot to do with cleaning up this messy manuscript, and I am grateful for every minute of it—as well as for your optimism which I did not share. Love, Andy White."

There was tree-trimming, last minute gift-wrapping, and a final checking over of many lists of lists (with holiday jitters on K's part and the absolute certainty that she had forgotten a gift for her nearest and dearest) on Christmas Eve. Since the tenth of the month, she had been opening presents as they arrived in the mail, and she was trying valiantly to keep up with acknowledgments so there were a few of those to be written, too.

When I had made, finally, the last of a dozen trips upstairs and down and was ready, with her blessing, to assemble outer wraps and depart, I discovered a package of familiar size and contour laid on my briefcase. The shape of the box said plainly that it was one of the Deer Isle boutique specials. Apparently EB had wrapped it himself; the inept male touch in such circumstances is easily identifiable. The card on top said "Merry Christmas, love, and thanks." The uniquely beautiful silver necklace inside would be, next to my engagement ring, my most precious item of jewelry. Dotty, Harriet, Corona. Me, too? I was flabbergasted.

·ↄ EIGHT ϱ··

The New Year required too many additional notes of thanks, too many descriptions of the family celebration, too much general correspondence for K to surmount with equanimity. Frequently she handed over a batch of letters with a telling commentary: "Answer them any way you think best and I'll sign them. They needn't be long—half a page will do." Certain adjectives seem to have found their way into the English language for the express purpose of describing her: she was tenacious, she was indomitable, she was uncompromising. Although her vision difficulties were slowing up all her work, she was doing her best to surmount them. She didn't complain; she simply sent more notes to the office. "Isabel, just say we can't." "Tell these children folders have been sent." "Tell them my health is poor." Saddest and most frequent: "You know what to say." Whereas in healthier days she had demurred occasionally at having to intersperse her own projects with assignments of her husband's, in 1977 she seemed to seek out eagerly everything of his that came her way. "There's nothing here from Andy; I'm sure he spoke yesterday of two items that would need attention. Just run in and ask him before he goes out somewhere."

He obliged as often as possible and several times put into K's hands a letter so polished that it required only a date and his signature: "Do you have time to edit this, K? Perhaps I've been too garrulous, running on about the Mount Vernon days." On one such occasion I was the lucky go-between in an account of an encounter with a cow that was, perhaps, purposely made flippant.

"What do you think about this one, K?" he asked, sliding a letter with an attached sheet onto her table. "He seems to have acquired a farm so maybe I ought to tell him about that cow I had once. You remember? We got on pretty well together until she fell over on me one afternoon. Had a slipped hip." The nurse interrupted briefly with a daily mid-morning dosage for K, giving me time to ask, "Did the cow really fall on you, Mr. White, or is this going to be humorous?"

"Did you ever have a cow fall on you? Believe me, it's no joke."

"Well, for heaven's sake, it's a wonder you didn't suffer from more than a slipped hip."

"What?"

"Isn't that what you said?"

"*Her* hip, not mine."

"Yes," K put in crisply, setting down her glass, "that's what you said, Andy."

"Well then, you'd better add 'She was drowsy.' "

"I certainly am *not* drowsy, Andy. As it happens, I had a very good night."

He looked for a moment as though he longed to be away in some peaceful pasture, regurgitating meadow grass and clover with that long-departed cow, but he smiled at his wife and finished comfortably, "I know you'll get it right, my dear; after it's typed, I may just add a paragraph."

Dinner guests at the Whites' on Thursday altered the inviolate custom of Thursday evenings, so there was no opportunity for their careful reading of *Time* magazine. I was first with the good news, therefore, next morning: "It's in ninth place on the best-seller list!" I cried joyfully to EB, brandishing my own copy of *Time* at him in the upstairs hall. "Best-seller list, best-seller list," I chorused to K, dispensing with the formal greeting and requisite polite query about her health.

"*Time* doesn't mean anything that way; subscribers depend on it for news and editorial comment, not for books," reproved K, our resident specialist in literary prestige.

"It's just a flash in the pan," added EB in his glummest manner. "Probably the backlash from holiday orders."

It almost seemed as though they wanted the book to fail. If not, then they were reacting in the manner of fatalists who dared not dip a spoon into a dish of good luck for fear spoon, dish, and luck would fragment at the instant of partaking. It was some small comfort to have K mention the *Time* rating, even if apologetically, in several letters she wrote that Friday. Then everybody was permitted to be jubilant when the January 30 issue of the *New York Times Book Review* placed the *Letters* in the number eight spot on its list.

In February those of us closest to K were exasperated, as was the groundhog. He saw his shadow and retired underground, abandoning us to six more weeks of winter. K went once more to Blue Hill Hospital with respiratory problems, which may not have been caused by the harsh weather but certainly were not helped by it. When she returned home there was not enough leisure in which to recuperate. Once more, the weary, muddled outlook. "In your spare time, Isabel, start a shelf list of all the books in the house." I nodded agreement but felt sick at heart. The shelf list had been completed before I started working for the Whites and it was my responsibility to make sure that each time a new book came into the house it was added to that general list; after that, under K's aegis, the title appeared on the Bryn Mawr starred list, with that listing being made only if the book had a specific *New Yorker* connection. "Be sure now that you state the condition of each book," she added, compounding the problem. Neither the general shelf list nor the college list ever had been concerned with how a book looked—new, old, with or without dust jacket, tattered or uncut pages—none of that had to be taken into account unless a book was being offered for sale, as the chatelaine of books herself had often expounded. Her voice followed me down the hall, "We have to have an up-to-date shelf list to make it easier for the children when we die."

It was difficult to decide whether to show her the current list, kept in a carton under the highboy (a list so up-to-date that the *Letters* and all December and January acquisitions had been entered in it) or to linger a while and hope she might forget her request. It had happened before, it might happen again. It would be pure folly to hand over the carton as verification of an existing shelf list. Once she got her hands on the list, she could easily strain her weak vision reading it all through; then she might be tempted to edit most of the entries and have them recopied. Nothing would be gained, much of her time and energy would be lost. The arrival of the Whites' granddaughter Callie for a few days' visit turned K's attention in happier directions and it was logical to postpone decisions about list-making while a guest was in residence. Later, searching memory and journal, I could uncover no further reference to the list; there must have been so much else to occupy K's mind that the reality-unreality of a shelf list died aborning.

EB was falling behind on "Newsbreaks" for *The New Yorker;* he spent much of the latter part of February trying to catch up. One submission amused him enough that he wanted to share it. "I'm going to caption it 'Clear Days on the Kiss and Tell Front'," he announced. That caption offered an opportunity I had long sought.

"Who thought up that familiar *New Yorker* slogan about the 'Kiss and Tell Front'?" I asked.

"I haven't any idea. We've been using it for years."

"I'll bet you have. Since about 1932, for instance?"

"Well, no—maybe not as far back as that. Why?"

"I'm asking because I remember where the phrase 'kiss and tell' originated, and I wonder if you know?" Unselfishly pleased that somebody else knew something in his field that he didn't know, and liking nothing better than a challenge, he asked for a clue.

Not so kind as he, I offered the one least likely to help him. "A policeman named MacMahon."

"Well, that indicates there has to be a crime somewhere but I can't seem to place it. Boston or New York?"

"North Carolina locale but New York people, or at least they were well known in New York circles."

He shook his head but obviously was enjoying the game. "One more clue?"

"Tobacco."

It was too obscure. He looked so abject over his inability to recall a notorious crime that had added a picturesque expression to his caption world that I relented: "Tobacco heir, name of Reynolds. Libby Holman married him."

"Aha, I do remember that. She was the last of the so-called torch singers. We didn't hear them described that way after her era, did we? Anyway, it was a murder, I think, but where did MacMahon come in?"

"He was Libby Holman's special friend—a speck too special,

the authorities decided. The newspapers labeled him 'the kiss and tell cop.' "

"Odd that you should remember that one murder out of so many over the years."

It was less odd than he supposed; I remembered because the entire subject was *verboten* in our house. The section of the now-defunct *Boston Traveler* that carried the daily account of the trial was strictly off limits for us youngsters, even though my older sister was in high school. Adult guests who spoke of the trial in our presence were quickly hushed and steered onto safer, more moral topics. The prohibition naturally whetted our appetites for forbidden fruit; when our parents' attention was safely engaged elsewhere, we delved into the stack of old newspapers in the shed and devoured every word. We were haunted by the photos of Libby Holman Reynolds, attired in demure, almost severe dark dresses with wide white collars and cuffs. She looked ever so seductive, we would have said if we had known the word, and at the same time innocent and appealing. Even a child could sense the lethal combination. We half believed her to be guilty but still we loathed MacMahon for his ungentlemanly disclosures. It might all seem ridiculous to today's children, nurtured on television's lurid fare and exposed from infancy to a permissive sexual atmosphere, but to youngsters of that era, glimpses into the grown-up world of crime and intrigue were rare indeed. How impossible to imagine Libby Holman growing old! EB could grow old, I could grow old, but Libby Holman should have stayed forever young, forever sultry-looking, forever delicately garbed in a dark dress with a virginal white collar.

On the last day of February EB and I exchanged a few pleasantries about assisting our luck by the old folklore system of remembering to say "rabbit, rabbit" the first thing next morning. He was suffering from what he described as a dropped stitch in his lower back, so he was not comfortable and by extension not very cheerful but he managed a wan smile when I decided I was going to experiment with "March hare, March hare," this time.

K, coming very slowly and carefully down the stairs as though afraid of losing her balance, a posture that had become more marked since the new year, asked immediately for the mail, so I volunteered to do the fetching. In the kitchen Edith issued a friendly warning about the geese, who had been wandering freely, and squawking bad-temperedly, around the yard for an hour or more. When at liberty they were strongly inclined to be vicious, and sometimes pursued staff or strangers with unholy glee, threatening to attack. I told her I wasn't afraid, and of course I wasn't, never having encountered the creatures outside their fenced-in corral, but she came out with a broom, just in case. The instant I drew abreast of them they began a fierce hissing and flapped their wings, appearing to be fully prepared to begin snacking on my tender flesh. Having assured myself that Edith was out of hearing (she was shouting polite admonitions at them from the steps, brandishing her broom in accompaniment), I said in a low but nasty tone: "Back, you little bastards or I'll kick your teeth in!" and lo, they executed a rear march maneuver worthy of a drill team and fled around the house in the opposite direction from the mailbox. How triumphant I felt, as well as a little surprised. Were they just a bunch of bullies, after all, afraid to stand up to a menacing voice? Perhaps it had been a sobering occasion for them, being scolded in vulgar, if not actually profane, language. Heretofore they had been addressed in mild and courteous accents by Henry, a soft-spoken man and a non-cursing Baptist, and by

EB himself, who rarely raised his voice to any species of fish, flesh, or fowl.

"I saw the geese out there," he remarked, accepting the mailbag. "I hope they didn't give you any trouble." Not a bit, I reassured him. He emptied the contents of the bag on top of Jones, who had been enjoying a midmorning siesta in the middle of the loveseat. "I suppose you talked turkey to them," he added thoughtfully.

As his annoying backache showed no signs of abating, EB visited Doctor Britt to see if any relief could be promised. Apparently X-rays were advised. "Well, what happened?" demanded K, all animation and interest, when her husband returned.

"I had a tender spot around the kidneys so they took X-rays," EB responded apathetically.

"Well," stated K, forthrightly, "many persons have got along just fine with only one kidney so no doubt you'll be able to!" Then she ticked off a few names of recovered victims of kidney surgery.

"Thank you K, but it hasn't come to that yet, nor is it threatened. I'm going to try to keep the set I have for a few years more," and he stumbled upstairs, muttering to himself.

K's own greatest fear was that she "would no longer be useful to Andy if she couldn't take care of his fan mail." There was a simple pattern emerging during the early weeks of her failing vision: EB would leave a fat stack of letters for her attention; then, a few days later, the heap would have dwindled remarkably, without K's having dictated many replies; soon after, a group of them, with EB's own answers appended, would appear on my desk. Obviously they had been culled from the bottom of the heap, where K wouldn't miss them. Often, too, in the winter of 1977, he would give me a handful of letters and say quietly, "Can you just take care of these yourself and put them right in the mailbag, not on the table?" Of one such missive he enjoined: "Send thanks but not so many thanks that she writes back."

A food faddist had written to EB on the subject of lecithin and its efficacy in controlling cholesterol levels. Roosters among a flock of hens, according to the writer, promoted the substance lecithin in eggs. On a blustery March morning EB spoke to K of the one Buff Orpington rooster in his flock of hens. He hoped one was enough? She thought another might be in order—one could never be too sure. He came into the office with a letter to be typed. It was my first encounter with that breed of poultry outside the radio show "Fibber McGee and Molly," in which one of the human characters (who sounded like a gossipy, big-bosomy type) bore the name Bufforpington. EB seemed to be in an approachable mood so I checked up on the letter, inquiring if he and the faddist seriously subscribed to the lecithin-rooster theory.

"Yes, I'm fairly sure it works; I've read about it elsewhere, and that's the only reason I keep roosters."

"I supposed roosters were around to keep the hens happy, aside from the business of fertilizing the hatching eggs, of course."

"Who needs a happy hen?"

"Well—doesn't the egg taste better if it's been laid by a whiffy hen?"

"Whiffy?" I had made a blunder; he was enmeshed in vocabulary now, not poultry, and I had to stumble out of it somehow.

"Whiffy. Well, chirpy, upbeat, tuned-in-to-the-world. Eggstatic?"

Reproof was writ large all over the usually benign countenance. "A bit of idle chatter like that, my dear, if it happened to come to the attention of the Department of Agriculture, could set off a bunch of experiments that might eat up millions of taxpayers' dollars. Do you want your own hard-earned wealth to be chewed up in that fashion?"

On March 7 the Whites received an invitation from their friend Doris Wolfers to have lunch at her home on Naskeag Point and view her latest montage creations before they were shipped for exhibition to a New Haven art gallery. K, not having been out of the house socially for a long time, was looking ahead to the outing with anticipation and anxiety. Much discussion ensued between living room, Andy's study, and with Doris on the phone. Was Andy too busy to spare the time? Could I change my work day from March 9 to March 8 because K would want to rest the morning of the ninth before going out. Would the weather be a risky factor or could they take a chance on it? All problems finally being settled to everyone's satisfaction, the invitation was accepted. March 8 was a warm, spring-like day. The more ambitious of the avian population had signed in from the south and there was some twittering in the apple trees; the last of the snow was slushing itself off in mushy streams and a few blades of green were visible among the brown grasses of winter. The ear attuned to it could pick up the musical drip of sap into buckets on maple trees. "What a heavenly day!" I enthused to K at noon. "I hope it will be exactly like this tomorrow when you go out." There was a short silence while she looked at me blankly. Then she asked, "Am I going out tomorrow?"

As the month advanced, the sunshiny days were few; the weather retreated into its more familiar pattern of March winds shaking the house and March snows fertilizing garden and fields. EB gave the impression that he didn't feel very well during those weeks. He looked disconsolate, sitting humped over papers at his desk, and his voice matched his step in weariness. A letter he wrote to one of his favorite correspondents, Kathy Hall of the Cornell Library Rare Book Department, sounded so despairing (even to its composer) that he had second thoughts about it and returned the finished copy to my desk with a new, more optimistic version clipped to it. The letter Kathy never saw was fulsome in its sorrow, dwelling particularly on his fears for Katharine's future. Discarded in my office wastebasket was a single line I wanted Kathy to see: "What a boon it would be if only you were up attic among the audiovisual materials." I hoped that perhaps he had third thoughts, and eventually appended it by hand to the typed copy. If so, only Kathy knows.

On March 19, a Saturday, an extra Town Meeting (to complete leftover business) was to be convened in the town of Brooklin early in the afternoon. Our family had no intention of attending it and, indeed, no special interest in the main issue: licenses for clammers. Between working mornings at the Whites' and afternoons at an additional secretarial position, plus an extra stint of typing two evenings a week for a friend, I had no plans for Saturday beyond the privilege of catching up on cooking and cleaning at home; but on Friday EB himself requested that I work on Saturday, and K chimed in heartily. I had found excuses for staying away two previous Saturdays. Had they maneuvered together and cleverly figured I wouldn't be likely to refuse his request? I hoped not, but then proved them right by agreeing to come, trying to conceal some natural reluctance. I raced through EB's projects as fast as possible because all signs indicated a long session of writing personal letters for K. Her dear childhood friend and roommate of Bryn

Mawr days, Eleanor Washburn Emory, had died, and letters of condolence to five Emory offspring would be of prime importance. At least the renunciation of my valuable Saturday was in a worthy cause; it wasn't going to be frittered away on the mundane. On Friday K had begun a rough draft of the sympathy letter: it spanned two world wars, three assassinations, innumerable weddings and funerals, some childhood high jinks during summer vacations in Chocorua, New Hampshire, a number of dormitory escapades, and other minutiae that I devoutly hoped she (or someone) would edit.

At 10:30 Saturday morning she began her slow, laborious journey downstairs, calling out from the landing, "Andy, is the mail in yet?"

Invisible to her, but able to make myself heard, I replied, "It's right on your table, Mrs. White. I think Mr. White is in the cellar." There was a moment of silence (appalled silence, it must be assumed) on her part. Then she spoke to the nurse who was standing at the foot of the stairs, monitoring her progress:

"That sounds like Isabel's voice."

"Yes, it is Isabel's voice," replied Linda cheerfully, smiling at me.

"Well," said K, descending into my view, "well, of all people, I didn't expect to see you today! You certainly should be excused on a Town Meeting Day. I hope you're planning to attend?"

All the details of work at the Whites' the following week stand out in memory with the clarity of a reflection in glass. Glance away from the light and, for the moment, the scene fades; look back again and there is each person and the entire landscape as faithfully reflected the hundredth time as it was the first. That week, because it turned out to be the last truly familiar one of all the eight years of weeks spent in that household (as well as marking the close of my association with K) is mirror-imaged in my mind with stark precision. I remember such insignificant details as the delicious cooking aromas from Edith's domain (EB liked to call them "the smell of plenty") wafting through the house. Something was being steamed in the pressure cooker one morning and Edith and Shirley were amused to learn I didn't own one, because I couldn't learn how to use it and was afraid of an explosion. (Microwave ovens were not yet popular and indispensable. If I had known anything about one I would have thought of it as an elegant place in which to burn Hansel and Gretel's witch.) Henry was mildly disgruntled over some directions issued by K for preparing a flower border. The directions were in utter variance with her orders of a week earlier, and he didn't see how he could undo what he had already done. I offered the sage advice I myself often followed in similar situations: wait a few days to see if she would forget all about the second set of instructions. I could advise Henry ever so glibly about undoing tangles in his department; future events would prove I was not as skillful at unraveling my own knots. My final memory of Florence Sherman, a nurse of K's with whom I had had many a friendly conversation over the years, centers around the ubiquitous geese. When I stepped out of my car in the parking lot one of those last mornings she was standing in front of her car, looking harassed. "What's the trouble? Flat tire?"

"No, I'm afraid of the geese."

I looked to where she pointed and sure enough, there came the battalion, bearing down on us in deliberate single file, honking viciously. We looked around the premises as far as we could see in all directions but there was nobody to come to our rescue. Florence was armed with no stouter weapon than a small purse, while I carried a sturdy briefcase, so it was up to me to offer protection. I placed her on the off side and we proceeded to charge their line as bravely as ever members of the Light Brigade charged whoever it was in their heyday. The briefcase served as our shield; though the geese gave us a lot of lip (bill?) we returned an equal amount of the same and they did not press the issue but doubled back toward the barn, hurling expletives at us all the way.

Letters typed for EB on Monday and Tuesday of that week were average. So was his attitude: "I swear I'll never write another professional word. Then I won't have to field so much fan mail." He spilled out the contents of the mailbag on his desk and eyed them ruefully.

"If there were no fan mail you and Mrs. White wouldn't need a secretary and I'd be out of work."

"No, you wouldn't. I know just what you could do. You could type the manuscript of my last book. I'd write one just to please myself and we wouldn't let the publishers get their grasping hands on it!"

K's letters that week were on only one subject. She wrote about her lost friend Eleanor, not only to Eleanor's children—that omnibus was in its third rough-draft stage—but to other correspondents who had neither met nor scarcely heard of the deceased. It began to seem like an obsession with her and I longed to have done with it so that her mind could be turned away from death and toward more sprightly subjects.

On Wednesday the twenty-third came one of March's unique goodwill offerings: a biting, driving, menacing ice storm. This time the phone was not silenced too soon; it did its duty long enough for me to call K to let her know I couldn't get out. She agreed that it must be so, but bemoaned the lost time. "We'll have to get you here some way tomorrow because there is so much to be done and we really must try to make some progress on the letters to Eleanor's children."

The office desk was inundated with work the next day and there were letters to be transcribed that had been left in my notebook Tuesday. On top of the heap of handwritten messages for me to copy was a letter to Carol Angell. Roger was away in the south doing his annual report of baseball spring training for *The New Yorker* and K was good-hearted about writing extra letters to Carol in his absence. Doubtless Carol's letter would be the most important one of the group so I struggled through it first. By chance the written draft had been completed just before Wednesday's severe storm struck, and that meant there would have to be an addition, because K was never one to leave storms unnoticed. She reported them all with verve and gusto to each correspondent and she would insist, I knew, on adding a storm postscript to Carol's communiqué. EB was bringing in more and more of his own work to be done and it seemed that there would be no time to do more for K so, hoping to save my time and her own peace of mind, I added a brief storm postscript to the letter for Carol, then went on to EB's correspondence.

When K came downstairs she was unhappy to learn that her husband was going to preempt most of her secretary's morning. She wavered for a moment, as though she might be going to break the long-established precedent of putting his work first, but then thought better of it, and propelled herself with a deep sigh to the living room.

So many small happenings might have stood between the two of us and what followed, such as a chance remark of hers about something she had read and wished to share; an inquiry of mine about her health; an interruption in the form of a phone call or a stray visitor (two- or four-footed variety) at the door. But nothing intervened and it truthfully could be averred that the dimensions of the weather on Wednesday were the means of reshaping our destiny on Thursday. If the ice storm had not occurred, I might have seen K through to the end. However, I was not more than a third of the way into the stack of EB's correspondence when her peremptory summons sounded from the living room: "Bring in Carol's letter; I shall have to dictate a postscript about the storm. Are you doing anything important? We'll simply have to get all those Emory letters out today."

"I have a lot to do for Mr. White, Mrs. White, and I thought you might want to finish off the Emory project if there was a minute to spare, so I added a few lines about the storm to Carol's letter to save time." I handed the typed sheet and envelope to her. "Do you want to look at it and add anything I've left out?"

She snatched the letter from my hand with the air of one who had found a perfect excuse for venting some pent-up anguish on the nearest object. *"Well!"* in tones of red-purple-black, "you have absolutely no authority at *any* time to add *any*thing to my letters!" What a mild reproof it seems now in the face of many deserved and undeserved tongue-lashings that had come my way over all the eventful years. Perhaps it was her strident tone of voice and the deliberate misinterpretation of motive that touched a deep core of anger and dismay in me that morning. She sealed her fate—or mine—with the next terse statement. "Take this in to Andy while I decide what to tell Carol," she said, as she put an envelope down on the table.

Crossing the hall to Mr. White's sanctuary, I said to myself, "I might as well tell him right now that I've reached the limit of my resources. I wasn't planning to stay through another

Christmas season so what difference will a few months make?" The words I used, as quietly and evenly as I could speak them, to EB at his desk, will not come back to mind no matter how stubbornly I seek them. Perhaps that proves how much sympathy and distress I felt for him, how much animosity, at that moment, toward her. It can be assumed that I spoke the simple truth: I no longer had enough patience to surmount the confusion her work represented and I resented not being permitted to go ahead on my own and help where I could. I have tried ever since that awful day to blot from my consciousness the stricken face he turned to me but nothing will erase it, not even the handsome portrait of the younger E. B. White now looking kindly down at me from the wall of my study.

He made the inevitable reply: "Please think about it at least overnight. Perhaps things won't look so grim tomorrow." I was beyond speech then; I just shook my head and went out. I was late finishing work and had to make a hurried exit, well after twelve. EB was not, according to custom, sitting in the living room with a pre-luncheon martini. I quietly told K what I had told him, and added that I would of course serve out three weeks' notice while they searched for a replacement. K had no opportunity to protest (for all I knew she may not have wanted to) because I waved farewell, saying "I'm late, I must run," at the close of my resignation speech.

Predictably on Friday she was ever so distressed and ever so gentle; at one point she shed unaccustomed tears and it was difficult to restrain myself from saying, "It was all a mistake, let's forget it and begin again," but the prospect of total release was such a rapturous one that I wavered for no more than a second. When she remarked forlornly, "Surely we can sit down and discuss this misunderstanding," I knew I would be lost if I agreed.

"If we discuss it, Mrs. White, inevitably we shall be critical of each other. I'd rather not have that happen; I'd rather leave with no hard feelings or harsh words. Please let us say good-bye as friends."

She made one final effort to reverse my decision. "Is it an irrevocable decision or may we hope you will change your mind next week?"

"It is absolutely irrevocable. Please begin looking right away for a replacement so I surely can leave in three weeks, if not sooner."

EB stopped me midmorning on the stairs to put the same question in nearly identical words: "Is this decision irrevocable or may we hope for a change of mind?"

It was, and he couldn't. I felt far worse for him than I did for his wife. The heaviest part of the burden would fall on him. Even the most proficient, best-trained secretary in the whole state of Maine would find the first months with them difficult. While their secretary was trying to learn the ropes (and good luck to her, poor dear) he would have to do much of his own typing, as well as much of the general correspondence that he might otherwise have surrendered to K. He did not take kindly to change under the most ideal circumstances and this was an unkind change under most imperfect ones. He had rallied sufficiently by noon to introduce a brief discussion on a choice of wine for a dinner party, speaking about it in a purposeful "all is well" manner. K, meanwhile, was entertaining the possibility of finding some young, untried secretary, and asked if I had anybody to recommend. I was dumbstruck. Was she so unaware of the unusual demands she made on a secretary that she thought any young woman could put up with them or her? I shuddered to contemplate my three weeks in limbo as she conducted interviews and as I tried to bring a semblance of order for a successor out of the rabbit warren that constituted my desk and files.

On Monday, March 28, by fortuitous circumstance, K had a doctor's appointment. That meant an almost uninterrupted three-hour session of work and the opportunity to start sorting and labeling the many unfinished projects that leered at me like so many paper demons from every flat surface in the office. As had so often happened during the past eighteen months, on the day following the medical session, K stayed in bed. Having little energy for dictation, she was content to settle for four letters and to promise "we'll get to work on the files later in the week." There was small chance of the promise being adhered to, but I was willing to agree to almost anything that day.

On Wednesday there were again only four letters and no mention was made of files; with the audacity of a chipmunk confronting a tiger, I began sorting, stacking, and labeling without permission, rejoicing in the opportunity to begin on constructive work. Thursday brought a stroke of good fortune that turned me into a life-time convert to the "rabbit, rabbit" syndrome. "You'll be relieved to hear that Glyneta Andrews is willing to take over for you," announced EB, popping into my office before the cover was off the typewriter. I responded with heartfelt enthusiasm because I genuinely felt this was the best possible solution. Glyneta lived in Brooklin and was a sensible, practical sort of person who had known the Whites for years. She had filled in on typing for them for more than a decade, and often cooked when they needed a substitute in a hurry. My worst forebodings, doubtless shared by EB, had centered on the problem of introducing a stranger into the household. That was one apprehension that could be allayed. There would be no need to learn new ways, no adjustment to be made on either side. Only shorthand would be out; everything else would be the same and probably better. An enormous weight unsettled itself from somewhere far down inside me, giving a sensation of feather-lightness, as well as the inspiration to ask, "Is Glyneta free so she can start in two weeks, by any chance?"

"Oh yes, any time," answered EB casually.

The next comment was not premeditated, it was an instant reflex: "Well, then, would you be willing to find out if she can begin Monday? If so, I could just finish this week."

"Well—." He paused so long I was afraid I had hurt his feelings. Then, "I suppose that's what you'd rather do, wouldn't you?" He was pragmatic enough to recognize that serving out notice in this instance was tantamount to cutting off an arm by way of one finger at a time.

I sneaked into my office very early and unobserved on Friday morning, hoping to assemble all the flotsam and jetsam of the years into workable form for Glyneta. The five hours it took felt far longer. Each note on a folder explained what was wanted (if I knew) and gave details of progress already made; each was numbered in order of comparative importance. Several were labeled "put aside until there's nothing else to do." When it became evident that K had forgotten all about going over the files, I surreptitiously picked out a few duplicate and unnecessary folders and magazines and stuffed them in an empty carton under the highboy, in the hope that Glyneta would be less discouraged as she opened random file drawers.

When I carried the last letters in to EB, there was a sheet of paper in his typewriter; uncharacteristically he covered it with another sheet while speaking of routine matters. Never before had he treated anything on his desk or in his typewriter as private; everything was left plainly visible for me to read or not to read; he took secretarial discretion for granted. The note, therefore, had to concern me. I wanted most of all to avoid any ceremonious farewell, and the sight of the note was an encouraging sign. Perhaps he would entrust it to K and betake himself elsewhere when the clock struck twelve. But that was a mistaken supposition; it wasn't going to be that easy. When I had cleared my desk to a state of pristine neatness for what I thought was the final time, and gone into the living room where K had my last paycheck ready, EB was sitting in his regular place, fortified with a pitcher of martinis, rather than the usual single glass. K made a brief, kindly speech of friendship and thanks, and he handed an envelope to me, shook hands, and said unexpectedly, "If you ever need us, be sure to call on us." I made an uneasy departure. Clearly he had stolen my own exit line.

At home, when I opened the envelope, a check for one hundred dollars, with the notation "severance pay," fell out. The warm letter that accompanied it is as treasured a possession as is the silver necklace gift.

On Monday I mailed a reply:

Dear Mr. and Mrs. White:

Enclosed is my receipt for money received for secretarial work in 1977. Enclosed also is a news photo from our Sunday paper— I thought it would amuse you. [It was a photo of an elderly lady bending over and peering above her glasses at a long-necked goose, eyeball to eyeball. The lady bore no resemblance to our dignified K.]

The 'severance' check was generous beyond any expectation of mine. I anguished over it all day Saturday and Sunday; then I tore it into small bits and felt immeasurably better. At first I considered enclosing the bits here so that you, Mr. White, would have positive proof that you should mark 'void' across that stub in your checkbook but it seemed rather a dramatic gesture and I know how you like to keep it simple, so I refrained. I don't know how either of you regard a severance check; this is how I regard it: it is a sum of money owed an employee by an employer if the employer suddenly closes down the shop and has to say 'Sorry, your employment is terminated.' You didn't sever me at all, I severed you, with great regret. If anybody owes anybody anything, it is I who owe you the hundred dollars. I shall not offer to pay it because that might hurt your feelings. On the other hand, then, you must not insist that I accept such a payment because it would hurt my feelings. Please let this be the closing statement on the subject. Don't cast around in your minds for some way of making a gift in a different form that will be more difficult to refuse, something that can't be torn up; if you do, it will make me unhappy again. As a character said somewhere in Shakespeare: 'There's an end on't.'

My bookshelves are laden with many fine books that came from each of you. On the wall of my bedroom hangs a delightful Goulandris flower print (that by now you may have forgotten you gave to me, Mrs. White); I remember many happy conversations and quite a bit of laughter over the years. I treasure the note that accompanied the check. Thank you for everything.

. . .

·ᴥ NINE ᴦ··

In retrospect, the month of April 1977 seems to have been compounded of equal parts numbness and buoyant relief. The part of me that refused to believe all the worry and strain and confused encounters were over continued to function as though a return summons was imminent. The sensible part greeted each new day lightheaded, lighthearted, with a cheerful anticipation that is rarely felt by anyone over the age of ten. Glyneta, bless her, settled in with aplomb and did not have to phone for assistance or ask a single question, a feat nothing short of remarkable. K asked a few but she was tactful, always phoning at lunch hour when Glyneta had departed. For the most part I could give a ready answer to her queries, and it was gratifying to discover that often her true reason for calling was a wish to talk—as she and I had been accustomed to talking— about an article or story that had appeared in *The New Yorker*, or some other item of literary interest.

By the time we were well into the month of May, my concern for the Whites was no longer a paramount part of my existence. The concern manifested itself unconsciously when our travels took us by their house: I always found myself looking to the driveway to be sure the nurse's car was there, a signal that K was safe at home. Summer was the busiest season for us, as for most residents of coastal Maine, because we entertained many weekend guests and some week-long ones. My other secretarial position occupied my attention each afternoon, and our family was contemplating a drastic change that relegated most other topics to the background.

Russ, Ernest, and I had reluctantly concluded that we must sell our greatly beloved Brooklin property and move to the southern part of New Hampshire, where we would be not more than an hour's drive from close relatives in Massachusetts and New Hampshire. The decision was the result of much thought, argument, and anguish; we almost couldn't bear to move when the time came. We had sometimes regretted the great distance we had placed between ourselves and other family members when we initially moved to isolated Brooklin, but the selfishness of that move was not forcibly brought home to us until midwinter of 1977, when my sister in Massachusetts was struck by a serious illness and we found ourselves too far away to offer physical support. I had comforted myself through the worst days of breaking my bond with the Whites by saying, "Well, I'd have had to give them notice before Christmas anyway because I made that promise to Russ and Ernest." Now I could add, "And if we had to sell the house, it would be a case of giving almost immediate notice," but we were not sanguine about a quick sale. We had to be prepared for it to take at least a year and perhaps two or more, we told ourselves; therefore we could see no reason for making the matter public and upsetting friends and employers before the supposition became a fact.

There was one serious drawback to a sale: we had drawn plans and constructed most of the house ourselves and the whole structure had been designed for semi-retirement living of a very special brand—not just anyone's retirement living, but our very own. How were we going to find a buyer whose life-style harmonized with ours and who would be willing to live away from the mainstream of civilization on the coast of Maine and particularly in Brooklin, so far out on a peninsula? We could consider it a miracle if such a person or persons existed; a double miracle if they chanced to call upon our realtor and learned that our home was for sale. We did not expect that we would be treated to the triple miracle of being able to move from the property that summer or autumn. Despite our ill faith, the triple miracle came to pass: the property was listed with a realtor in Ellsworth at the end of June; he brought the first prospective buyer to view the house at the end of July, and by the middle of August this potential buyer had reached an affirmative decision. It was reached, unfortunately, just a few weeks later than suited my purposes, E. B. Whitewise, but one would hardly dare complain over that single flaw in such a speedy sale.

A lot of "what ifs" ran through our heads in June, once the momentous decision to list our property had been made. What if my afternoon employer heard that our house was on the market? Roy Barrette and his wife Helen were dear friends; we would not knowingly hurt their feelings. On the other hand, neither would we subject them to a year or more of suspense while we anxiously waited for a realtor to move our listing. At Amen Farm, their home, where I had spent all my weekday afternoons and some mornings for nine months, we fitted together hand-in-glove. Leaving it was almost as unthinkable as staying. I could not bring myself to speak of a future desertion until the sale was an accomplished fact. The secrecy shrouding the matter, therefore, extended even to close friends. Our realtor was admonished not to speak to any Brooklin client until he had consulted us; previously he had agreed to advertise our property in slightly disguised form in the county newspaper, and he carried out the promise with great finesse. I shuddered over the possibility that word might leak out, despite all precautions, to the Whites. They would have every right to say I had been untrustworthy and unfair in the reason I gave for resigning. They would attach little credibility to a disclaimer that the decision to sell had been made many weeks after the first of April.

In July I was bedeviled by worry over one awful contingency: what if our realtor phoned for an appointment to show the property while I was at work at Amen Farm? I developed an allergy common to any woman who has listed her house for sale. It consisted of a light rash on the back of the neck and a hollow sensation in the pit of the stomach when anything disorderly or untidy came into view anywhere around our house or grounds. Everything had to be display window perfect when a prospect appeared. At the same time we wanted to follow the comfortable, relaxed pattern of life we regularly indulged in. The two were mutually exclusive, so what was to be done? Finally I devised an emergency worksheet for the men to refer to in my absence.

We titled it "Code Charlie," in honor of our kind and friendly realtor, and it hung on the bulletin board in an obscure spot, blank-side out. It contained twelve admonitions to be carried out between the time of hanging up the phone after an appointment had been announced, and the opening of the door to an interested viewer.

1. Dust anything that has a flat surface.
2. Hide Tuffi's food dishes in the garage under something. [Tuffi was our cat; his food dishes ordinarily were treated with all the respect accorded our own.]

3. Put under your pillows anything in your respective bedrooms that doesn't look strictly neat. Do **not** toss into closets. Neaten your closet. Remember **"she"** will investigate **all closets!**
4. Sweep utility room rug—even if it was swept this morning.
5. Check spiders in shingle corners. [A mysterious directive understood only by ourselves.]
6. Wipe out all sinks with old towel and hang fresh towels in all baths. Put old towels in washing machine and close cover. Same with anything else that's soiled. Remember to do this or **I'll kill you!**
7. Put old newspapers and magazines somewhere—dresser drawer maybe? Or under my bed—the long spread will cover them.
8. Arrange chairs and tray tables on deck to look inviting (unless raining).
9. Sweep garage.
10. Use polish on door and handle of fridge and freezer.
11. Mow lawns and trim, if time.
12. Put on neat clothes in case you are in workadays.

P.S. I don't worry for a minute; I know you'll do us proud.

The postscript was a barefaced lie, included only for encouragement, but I doubt that I fooled them much. Our regular summer socializing went on; we wrote to distant friends about the decision to sell, cautioning them on the secrecy angle. We invented a reason for letting our boat go, and advertised it for sale; and we read hundreds of realty ads in New Hampshire brochures in order to have an idea of what the market offered and what towns would meet our requirements in case our flitting date came earlier than we expected. It was a wonderfully warm, sunny summer and we took advantage of the balmy weather to eat breakfast every morning on the deck, listening to the sounds of shore and sea, and looking out to the lobster boats and the faraway islands—in my own case, through eyes often blurred with tears.

Saturday, July 16, ushered in a spell of unconscionable heat. It was not the sort of weather we were accustomed to on the coast—usually the hottest day inland found us quite comfortable. This was different from other Julys: the heat engulfed us, there was no refreshing sea breeze; indoors and outdoors was stifling; at night, trying to sleep, we found it difficult to breathe. K's welfare was at the forefront of my mind during the weekend and again on Monday, as the heat wave showed no sign of abating. She had far more trouble trying to breathe in humid weather and it seemed likely the prolonged heat wave would sap her strength. An errand took us by the North Brooklin farm on Wednesday morning, July 20, and I was relieved to see that a nurse's car was parked in its regular spot, an indication that all was well. In the afternoon, however, when I needed to place a business call from Amen Farm to Joel White at his boatyard, the worker who answered said he was at Blue Hill Hospital, to which his mother had been taken. When, therefore, our own phone rang at 7 P.M. and we learned from a friend that K had died at five, it seemed a completely logical outcome to the fiendish weather, a sad ending preordained on Saturday.

I wanted then to go immediately to North Brooklin to offer sympathy and assistance to EB but it was nearly 8 P.M. before our phone stopped ringing. Until that night we had been unaware that nearly half the town knew us and knew where I had worked. Of that half, it seemed as though more phoned than didn't. Some had found out that professional connections had been severed early in April; others had not, and I didn't stop to explain unless pushed to it by a question about what K's health had been like during her last days. Finally I told my family and the phone, "Ring, if you must," and walked away from them and it. I had no clear idea of what I would or could say to EB and decided not to rehearse it. A spontaneous expression of concern was always better than one that had been planned, I assured myself, and that night nothing could have been more spontaneous than my expression. When, after knocking lightly, I stepped into the kitchen, and EB appeared from the north porch where Joel and Allene were sitting, one look at his devastated appearance and I turned away all choked with weeping, so that it was he who had to comfort me, instead of receiving the comfort himself.

He figured, ever so accurately, that I would not want to sit properly on the porch speaking platitudes to the younger Whites. "Let's sit outside where there's a little breeze," he suggested, "and I'll tell you how it was when K left us." We sat on the big settle that formed a segment of the entrance and he related how the humid weather had worn K down, how her temperature had soared to 101 degrees by the time the night nurse left at 7 A.M., and how he had summoned the day nurse at eight, an hour early, because he feared it was going to develop into an oxygen-ambulance morning. At the hospital, when K's temperature crept up to 105, he felt the first real premonition of death.

"I sat by her bed all afternoon and watched the pulsating of her heart on that chart on the wall, and I knew from the rhythm there wasn't going to be anything they could do. She wasn't suffering. She didn't know. Finally the wavering line just wavered out."

"I wish—" I began, then lost my voice again.

"Everybody wishes at a time like this. If we could only know when the last year, the last month, the last week, or the last day would be, there are so many things we'd do differently. But thank God we don't know. Who could bear it? You need have no regrets; you were infinitely kind to her and infinitely patient with her all those years."

It occurred to me at that moment to remind him that he was more fortunate in his loss than were many husbands who had relinquished dearly loved wives; in his published writings he had already eloquently informed the world how much she meant to him. Perhaps it was the wrong attempt at solace because he broke down and wept bitterly, although not for long. When he had recovered enough composure to speak, he reminisced a little about the younger K; talked of the burden her vision loss had placed on her and of how unhappy she had been the past three months when her reading was restricted. "This is terrible—but better," he finished.

He had talked just enough to restore my balance. I could ask firmly: "What may I do to help? That's why I came, to find out. Surely you'll need someone here for the next few days in the afternoons when Glyneta goes home? The phone will ring so much, there'll be telegrams, extra mail. Please let me help as a neighbor, not as an employee." It was such a reasonable offer, so little to do for anyone who had suffered a bereavement, but he seemed inexpressibly overjoyed, beyond the slight amount of kindness or devotion implied. I went home feeling less conscience-stricken than I had at any time since the last day I worked for him and K.

"Yes, I saw him," I replied to a question from my family, "and he made me feel so much better." This innocuous remark was greeted with some degree of mirth but I was so obtuse about it that they had to explain why they smiled.

The next day was as blistering hot as the previous four had been, with a gray-blue haze hanging over nearby Flye Point Lighthouse and distant islands; on the incoming tide the waves lapped indolently against the shore. A feeling of somnambulism permeated everything on land and sea. Whatever moved at all, moved slowly; even the gulls were lethargic, too limp and indifferent to utter their familiar shrill complaints. At last, on Thursday afternoon a violent thunderstorm sent the temperature plummeting and restored normal July weather to the area. If the storm had come upon us Wednesday morning instead of Thursday afternoon, K might not have succumbed, but such a conjecture was of little value. No one who knew her would ever believe she had rendezvoused willingly with death but at least there must have been less reluctance on her part to venture into the shade than once there had been. The slow-growing cataracts were threatening her with total blindness, and the shape of that personal shadow was more menacing than the prospect of death. "I could not bear to live in a world of perpetual night," she had said one day when the doctor's verdict had been less than optimistic.

At Amen Farm my book cataloguing and secretarial schedule was rearranged for several days so that afternoons, when Glyneta would not be at the farm, I could be useful to EB. That first afternoon when I approached the kitchen door, Jones was at hand but he did not bark, and that was the beginning of the strangeness of everything. The familiar rooms that I knew almost as intimately as I knew the rooms of my own home looked unchanged but at the same time utterly foreign. The core and the axis, the heart and excitement, the reason and the problem that accounted for those rooms, was missing. For the first few hours K's ghost was everywhere and I could believe only in the rumor, not the fact, of her death, in spite of having said two dozen times on the telephone, "Yes, Mr. White is reconciled to it; it wasn't just that her general health was poor—he told us that much of the savor had gone out of living for her when her reading was restricted." Everywhere I looked in the office there was a pamphlet or address or newsletter from an organization for the blind. At the same time there was almost nothing visible in K's own handwriting, an unusual circumstance no matter how sick she had been, no matter how efficiently Glyneta had worked.

Persons who telegraphed or phoned in the first few days of learning the sad news later wrote proper notes of sympathy to EB; again, it was the perfect excuse for longtime EBW fans who had written before to write again, this time to express their sorrow. *New Yorker* magazine staff and associates on all levels, denizens of the literary world and even of the political one; relatives, friends, neighbors, all were about to become articulate in K's behalf in the next few weeks. From the early sample I saw that weekend I felt compassion for Glyneta and her employer. How were they going to keep pace with it?

I worked until noon on Saturday (the day of the private graveside services in the Brooklin cemetery) engaged in a task that gave one more proof, if any proof was needed, of EB's perception and compassion. At 9 A.M. he brought in a list of names he had scribbled on scrap paper. "These are the ones who knew K best and corresponded most. They'll want to know all about how it was with her since Christmastime, and about her last day and the kind of service we plan. So take your time, go down through the list and select the ones you would most like to write to, and just tell them everything in your own words. Say at the beginning that I asked you to do it because you wanted to help."

Four letters and one hour later, I was crying all over the typewriter and some of the pages looked a bit the worse for salt-water spots, but not for anything would I have been anywhere else in the world engaged in any other task that morning. The specter of death receded gradually from the room, the house, the garden borders, and then to some unseen horizon beyond the cove, banished momentarily by the happy memories of K I was able to dredge up. There were an infinite number of unimportant but funny-crazy episodes, often connected with her health, that we had laughed about together. It was sad, but at the same time uplifting, to be busy letting others know how brave she had been in facing up to her infirmities during all the time I knew her. It was a panacea of sorts for much of the bitterness that had built up over the years. The bitterness had been corrosive but the process of summoning up the best of K for her friends' edification was healing. There had been many good days and they began to blot out the bad ones when the time came to reassemble memories.

I was plying a handkerchief with vigor during one interlude, unaware until EB spoke that he had entered the office from the living room. "I'm so sorry; the last thing in the world I meant to do was to have you grieving over this."

"Just don't look at me. Don't give it a thought. I was never so happy," I wailed on a long, sustained sob. What a dreadful thing to have said, what a stupid choice of words at such a time! I turned around in despair but he was smiling.

"Don't look so miserable; I take your meaning fully. I've been untangling your syntax for years."

There were a dozen methods to use in recapitulating the tribulations of July 20; different versions could be written to different friends of K's, with opening and closing sentences that befitted not only the occasion but the degree of friendship or perhaps particular personal circumstances.

To Buckner Hollingsworth in Vermont, a noted author of books on gardening, and herself the victim of greatly impaired vision, went the longest, most carefully worded letter. A few weeks later, I was surprised and touched to receive personal replies, directed to me in care of EB, from her, from author Elizabeth Lawrence, and from several others. On their part it meant writing twice, once to him, once to me. It proved, perhaps, that nothing was too much of an undertaking for them when it concerned their lost friend Katharine.

It was past noon when I finally put aside the last page and covered the typewriter. I had no idea whether EB intended to be present at the graveside service or not, but it seemed tactful to leave promptly and abandon him to the sorrowful recollections of that hard afternoon. I learned later that he stayed at home, having placed in Roger Angell's capable hands the eulogy he had written for the dear love of his life. There was no opportunity for me to creep out that day; EB had anticipated such a move and was on guard in the living room. "Don't hurry, please; I want to have a serious discussion with you."

He didn't need to utter another word. Even if I had wished to do so, how could I have refused him on that day? I sat down on the arm of a chair and heard him out.

"There's going to be an enormous amount of condolence mail to deal with; far more, I'm sure, than Glyneta wants to do. In fact, she was rather filling in for us until we found a substitute for you. She never has thought of this work as a permanent position. As you may remember from times past, she didn't and doesn't really want to be tied down. And we'll be coming to K's bequest of books to Bryn Mawr, and you're the one who knows all about that. . . ."

There was a slight pause while we looked at each other. I had known my answer to the question he hadn't asked before he began laying the groundwork for asking it. Somebody had to help him clear up all the tangled ends that had been left dangling in April and that were becoming more unraveled by reason of K's death. Nobody could expect Glyneta to have absorbed in three months all the intricate facets of K's personal wishes in the realm of bequests, and to have finished cataloguing all her jumbled affairs. There was a distinct obligation here that had to do with length of service.

"Of course I'll come back, Mr. White, and help you get everything straightened out." There was no question in my mind but that he meant "until everything is straightened out and forever after." But for him to put it into words would have underlined the obvious: I could work for him but I had been too sensitive at the end, when I should have been more understanding, to work with K. His affection and admiration for his wife and his loyalty to her, even in times of deep stress, in her lifetime and to her memory after death, precluded his saying or intimating that I could continue with him even if I had failed with her. Who could help but admire him for phrasing it the honorable way?

I thought about it all the way home. This new situation meant that another trauma loomed ahead if a sale went through; but much as I dreaded the second announcement of a resignation, I was anxious to sell and get it over with. There's an unsettling aspect to the sale of a house that goes beyond conferences with realtors, beyond waiting stoically while groups of strangers pry into a home's most private enclosures, placing mental price tags on the owners' most cherished possessions. The agreement to sell is a miniature dispossession all in itself. No longer are the dwelling's few odd quirks, part of its character and aspect that one has learned to live with, to be taken for granted. The squeaky door, the infinitesimal crack in the ceiling, the flaw in the wallpaper, the loose brick, the dripping faucet—all must be repaired to satisfy the critical inspection by a prospect. The very disposition of the house changes before one's eyes. It can no longer be looked at with a benevolent expression, with allowances for slight discrepancies because it is home; rather, one seeks out small flaws and exaggerates minor inconveniences, staring with the unfriendly gaze of the stranger upon something that has been dearly loved, something with faults one has learned to accept. Daily living loses its savor while the family operates on a cycle of "I wonder if we'll be barbecuing here on the shore next summer;" "Will this be our last Labor Day picnic and final apple crop?" "Was that our final Christmas here and we didn't even know it?"

·❧ TEN ❧·

K's will, of which EB was executor, promised to be extraordinarily complicated for an instrument that dealt chiefly with household possessions. EB's lawyer came from Blue Hill on July 25 to engage in the first of several grueling sessions as the two men began the long process of deciding what values to set on books, furniture, china, and jewelry. They could do little of the appraisal themselves—experts in the field had to be retained for that—but it appeared that just setting the wheels in motion would be no easy matter.

There were no letters to be copied on my desk that day— sure evidence that EB had not slept—but there were two names, with a request to write a letter of my own to each. The first was routine and unexciting: an apology to Harry Cloudman at Macmillan for a necessary delay in the revision of *The Elements of Style* on which EB was working. The second, though, was in the nature of a privileged assignment, an explanation of K's death to go to Margaret Fishback, a writer of exceedingly humorous light verse, who had sent four of EB's own books to him with a request for autographs. Recalling how I had laughed over her light verse in periodicals of the 1930s and later, I labored over that communication with all the care and attention a student lavishes on a doctoral thesis. Then I packaged the books, taking them to the post office en route home, and wishing all the way for the magic opportunity to accompany them in order to catch a glimpse of, and to exchange a few words with, the addressee. We would both be sorrowful over the news I was bringing, but I was positive she'd know how to lighten my heart.

EB's birthday on July 11 had engendered a volume of mail to add to the ever-growing amount of correspondence that was still coming in from readers of the *Letters*. The phenomenal response from readers made me eager to tabulate the exact number of letters EB received, but by the time I was back in harness at the big farmhouse, the opportunity for tallying had long gone. When it became evident that birthday mail had been overflowing into *Letters* fan mail, and that the latter was going to mesh with the notes of sympathy, EB devised a partial solution. He composed a rhymed stanza of thanks that alluded to his birthday and the book; he composed a second one that acknowledged messages of condolence. A few hundred of each were printed in black type on correct, somber gray stock, and although it required a while for the printer to catch up with us, eventually he did, and thus we saved an immeasurable amount of time. The cards needed only initials or, in some cases, the informal signature "Andy." If much more was required, he dispensed with the card and wrote a formal letter.

"Will they be acceptable? Are they in good taste?" he wanted to know, the day he was ready to send them to the printer. I admired them, especially a light touch in the last line of the *Letters* rhyme, where the perfectionist had deviated slightly from textbook grammar. It was not enough, however, to reassure him in the hope that the reassurance would comfort and help him and thereby spare him the trouble of writing innumerable letters. The somber gray cards would find their way into hundreds of homes across the United States; a few would be sent over the northern border; a few more to Europe. It wasn't enough for the card to be a clever example of how to express a polite mass thank-you. It had to be right. And it was. I read once more the card referring to the loss of K and tried to put myself in the place of an elderly dowager from Beacon Hill or Louisberg Square who might have been a classmate of K's in the long-ago days at Miss Winsor's select school.

"Yes, I feel certain they're acceptable. I'm sure Mrs. White will approve." It was several seconds before I realized I had used the wrong tense—not, in fact, until I glanced up to see why EB was so silent. He did not refer directly to the error but it was easy to follow the pattern of his remarks.

"When I'm upstairs, it's easy to believe K's somewhere down here. When I'm downstairs, I'm lulled into thinking she is up in her bedroom. What I have to guard against is coming down to the living room and then going right back upstairs again." His sigh was so profound it could be felt like a gust of cool air that blows unexpectedly into the afternoon of a warm August day.

On one other occasion, as we sat at the dining-room table sorting sympathy messages and counting and stamping envelopes, he spoke of the verse on the condolence/acknowledgment card and worried that K might not have approved had she known of it. I told him that she and I had often discussed matters of good taste versus poor taste, and I was positive what her reaction would have been to the sentiment he had devised. "She would have liked it so well that she would have wanted to send a copy to *everybody,* not merely to those concerned— and then she would have slipped a long personal letter in with each card." Whereat he laughed until the table wobbled, and I joined in, and we both felt remarkably better for the exercise.

He was not, we all were relieved to see, prolonging his anguish by insisting on keeping all things associated with K exactly as she had left them. He exorcised a troublesome spirit for the staff by getting rid of the hospital bed (with the kindly assistance of Allene White) as well as various medical appurtenances that had been necessities in K's room. Then from the attic Henry carried down twin spool beds and Shirley dressed them neatly in white hobnail spreads. She arranged chairs and lamps for reading comfort; and presently the space that had been a focal point of invalidism in the house became a sunny guest room, with K's valuable collection of original prints decorating the walls, and the connecting bath untouched—as much a convenience for a guest as it had been for a former occupant. I no longer tiptoed across the floor, as I had done during the first week when I had to search for something in the desk or highboy in that room, nor did I have to restrain an impulse to glance in (as though expecting an order to be issued from an occupant of the bed) each time I stepped into the television room nearby in search of books. It was too late, of course, as are so many circumstances in our brief existence, to sit by the bed and offer help and solace to a brave octogenarian, as I longed to do. EB went one step further in his own determined acceptance of the new order of things. He began referring to K's former domain as "Nancy's room" immediately after Nancy's first visit.

When his ministrations were completed in the living room it looked, for a while until we grew accustomed to it, the way it had looked during K's tenancy when guests were expected. The large table was immaculate, with only a lamp, ashtray, and a few snapshots of the family on it; the bench she had used as a desk was banished to my office. Whenever there was an idle moment I sorted out the paraphernalia that covered it, arranging it for EB's later inspection. Now and then I surreptitiously tore into small scraps some barely decipherable note about medication, menus, or garden that was of no value and that would have been harshly poignant had EB come across it himself.

Often during those mornings on my way to work, I met him heading toward town in the Mercedes, sometimes with one of the dogs perched beside him, sometimes alone. It seemed unlikely he could have an errand each day at the store, and he was back again after a short time. Finally Henry supplied an explanation: each morning EB took fresh flowers from the garden to place on K's grave, which was in a forlorn corner of a new part of the cemetery, its harsh outlines unsoftened by trees and shrubs that over the years had helped to mitigate the stark aspect of the older section.

The news of K's death penetrated far and wide, and I was surprised by the number of persons who paid attention to it, and recorded on paper words that conveyed their reaction to it. The majority of those who expressed sympathy to EB were persons acquainted with K only as she had appeared between the covers of the *Letters*. All of them stressed the same fact: they had just begun to know her through her husband's correspondence and were troubled by a sense of personal loss, so explicitly had he evoked her character and revealed his devotion in his messages to her. It was taken for granted that the literary great and near-great would write to EB about his wife, extolling professional qualities they had admired in her. Their expressions of sympathy followed a natural line of social and business association with one or both Whites that had begun with the early days of *The New Yorker;* but only the publication of the *Letters,* coming exactly when it did in the last year of K's life, could have called forth such a general outpouring of concern from one end of the country to the other.

I was mildly surprised to hear from many of my own friends, most of whom wrote, "I really wanted to say this to E. B. White himself but felt it would be a burden to him, so I'm writing to you instead." One friend, inexpressibly dear, did write to him and mentioned in the letter that she was acquainted with me. I came across her note one day when I was typing envelopes for the printed cards and was touched by EB's notation across the top: "Isabel's friend; be sure to include personal letter." His stock of deeds of kindness to his staff, of which innumerable examples could be recited, was replenished, rather than diminished, by grief.

July 29, a Friday, was a mixed dish of a day indeed. K had been gone only nine days but already it seemed to me, contemplating the mass of sympathy letters engulfing us, that we had been constructing words and phrases and paragraphs about death and dying for weeks and weeks. It was as though we had been sentenced to dwell forever in the valley of the shadow and there would be no release ever, no escape into the world of sunlight, where jokes could be told and laughter dealt out liberally, and old memories recalled without stirring of pain. I reported early, wanting to get on top of the heap of work that had been littering my desk when I left on Wednesday. Fortunately, in spite of my haste, some housewifely instinct held me at home long enough to polish a counter, wash a mirror in the master bath, and to put in order a desk so untidy as to rival K's own in her best moments. There had been some excuse for her untidiness. There was none for mine.

EB said, approving: "You're here early, good! I almost phoned to ask if you could spare an extra half hour. Here's a big batch that could use your personal touch. Sign 'Secretary'

and then let me have the pleasure of reading them, please."
What a delicate way of saying "I almost trust you but I'd feel
safer if I had a chance to glance at what you've said." Truly,
there was no bottom to the deep well of the man's tact.

When the phone rang at 10:30, EB was outdoors, but within
my line of vision, in animated conversation with Henry. The
caller was my husband. "Code Charlie," he whispered in con-
spiratorial tones as though he feared all parties on our four
party line were listening in. "I'll have to go it alone; Ernest is
golfing with Win. What shall I do with the chicken?"

"What chicken?"

"Defrosting, on the counter."

"Shove it in the fridge. Wait till you hear their wheels on
the driveway." (As though the poor man had nothing else to
do but listen for the sound of approaching realtor and prospects.)

"And the bra on the clothesline and the lobster table out
there?"

"If it isn't dry, throw it in the dryer and be sure to shut the
dryer door. Drag it out in back of the garage as though it were
junk." A mixed-up response to his question, of course, but the
table on which the crustaceans got subdued with a cleaver
wouldn't fit in a dryer, and who would throw a perfectly wear-
able piece of underwear out behind the garage? I trusted him
fully.

After that interlude I was inspired to type at nearly twice my
usual speed in order to keep my mind off what was transpiring
at home. How I longed to be there overseeing the cleanup and
making sure of the infinitesimal details the best husband might
overlook, even with list in hand. EB managed to get into his
study, sort the mail, and cross the hall to my desk before I was
aware he was indoors.

"You're typing as though the devil were sitting on your shoulder. That machine won't last out the year at this rate."

"Oh dear," I thought, "if only you knew what was going on behind your back at our house," but I said only, "No time for small talk, there's so much to be done."

Anxious above all things to get home on time, I began assembling my belongings for a quick getaway while EB was still out on his regular pre-noon jaunt on his bicycle, but once again he fooled me and strolled in with a question just as I covered the typewriter and picked up my purse. It was a long question that required a long reply; I was so late getting home that I had to eat a quick sandwich lunch while the prospects were walking through the house. I had time to be introduced, to give them a brief welcome, and then to apologize as I ran off to my second job. I learned later that the busy-ness of the lady owner was highly interesting to the lady prospect. With her husband newly retired from the foreign service, where her own days had verged on being tumultuous, her chief concern was "What did one do in a small town like Brooklin?" As I dashed in late (thanks to EB) and dashed out early (because of Amen Farm) she was solidly impressed with the possibility of a two-segment career being pursued in the context of a coastal hamlet.

Our prospects returned the following day, sans realtor, for a more leisurely inspection, this time accompanied by their son. It evolved that my opposite number was, of all incredible coincidences, an experienced secretary. That made our house offer truly unique: if she and her husband accepted it she could, with any sort of cooperation on the part of my two employers, be assured of steady employment as well as of a dwelling. Privately, our family decided that any employer, after a few minutes of listening to her cultivated accents and one glance at her winsome face, would surely hire her; would be likely to pull back a chair and seat her at a desk with alacrity.

It was indicative of my state of excitement that I neglected on Sunday night to say "rabbit, rabbit" in the small hours after midnight. Of all times to forget it, when we were anxious to burn our bridges and have done with it; how could I have been so stupid, I asked myself when I looked at the calendar Monday morning. EB was in a slough of despond that would require more than a rabbit to defeat. He had a number of reasons but chief among them was the anticipation of another session with his lawyer. "You won't want me, then," I started to say when preparing to leave but caught the words back in mid-sentence when his expression went suddenly from cheerless to abject. The sentence was amended to a tentative "I can come tomorrow as well as Wednesday in case there's anything I know of the estate that the lawyer might ask about."

"Yes, yes, do come if it won't spoil any plans. Everything that's asked will be about something I don't know. If there are two of us looking ignorant it will be only half as bad."

The will had little validity in EB's mind, he confessed weeks later, because he still could not quite believe in K's death; also he was beset by a strong fear he might do something not in accord with her wishes. "Are you sure she meant—?" he asked repeatedly. "Do you suppose she planned—?" "Do you interpret this the way I do?" He was haggard by day and working himself into a fine state of insomnia by night. I wanted to shake him fiercely and push home the truth: this is all superficial, she no longer knows, the living are more important than the dead.

There was a pleasant interval when his step-granddaughter, Alice Angell, came to stay with him, to fill in the gap that had been left when Roger, Carol, and little John Henry departed for New York. A quiet person, soft-spoken, with a reserved manner that matched EB's own, and an air of reticence, Alice had a tranquilizing effect on him as she flitted unobtrusively around the house or went down to the shore to swim. She required no entertainment, but when he needed a companion she was pleased to talk to him. One morning when everything (lawyers, appraisers, K's personal effects to be sorted) all seemed too much for him, he stretched himself out on the big sofa in the upstairs hallway; after the mail arrived, Alice's soothing voice could be heard reading aloud to him some interesting excerpts from the gleanings of the morning delivery. She was a restful presence, filling some of the emptiness of the somber house in the night hours especially, when the staff had left and it became too large a dwelling place for one bereaved man.

High blood pressure was attacking sporadically and the best remedy, lying down to rest for an hour or two at a time, was not at all to EB's liking. "How can a man rest when there's so much to do? It buzzes around in my head the whole time I'm supposed to be relaxing. What do doctors know about their own advice? Did you ever see one stretched out at ease in his office when his waiting room was full of patients?"

"No, I never actually caught one napping, but sometimes I've had to sit so long in a waiting room that I suspected that's what he was up to."

That brought a reluctant grin, followed closely by the admonition that one telegram had to be acknowledged with a letter that morning else he might lose the good opinion of two valued friends. He was particularly anxious about it because its destination was a foreign port. His beleagured mind would not, for the moment, accept the proven speed of overseas airmail; he was convinced the message would be somewhere out there in an unfriendly environment for weeks before it was delivered.

He had been turning the telegram over and over in his hand as he spoke. Finally, with an air of bowing to the inevitable, he laid it on my desk. "You know her, too. And you know my style. Want to give a try at a good imitation?"

It was a new and unexpected assignment, akin to those a student sometimes comes across in college, when an inspired professor dares a class to do a bit better than its best, the dare is accepted, and he is presented with a *fait accompli* that justifies the daring. All I remember of that letter is the phrase "being badgered by lawyers, appraisers, and probate clerks." When EB came to it he laughed—a lovely sound from that lonely room—and commented, "I like the idea that I'm being 'badgered' by the law. Remind me to use that word to everybody who is kind enough to inquire about my health."

In an unaccountable switch of symptoms, one aspect of his health changed drastically, if briefly, soon afterward. The high blood pressure that had been plaguing him vanished overnight and the reading two days later was inexplicably low. He spoke of it as soon as I arrived; I agreed that it was indeed a surprising turnabout. "What can you do about it when it's low?" I inquired sympathetically.

He assumed the deadpan expression I had come to recognize; it was a prelude to a humorous or sarcastic retort. "Stop taking medication for a high."

He was methodical to an amazing extent. Everywhere one looked were small cartons, folders, assorted boxes, each neatly labeled in large black crayon letters that were visible halfway across a room. "Lawyer," read the labels, "Appraiser-furniture," "Appraiser-incidentals," "Jewelry Bequests-specific," "Jewelry-miscellaneous," "Bryn Mawr-to write," "Ask Roger," "Ask Carol," "Ask Joe & Allene." Small wonder that the healing process was slow in starting. K had provided selflessly in her lifetime for all persons and causes dear to her, and in death she could not be forgotten; indications of her providing were to be found in nearly every room. One day EB would be exuberant, reminded of a funny anecdote connected with an old Canton platter or an antique silver jug. Another morning he would be dogged by a headache and sunk in gloom, fingering an objet d'art that held sentimental memories of K.

"There are at least six letters here I ought to answer myself. If I don't get started, I'll never get caught up." He was down at his desk earlier than usual, not only down physically but in spirit. "There are two packages that must be wrapped right away but I don't have enough ambition to go after paper and cord."

"Well, what do you want me to do? Supply the ambition or wrap the packages?" He thrust them quickly into my arms. "I was hoping you'd rise to the occasion and you did. When you finish, I'll have a nice reward for you. I'll let you write three of the letters in bogus E. B. White."

Presently there was a reprieve from negative phrases on aspects of death, but only for me, not for long-suffering EB. As a witness to K's last will and testament, I had to declare her signature on the document bona fide, an insignificant matter of answering "yes" to a single question and requiring about five seconds for the will to be validated. However, the question had to be asked and answered at the county seat Office of Probate in Ellsworth; that meant a round trip of sixty miles for the matter of a five-second declaration. Satisfying the law involved a scandalous waste of time and fuel.

One day in a moment of indulgence (any departure from acknowledging messages of condolence was an indulgence) EB had introduced the subject of haiku, the deceptively simple

Japanese form of poetry that extolls nature in three unrhymed lines of five, seven, and five syllables respectively. We were in agreement that only Orientals could handle the form successfully; that imitations by Occidentals were dull at best. "I feel so circumscribed by the form that it's a waste of time to attempt to fit a thought into it," was his complaint.

"I can't keep it from rhyming," was mine.

"That's right," he agreed, "once you've written 'blue' you want to add 'hue' or 'dew.'"

"And rhyme 'fog' with 'bog' and 'house' with 'mouse'," I supplemented.

Two mornings later, under the apple tree I came upon a slim mouse, looking to be so lately done in that I could visualize its whiskers twitching. On an undefined impulse I secreted it in a paper tissue from my pocket and carried it into the house. Into a medium-sized manila envelope the mouse went, with a tag attached that said, "What's inside rhymes with 'souse.' Don't open it. Just guess." I laid it on EB's desk and bent my head innocently over my papers.

The telephone rang. An address and a list were wanted, and a lot of time was consumed dictating them over the phone. Back in my office again, I found on my typewriter a tiny sealed envelope, of a size to hold a calling card. The sheet of paper under it bore the message "Rhyme with 'stopper' or 'popper' and release outdoors unless you want it jumping all over your desk."

EB was pleased and comforted by an unexpected message in the mail. A monk from St. Anselm's Abbey in Washington, D.C., spoke of a mass that had been offered there for the repose of K's soul. "How that would have enchanted her! What a pity we can't be aware while still alive of all the fabulous words that are going to be written when we aren't. How my dear Katharine would have bustled around attending to all this minutiae and enjoying every minute of it."

K, reported the abbey brother, was remembered by him because of some correspondence exchanged at the time Harold Ross died. The brother had written a letter to *The New Yorker* to praise Ross and to indicate that he (the priest) had gone alone to the funeral chapel in New York City to pray for the *New Yorker* editor. K herself, doubtless much touched, had answered the letter kindly and the recipient had never forgotten.

By the third week in August we had apparently turned a corner. Kind hostesses who had been urging EB to join them for lunch, for cocktails, for dinner, and had been finding him unwilling to make the effort to be social, suddenly began receiving affirmative replies to their continuing invitations. Almost at once his 9 A.M. conversations took on a new, animated tone. The topics ranged from snatches of local gossip to erudite comments on world affairs that had come to his mind overnight as a result of the previous evening's conversation. He needed to talk; he was too much alone with a tendency to introspection that saddened his evenings and blighted his nights. I quickly got into the habit of arriving earlier in the mornings and moving ahead swiftly on leftover work, thereby releasing time to interrogate him about any social doings of the preceding evening. Cooking being my forte and a chief interest, it was pleasant to stress that aspect of his partying, and sometimes it seemed that he was pretending absymal ignorance of a menu in order to prolong any conversational encounter and to postpone the commencement of the less happy business that awaited.

"Well, what did it taste like? Surely you know whether you were eating salmon or crabmeat or lobster, even in a wine sauce and served on a shell?"

"Not I. Might have been Maryland terrapin for all I could guess. When women start putting some of their famous concoctions together, how is a mere man supposed to know what they've been up to?"

"Was it the main course or an hors d'oeuvre sort of thing?"

"It was the main course if you discount a slab of roast beef big enough to choke a St. Bernard—"

He was renowned for having a small appetite, so he must have paled under the provisions of the groaning board that night.

"Dessert?"

"Chocolate parfait but I couldn't face it; I was overstuffed. I told her I was on a diet—no sweets."

"It will be just your luck that she'll be entertaining your doctor some evening and she'll find out what a fabrication that was."

"Ummmm—well, he's going to drop in this afternoon so I'll put him on his guard. He's never to deny a word I've said unless he wants punishment in kind: in other words, he'll be forced to eat a meal I've cooked myself. It happens he's a friend—but wouldn't that be a fine way to get rid of one's enemies?"

Many fan letters that found their way to North Brooklin were unimaginative and repetitious, through no fault of their originators, perhaps. They couldn't be held responsible for what we had read before, and before that, for years and years. Once in a while came an exception of which K herself might have remarked (and EB and I usually echoed the sentiment), "It would be interesting to meet the person who wrote this." Late in August such a one surfaced out of the hordes of sympa-

thy mail. The writer, who lived in Manhattan, was not com-
miserating with her favorite author for the loss of his wife. She
was recounting instead the tale of her attempt to purchase a
copy of *The Second Tree from the Corner.* It had begun at the
Doubleday bookstore on Fifth Avenue. The young clerk,
searching the stacks for the book, held her order in his hand;
it had been delivered to him from a superior abovestairs, and
a notation at the bottom, which EB's correspondent chanced
to see, said, "This is not a humor book."

"I told him 'The hell it isn't!' " recounted the EBW fan, but
she was unable to convince the clerk; therefore the search
proved fruitless. Deciding to proceed along Fifth Avenue to
the Scribner bookstore, our protagonist had advanced several
blocks when Doubleday's young clerk appeared in hot pursuit,
with *The Second Tree* in his hand. He was not only triumphant, but actually smiling, having at last seen the humor of
the thing, explained the jubilant correspondent.

"I believe she's a Kathy Hall-type with maybe a dash of
Dotty Guth thrown in," mused EB. "Probably she has a dog
she takes for long walks on Riverside Drive, and she cares more
about books than about fashion. They had her in mind when
they wrote that old proverb about having two pence in the
pocket and spending one for bread and one for beauty."

Came a marvelously sunny day, full of fragrant flowers and
the clean scent from second crops of new mown hay, not at all
the sort of day to be thinking of tombstones—but there were
several drawings spread out on EB's desk and he was trying to
choose among them the one most appropriate to be used in the
cemetery; presumably, for his own grave as well as for Katharine's. It soon evolved that it was not to be a family stone—it
was to be K's personal one. "That's the way she said she wanted
it. Besides, mine's going to be a teensy-weensy one," and he

held up his hands to indicate a marker about six inches over all.

He asked an opinion on the selection and I offered it quickly because one of the drawings was outstanding compared to the others. It was not ornate. The designer had achieved a classic simplicity but, more important, he had camouflaged the newness that is so disturbing in a cemetery where a newly cut stone is placed. "That reinforces my vote," EB agreed, with satisfaction. "As soon as Joe and Allene have cast theirs, I'll send a confirmation."

I underlined one of the reasons for my selection: the design and shading had been so cleverly applied, they were going to obscure the newness of the stone.

"I noticed that, too. Strange, isn't it? We all want our markers to be moss-grown. We can't bear that any death should be recent."

" 'In the midst of life we are in death.' My least favorite of all quotations. If loved ones have to die, I want it always to be day after next week, never in the past or present," I added.

Jones, swiftly pursuing something intriguing in a dream, suddenly moved his paws an inch too far in the wrong direction and slipped off the sofa. He created a splendid diversion; he returned us, laughing, to the mundane present.

Not long afterward, EB and I found ourselves in firm agreement on a related subject, the euphemism that informed the world about one of its denizens "passing away."

"It's the most stupid phrase imaginable. It doesn't make Katharine's death any easier to bear or any less real to me if I say she 'passed away' instead of 'she died.' "

"I wonder who dreamed it up, anyway? Who was the first person to combine those two good words into such an obnoxious phrase?"

"I have no idea—it's been going on ever since I can remember. What puzzles me is that even clergymen use it. They, of all people, ought to know better."

"They think it's comforting. It's generally supposed to have a gentler sound than the word 'died.' I suspect an undertaker invented it."

"Yes. A very obsequious one. The kind who never outgrew those ghastly funeral urns on tombstones."

"I'll bet his father was an undertaker, too—and spoke of 'the dear departed.' "

"And his grandfather wore a watch containing a lock of hair from the corpse."

"What about being a 'survivor'? Does the implication there disturb you?"

That question brought the dialogue momentarily to a halt. He had glossed over the word in hundreds of obituaries and paid no attention to it. Now he lifted it out of its context and examined it from other angles. "It's almost as bad as 'passed away'," he mused. "Odd, I never thought about it before. It places the deceased first in the scheme of things, doesn't it? The family members lose their natural identity just because someone has died. They exist only in relation to the dead."

"And they become survivors," I finished for him. "When a baby dies, it seems to be the ultimate in stupid rhetoric. I hate the idea; I'm a crusader against it. Woe to the news editor who turns me into a 'survivor' when a member of my family dies!"

"The way you worry about things before they happen, Isabel, I have no doubt that you'll have the obit for yourself or your loved ones all written and ready to hand to the newspaper before the ambulance gets to the door." He walked off to fetch the mail, whistling to Jones and Susy to follow along.

·⚬ ELEVEN ⚬·

A s soon as events began to flow in more normal channels at the farm, they abruptly overflowed their banks and began to surge in an abnormal flood at home. It was hard to keep everything on an even keel at work when I had left things in such a turmoil behind me. Lorraine and Arnold Hanson, our prospective house purchasers, had been out of Maine for two weeks on various missions right after negotiations on the property were started, but now they had signed an agreement and made a substantial deposit. We still hoped to keep the news out of the public domain until after Labor Day, when I would have to speak of it in order to secure permission from both employers for time off to journey to southern New Hampshire in search of a new home. We were nearly overcome with gratitude for the ease with which the selling had been managed; and for me, the added bonus of the prospect ahead: announcing at Amen Farm and in North Brooklin that there would be a replacement secretary ready to take over when I departed. Nevertheless, there was a sort of fragmentation of life during the interim. Dutifully making notes for one employer mornings, and for another afternoons, trying to anticipate the needs of both so that I could fill them before being asked, I was at the same moment shaken and unhappy over the impending announcement.

Toward the end of August, I followed EB around busily labeling furniture, dishes, and jewelry with small numbered tags for the benefit of the appraiser who was coming from New York. EB's lists were varied and meticulous. Did all executors of wills go to such lengths in connection with an appraisal, the staff wondered? The house looked as if an auction was imminent and the labels that were pasted on objets d'art and even on silverware brought woe to the soul of the housekeeper. Shirley was disheartened by the nearly one hundred sticky marks that would have to be carefully removed by various methods from various surfaces when the miserable business was concluded. Midway in the tagging process, EB posed a serious question: did I have any use for hairnets? Unfortunately I did not. What a pity: he pulled open a dresser drawer to reveal at least fifty unopened packages. Each envelope held the regulation three nets. What an overwhelming number to attempt to give away! I was reminded of an old story about a very nice lady who was inordinately fond of pancakes and who, therefore, kept a trunkful of them in the attic. On careful consideration, though, it seemed not quite appropriate to relate the story to him.

The scenes choreographed at home concerned appraising of a more complicated sort. What furniture should we transport to our new environment; what should we give away or sell at a yard sale? How could we reach a decision until we knew the size and general decor of our new home? What few items could we begin to pack unobtrusively, trying not to arouse suspicion about our departure plan? What arrangements could we make now, in August, before purchasing a house in New Hampshire, to insure that we could vacate our Brooklin house by October 14, as promised? Even if we found exactly the property we wanted in New Hampshire, there was no guarantee the occupants could move out by the day of our deadline in Brooklin. Soon there was a new game to substitute for the old routine of counting sheep in the sleepless hours after midnight. Count the houses and the people: we had to vacate our present dwelling so the Hansons could move in. Somewhere in New Hampshire, a house awaited us. All we had to do was discover it and persuade the occupants they wanted to move out as soon as possible after October 14. All they had to do was to find another house and convince its owners they wanted to vacate *it* by October 14. But those owners had to find their next house and convince the owners it was essential they move in by October 14, and those owners had to . . . . What a treadmill we were on, and what nightmares emerged from that sort of counting. Clearly the entire project was not feasible. Nobody, except ourselves, was going to vacate anything in mid-October. We had better begin thinking about temporary shelter for the autumn months. It was at least as important a factor of the transition as was the purchase of a new home.

One week to the day before we wanted our plans to become acknowledged fact, the matter was taken out of our hands. I was late getting home for lunch that day because EB had unearthed another carton of material, previously overlooked by everybody, that had to be sorted and assigned to one of K's literary legatees. With a sandwich snack in hand, I was rushing out to my afternoon assignment when the phone rang and a dear friend said, "I know you're busy and probably on your way to work, but I thought I ought to tell you: they're circulating a mad rumor at the general store that you people have sold your house. You know what a tendency there is to gossip in a small town; hadn't you better send Russ or Ernest up there fast to straighten them out?"

"Of course," I told her, "right away. Thanks. I must run," and hung up the phone, having told *it* something under my breath that wouldn't bear repeating here. I paused just long enough to alert Russ and Ernest to hurry in the opposite direction from the store—down to the friend's house to confess; then I sped off to Amen Farm to do likewise. There would be at least three other places we would all have to visit, to explain and apologize, as soon as I returned. I could only cross my fingers and trust no word would reach EB before morning; I was of no mind to carry the message to him at night when he could brood over it till 4 A.M.

I had found him to be an undemonstrative person, and his demeanor was not markedly different from what was to be expected when the announcement was made, but the bitterness of the tone in which he said, "Well, I felt in my bones when you came back in July that it was too good to last," made me feel that I had done something wholly reprehensible. Perhaps I had. He evinced almost no interest in the prospect of a ready-made replacement right at hand to step into the secretarial slot, but that attitude also was typical. One thing at a time, let's try to take it easy, never plan too far in advance just in case, was his motto. His chief concern that morning was for the three of us in my family who were so incredibly naïve as to think they could search out and find a new home in New Hampshire in the space of the five days following Labor Day. "People have searched five years without uncovering the right parcel to purchase," he assured me in accents that presaged doom.

"Your tone of voice is exactly like the one my mother used when we were children and had been playing dangerously hard.

'Don't come crying to me when you're hurt!' she'd warn us—
and we always spoke of it as her Doomsday voice."

"Well, I hate to see you off for New Hampshire on a pessimistic note but I think you were a bit hasty when you agreed
to move out in October. Once you've built your own house it's
almost impossible to be satisfied with one someone else has
built. Furthermore [fixing me with a reproachful stare] I
thought you spoke to us repeatedly of how much you loved
living by the sea."

Of course I loved the sea; the prospect of leaving it was
building up a lump of lead in my chest; it was slowing my
formerly brisk pace to a creep, and converting my firm muscles
to mush, but the choice of going or staying had been taken out
of my hands. It was of no use to reiterate what I had told him
already about my sister's illness. He had dwelt most of his life
halfway across the country from some of his own brothers and
sisters; he had never felt the close-knit ties nor sense of depen-
dence that I did, and there was no way to make him understand. Also, he was certainly justified in his prophecy that we
couldn't find the sort of dwelling we really wanted in a week
of seeking. What he failed to take into consideration was that
we were prepared to make many compromises; and the fact
that our luck had run so remarkably high in the sale of our
Brooklin home was giving us hope that the luck might hold
again in the purchase of another.

When the news of the sale had penetrated to Sedgwick in
one direction and Blue Hill in the other, losing much of its
impact in the process, the aspiring lady secretary who was soon
to be chatelaine of our home, wrote to EB and to Amen Farm,
setting forth her qualifications (impressive ones) for employment and offering to present herself for an interview with each
of them at their pleasure. When both employers chose to reply

cordially to her message on the same day and I had to type the two letters to my probable successor-friend, I was overcome again with a devastating stab of fragmentation. Part of me yearned to find the New Hampshire house, secure it with the proper negotiable instrument, and move into it as fast as possible. The other part refused to believe that all the happy Brooklin associations were coming to an end, that we were going to turn our backs on the sea, that our life-style was going to be vastly altered. Now that it was too late to undo what had been done, the really harsh question was, "Did we mean it when we said we'd give up all this?"

The book, *Essays of E. B. White,* which caused some confusion the previous year in regard to its publication date, arrived presently in the mail with as little fanfare as if it had been ten copies of an old book on reorder. I was delighted to see the package and quickly unpacked it, anticipating the same satisfied reaction from its author, but when I held the top copy out to him, he waved it away. "This is the first one without K—there's no fun in it."

When his sense of duty began to unseat his sensitivity, he composed a note to accompany the first copy on a journey to Washington, D.C. In compliance with a request, it was going to Blair House, where it would join other distinguished books being assembled in the library there. Four other works EB had written went into the package with the *Essays,* and the covering letter, addressed to Assistant Manager Peg Murray at Blair House, contained a snatch of typical EBW humor. He had heard that the library was located next to the king's bedroom. Did the king read in bed?

A second copy of the *Essays* was lying on my briefcase at noon. EB was nowhere in sight, but on the flyleaf was written:

"For my dear departing Isabel with love and best wishes for happy times away. Andy White., N. Brooklin, Sept. 2, 1977." It was too poignant a message to take joy in and I went sniffling off to my car.

Labor Day was bright, sunny, and busy, in no sense a holiday because I had volunteered to work for both employers. It seemed little enough to do in return for their having granted the remainder of the week for our house-hunting. How quiet and lonely it seemed at EB's house. No staff, just ourselves; not even anyone scheduled to prepare his evening meal, but at least he had received an invitation to dine elsewhere and was "thinking of accepting it and getting away from this tomb." At noon he remarked glumly that he assumed it was of no use to ask me to join him in a martini because if I did, I would be late for work at Amen Farm. I had rejected a few other martini invitations in past years but suddenly that day time seemed to be running out. Our family was committed to living a long day's journey from Brooklin and neither EB nor I were good or seasoned travelers; when we parted it was likely to be a permanent severing of the relationship. There would be no more imaginative and exhilarating conversations sparked with his special brand of humor; no more puns delivered carelessly in passing; no more literary gems to copy. So I said, "Mix them right up, please, and I'll make two phone calls and explain the delay." Only a word was necessary at home, and scarcely more than a sentence to Amen Farm, where I promised to give an extra hour at the other end of the afternoon.

We sat serenely on the north porch and talked, like the Walrus and the Carpenter, of cabbages and kings. I learned some new facets of EB's childhood, his siblings, and his parents, some of them episodes of no great significance, that he confessed he hadn't thought of in nearly seventy years. It was light and amusing miscellany but as far as memory goes now, fleeting. His philosophizing had to do with his youth and his and K's first years in the big farmhouse, and those statements stayed with me long enough to be recorded. "Everything was harder, more of a challenge then, than now. I had a family to support and I hadn't yet made my mark. I ought to have been worried all the time but I don't think I was. And now it seems to me I'm never free of worry. I wonder why?"

"Youth knows everything and is confident of being able to bend life to its purposes. You've arrived now, and you know better—all the time you thought you were bending life, it was bending you."

"Do you believe in any form of predestination, Isabel? Do you think some force shaped the whole structure of my life and brought it to this week, this day? Was I just swept along with it like seaweed on the tide?" He had put a twist of lemon in his drink; having taken a few sips awkwardly around it, he fished it out and sat curling it over one finger. In the other hand he held an unaccustomed cigarette (he rarely smoked). Although it was nearly its original length, he began stubbing it viciously in the ashtray. His aspect was that of a man who sought reassurance that he had a firm hold on the rudder and was going to succeed in guiding his own ship of life into calm waters.

It wasn't possible to merge honesty and comfort in the same reply so I opted for the truth. "I can judge only from my own experience; personally, I've always felt a sort of tugging in the atmosphere that was almost palpable when a decision had to be made. Often I fought the pull and tried to go a different way, but some small circumstance intervened and prevented it. And each time the move or the decision was the right one as things turned out."

"As I've insinuated all along, I think you're being too precip-
itate about a move away from Brooklin. Have you felt some sort
of electric force intervening around you on this one?"

I looked closely to see if he was teasing but his countenance
was ever so solemn. "Yes, exactly. When our house was sold
to the first prospect, within a few weeks of being offered, we
all felt it was sort of a confirmation of fate or whatever it's
called. And that's why we're not afraid to allot only a few days
to the finding of a new home. I have a sensation that's almost
disturbing about the next house. I feel it's right there waiting
for me to open the door and walk in."

He shook his head. "I suppose I subscribe slightly to the
theory. I believe in it, you might say, on the long-run basis, but
usually the only way I can trace how fate influenced any decision of mine is to look back and follow through the pattern.
You seem to be doing it the opposite way—you trust to it in
advance."

As so often happened when the substance of a chance remark hinged on the years ahead, EB turned sad. "Have fun in
your future; you deserve it; but don't expect me to be around
to applaud."

"I don't expect it. If you last through the appraisal, we'll all
be amazed."

He tried not to laugh, turning to pick up the martini pitcher
for refills. I was surprised to find I had drained my glass and
was nibbling on the olive. At that rate, it would mean finishing
off two of them in an hour, and even though he had mixed a
mild libation in my honor, I was not accustomed to imbibing
more than one pouring-out of any alcoholic beverage. What if
I had to request assistance in driving home? Or fell ignobly
asleep in the midst of afternoon duties? As though he had read
my mind, he went out to the refrigerator and brought back a

bowl of celery and carrot sticks that must have been prepared ahead. "Can't have you staggering out of here," he said, offering a napkin and a small plate. "I wish you liked caviar; I'm fond of it but I had some last night so I won't want a repeat soon and there's almost a jar of it going to waste out there."

It was too much. For eight years I had filled in order blanks or written letters to Maison Glass in New York City, attending to the purchase of this favorite delicacy, imported beluga caviar, that mouth-watering delight I had tasted only twice in my life and coveted ever after. In my great greed, I was reduced to stuttering: "Who t-told that awful falsehood?"

"What awful falsehood?"

"That I didn't like caviar. I adore it. Even if the rule says you can't love something unless it can return the love, I still adore it."

"Well, you poor child," and he was off to the kitchen again. He brought back the whole ten-ounce container, from which only a smidgeon had been scooped, and set it down on the tray table beside me. Then he opened a drawer and took out an after-dinner coffee spoon. "Eat away," he invited, much pleased with himself, "and what you can't finish here you can have at home tonight." What a heavenly session. Not only wonderful, expensive, real caviar but—the ultimate in bliss— more than enough of it.

Reluctantly at 1:20 we concluded the cocktail "hour." It was going to be a close squeak getting home in time for lunch and off to the afternoon tour of duty, although lunch was not exactly essential for one who had sipped the best gin and dined on the best caviar.

"This is our real good-bye," I said at the door, "because when the last day of work comes there'll be the rest of the staff around to share in the farewells."

"In that case I'll make the pretty speech I had been saving up for that sad occasion. You've been almost as dear as a daughter, Isabel, though just a trifle old for that relationship, and a lot dearer than a sister, though far too young for that one. This seems like too much of a loss, on top of the other." I gave him a quick kiss on the cheek and fled, clutching the jar of caviar as though it had been a blue-ribbon award from the county fair.

·ᢒ TWELVE ᢒ·

We left Brooklin in the early dawn of Tuesday and met our first realtor in a southern New Hampshire town at two in the afternoon. He and our second realtor showed us a total of five houses before we collapsed at night. None of the properties interested us; they were, in fact, nearly impossible from every angle. We didn't panic, though, because we felt reasonably secure with four days left. Next morning, in a different town, we saw two houses and purchased the second one. Its big drawback (there had to be at least one in the very nature of the transaction) was a December 1 possession date. But there was no question of buying or not buying. The snapshot in the realtor's book had pleased the two practical members of the search committee and set my romantic heart aglow. The exterior had country charm; the interior was imaginatively laid out and offered an unusual amount of living and storage space. There was a deck overlooking a pond and deep woods, a screened family room for summer use, and a small bedroom off the kitchen that was immediately preempted for my office. The curved brick walk to the entrance was one I had trod many times in dreams. Because I had rehearsed our passage from driveway to door in imagination so often, the only thing remaining to do was to walk onstage in a scene that was already set. No waiting in the wings; we had only to declare ourselves and hand over a deposit.

In two days, mission completed, we were back in Brooklin and when relating the news, I fear I bragged a little to EB. At the same time I could promise to stay with him until Thanksgiving, and that was an agreeable commitment for us both.

I didn't take time that day to explain to him that we were assured of living space in Brooklin as long as we needed it. Within walking distance of Surfside was the summer home, occupied only from June to Labor Day, of two friends. Robert Heaton, a professor at Rutgers, and Jackie Heaton, a public school music supervisor, repeated their good-bye ritual every year: "Remember, now: our home is *yours*, for guests or yourselves, any time and all the time."

I showed him the snapshot of the new house, given to us by the realtor. The picture had been taken in June when everything was at its best. Roses climbed along the rail fence and salvia and geraniums were brilliant under it; the lawn was early-summer green; majestic pines lined the driveway. He stared at it so long without making any remark that I began to wonder if a long, low, cedar-shingled ranch with blue shutters was his least favorite form of architecture. Finally he handed it back. "That's about the prettiest house I ever saw that I hated so much."

Kathy Hall was back in North Brooklin in the middle of September to help us assemble K's genealogical material and to lend her library expertise to the task of sorting and arranging the Bryn Mawr collection, to make it easier for the Bryn Mawr College Library to deal with the bequest when the time came. When Kathy went away so did the few days of superior weather that had accompanied her. It rained so hard for a day and a half that a choice apple tree—a big, solid one outside the north porch terrace—was uprooted and had to be chopped down and hauled away. EB, deeply disturbed ["Everything I love is dying this year"] would not resign himself to the loss until he had consulted two arborists about the possibility of surgery to restore the ancient landmark.

While his mind was still engaged on the storm damage, it had to be turned to personal bequests of jewelry and other small items in K's will. Her lawyers affirmed that such items could be delivered to beneficiaries any time after the appraisal, but the trick was to read a description in the will and then match it to a selection of jewelry. There were several valuable earring and brooch sets and a few gold and silver necklaces composed of jewels so similar to each other that they weren't easy to identify from her description. Bequests to family members were individually listed; another group of adornments was marked for friends in general but no specific assignments had been made. It was shattering to learn that K had nobly forgiven my desertion: a pair of hammered silver buttercup earrings was given to me.

EB was conscientious about the sorting process. Before I came on the scene he had small boxes ready, identified with the name of each donee, plus duplicate lists of bequests. However, after we had matched names to jewels and checked off the lists, he took a rather cavalier attitude toward the wrapping and mailing. He would insure them all, of course, but no need to be so fussy about the packages; if the post office chose to be careless it was their loss. To my dismay he insisted on sending a pair of fine crystal candlesticks to Carol Angell in New York. In vain did I urge caution and delay (she would be visiting in late autumn; let her carry them home in lap or suitcase) but he was not to be dissuaded. When I had them ready in a large box, surrounded by mountainous wads of newspaper for protection, he took exception to the size of the package and found a smaller carton for them.

"We'll fool the post office; this one won't look so important and they won't deliberately toss it around and contrive to break the contents."

It was dismal to learn a couple of weeks later that the candlesticks had not made a safe journey. "You may now say 'I told you so' or 'You should have known better'," said EB contritely, but it was no comfort to have my judgment justified; it was not I, but Carol who had been short-changed. Fortunately it had been possible to dissuade him from sending along the Canton china bowl and platter, else they, too, might have gone the ill-fated way of the candlesticks.

The assortment of mementoes K left behind her ran the gamut from literary-sophisticated to touching. In the latter category was her childhood sewing book, discovered among a box of old postcards, photo albums, and minor memoranda. There were miniature examples of a variety of stitches, some sewed on cloth and others set directly into the heavy paper of the pages. Everything had been arranged with meticulous care; the stitches were neat and exact. They brought to life more clearly than any words could do a vision of the sober, industrious girl Katharine Sergeant once must have been.

With the sorting of the Bryn Mawr books completed there need be no delay on the appraisal, which was to be done by a representative of the Seven Gables Bookshop; therefore it was time for the final, final, final typing on the starred list and a letter to be dispatched to James Tanis and his assistant Leo Dolenski about the bequest. How many times I had said to myself in years past, "This is the final revision." How many times K had reiterated, "We won't do any more to the BMC list except add a new book now and then at the end." I had learned to dread that statement because invariably it presaged a demand to see the early pages; once seen, they had to be revised. K gave them the same intense scrutiny she would have given to a list compiled by someone other than herself. One had to admire the consistency of her editing proclivities: she enjoyed editing her own work as much as she enjoyed editing that of others.

"After the appraisal," hinted EB, in a remark that was supposed to be expanded into a letter to Mr. Dolenski, "the responsibility for the move lies with the donee—a ribald name for Bryn Mawr." In addition, Kathy Hall received due credit: she had done a "masterly or mistressly" job of assembling the books. It was the first intimation that we might not, after all, be facing the chore of packing all those volumes and handing them over to United Parcel Service. I devoutly hoped Mr. Dolenski owned a station wagon or could borrow a panel truck, and that he was eager for a breath of ocean air.

At home we were also knee-deep in cartons, newspapers, labels, and acrimonious discussions about pricing goods for a yard sale. "I know a couple who just had a sale and made nearly two thousand dollars" offered EB, when I fussed about the complications of pricing.

"Two thousand dollars! What did they have—Picassos and first editions?"

"No, not even furniture; just accumulated junk from over the years."

"One man's junk is another man's prosperity, then, and we must be doing something wrong. We're swamped with stuff but it won't add up to more than five hundred dollars, including some furniture."

"Go over the whole lot again," advised EB, "and mark up everything twenty percent the way the stores do. Come on,

Jones, come on, Susy, let's get the mail." A door closed; it opened and he reappeared with the dogs in tow. "On second thought, don't do a thing. I'll buy up the lot and resell it myself."

In the last week of the month a *Boston Globe* associate editor informed EB of his election to receive the Lawrence L. Winship Annual Book Award for the *Letters*. One-hundred-fifty books had been entered for consideration, recounted the editor; seventy-five were in the competition to the end, and the committee's vote had been unanimous. Only one name on the committee roster meant anything to us, that of Charles Dickens's granddaughter, Monica—but what chiefly impressed EB was an innocuous error in the message. A secretary or typist had written *our's* for *ours,* and the slip had gone unnoticed by the editor. "No wonder everything literary is at such a low ebb!" stormed EB—storming, of course, in his usual mild manner. "Why should that man be allowed to have anything to do with editing a daily paper if he can't do any better than that? And how could his office staff have failed to catch such an obvious mistake? If *they* made it, why did he sign the letter without demanding a correction?"

The awards ceremony was scheduled as part of a book festival in October, and Corona Machemer and Dotty Guth were to attend. But the publicity-shy author resisted all maneuvers, including the *Globe's* generous offer to fly him to the spot or to provide a car and driver down to the city, and James Russell Wiggins's invitation to accompany him on his drive to Boston. None of these kindly suggestions swayed EB from his negative decision.

"I never could bear to sit around and listen to people making speeches about me or praising my books. There's only one thing the *Globe* could do that might persuade me to attend:

perhaps I'd go if they'd agree to give the award to somebody else."

On an evening when we had dinner guests from Brooklin and North Brooklin, the same topic—EB's shyness in regard to hearing his works being praised—was discussed. One guest made a salient comment: "What are you going to talk about if E. B. White chances to sit next to you at dinner? Do you say inanely 'What a handsome necktie you're wearing!' or 'I've often hoped to meet you so I could let you know how much I admire the hedge in front of your house!?' "

The weather in September generally had not been as good as it often was on the coast at that time of year. Sunshine was intermittent, the temperature cool, but at least some high winds prevailed and EB managed a few sailing trips with an assist from Joel. Nothing cheered senior Skipper White more than a long morning or afternoon on the water, and he bewailed the infirmities of age that were beginning to cut into the stamina he had for his favorite diversion.

At the end of the month I kept an anxious ear to the ground in connection with all his engagements, business or social, ashore or afloat, hoping to uncover exactly the right combination of circumstances that would put him in the mood to accept a dinner invitation. Our house gradually was being dismantled; before it reached a cleaned-out stage too advanced for charm, I wanted to ask my employer/friend to share its hospitality. "Either drink or drop the dipper!" my husband advised caustically so, after five days of stalking the prey I pounced, and was rewarded with a shy grin and immediate acceptance, although EB made it plain he was fearful of being wined and dined too lavishly. "You will remember, won't you, that I am a man of light appetite and simple tastes in food?"

"Yes, indeedy. Imported beluga caviar and filets mignon in

dry ice shipped from the Midwest. Tuffi dragged home a partridge yesterday so we saved it to serve under glass. It isn't quite pheasant but it will have to do." No amount of foolishness dissuaded him; he delivered what amounted to a harangue on the subject of his small appetite. It was infinitely amusing therefore to discover the following night that he took his dining seriously and in leisurely fashion, complimenting a dish, ready to have his wine glass replenished, accepting a second serving of a seafood mélange, and keeping pace with the three of us right through dessert. He was by no means the enthusiastic trencherman a hostess might boast of to her friends but neither was he the person of finicky appetite that his protestations conjured. We had to watch out for his allergies, of course; no clams in the seafood, no marigolds on the table. At the last minute I remembered K's aversion to that flower because of the violent sinus reaction it caused her husband. Out went two pottery bowls of marigolds; a few mums and some late hardy petunias were thrust into a pitcher as substitutes. The cat had been informed early on of another of Uncle Andy's afflictions (cats induced his worst suffering) and he was banished to the deck, where he sat for three hours regarding us all with a baleful expression.

EB was a versatile performer when he was the only guest and felt at ease; he had a fund of anecdotes but was careful not to monopolize the conversation. He asked questions that would draw forth opinions from my husband on tax matters, and from our friend Ernest on fruit-tree culture and other aspects of farming. "If Tuffi had been allowed in, I vow he'd have spoken to him about mice," said Russ, approving, after EB left. One item of interior decoration caught the visitor's eye, a frieze done in oil paint around one of the kitchen windows. It served in lieu of a curtain because we couldn't bear to use curtains where they would minimize a view of the sea. "Does it sound carping if I inquire what those two fanciful creatures are at the head of that parade?" he wanted to know.

"Of course not; carp is exactly the word there; it's a fish, isn't it?"

He sighed and looked at his two hosts with an expression of "How do you cope?"; then he pointed to the fat pink-red creature leading the group of crustaceans. "Does this one inhabit your shore? I don't believe we have them at Allen Cove."

"Of course you don't; there's no unicorn there either, is there? That first seabody is known as a shrobster. He's two parts shrimp to three parts lobster. I wish I could sink my teeth into him. And his pal is a sealrus. Need I explain?"

One of our fringed linen cocktail napkins was missing at the close of the evening; otherwise everything went off satisfactorily, and what's a napkin compared to fun and food? It turned up next morning, laid ostentatiously across the office typewriter with a neatly lettered note that begged forgiveness for having walked away with one-quarter of the September 29 laundry at Surfside.

Everyone who knew EB more than casually was aware that he disliked above all things being forced (or even sweet-talked) into appending his signature to the flyleaf of one of his books. Over the years that reluctance had posed a problem for his staff. They liked to present his works at gift-giving time but their friends and relations, not comprehending the depth of EB's antipathy to autographing, thought it a poor gift indeed that bore only a printed name on the cover and no handwriting on the flyleaf. Thoroughly cognizant of this, I had sneaked in a gift copy of my own now and then over the years for him to sign, always trying to space out the requests so that one would not follow too close on another, but in the fall of 1977 time was running out for signature requests. There were the months of October and November and that was all. Boldly, on a bright October morning I took into his office four copies of the *Essays* and eased him into signing them.

"Thank you for promoting my works," he said gravely.

"Thank you for employing me all these years so I could afford to buy your books," I answered meekly.

"It's been pretty nearly fifty-fifty with some enjoyment all the way, in spite of the bad times, hasn't it?" he asked, laying aside the pen and glancing up.

"Far more than that figure," I assured him, hugging the books to my chest and laying a hand lightly on his shoulder. "Good times outweighed everything else at least three to one. If only I could contrive to leave and to stay, too, I'd be the happiest woman on earth." It seemed, all at once, the right time to recall a humorous K commentary. Doubtless he knew this funny occurrence from the annals of her childhood, but he might have forgotten it.

"Something has just come to mind that Mrs. White once told me, and I always smile, recalling it. Do you recollect the Tammany Hall tidbit?" He shook his head so I launched into it:

"She was young enough to be sitting in her aunt's lap; she was into the typical query of the young: how were babies born? Her very proper aunt wasn't about to become involved in anything of that sort, so she dismissed the child quickly. 'You're too young to understand anything like that,' she said. A few months later the Tammany Hall scandal erupted in newspapers; sitting on her father's lap, the young Katharine spelled out the headline 'Tammany Hall' and asked her parent about it. 'You're too young to understand, my dear,' was his reply. Years afterward, until she was a senior in high school, she continued to believe the two hush-hush topics were closely connected."

EB laughed, as I had hoped. "Fancy an era when a young girl could be so innocent, right through her teen years, as to connect the birth of babies with Tammany Hall. That's what comes of growing up in the city."

October was such a frenetic month I scarcely knew where one job left off and the other one began. Once again, situations had an unsettling way of overlapping. The packing of K's effects and the acknowledging of messages of condolence was still going on at EB's. In a continuing sequence at Amen Farm, Roy Barrette (a gardener-cum-writer) was turning out rough drafts of a lengthy review of the *Essays* for a Massachusetts news-magazine titled *UpCountry*. Being keenly aware of his friend Andy's penchant for privacy, Roy did not altogether rejoice when the editors of *UpCountry* approached him for the review and a survey of the life of E. B. White. He wrote later, somewhat apologetically, to EB:

"When they asked me to do a piece about you and the *Essays* I tried to avoid it, but then, thinking they might get someone who would do worse by you than I would, I capitulated. I didn't show it to you beforehand because I don't think the condemned man should see the gallows before the trap is sprung. . . ."

Roy's friend Andy, a stern precisionist in all professional literary matters, could find nothing to fault and much to commend in the *UpCountry* production, and responded promptly with a letter of congratulation. I heard him say on the phone, a little wistfully, "Thanks for your kind and sober review. I

Isabel Russell

can't recall when I last wrote a piece and I'm not sure I want to, but I can remember what it was like to be assembling words in orderly ranks, ending with a period and some liquid refreshment."

Presently came Michael Papantonio from Seven Gables to begin appraising the Bryn Mawr book collection. Although he was quartered at the Blue Hill Inn and had to be hosted only for lunches, his sojourn left EB exhausted. On October 12 EB languished dispiritedly on the upstairs hall sofa and asked Edith to fix iced coffee at noon. A reply to a student who had asked innumerable questions about James Thurber was something he couldn't contemplate with equanimity. "Write it yourself and sign it; somewhere in it tell him because of the recent death of my wife I lack time and strength to help students with their work. If you see any question you can answer, go ahead."

Rain had threatened all morning; by noon it was spattering against the windows and invidious gusts of wind gradually increased in force until the glass became translucent. Heavy fog obscured the view of the sea; wisps of moisture draped the foliage like Spanish moss. All our world was water, and the big dark house grew momentarily larger and darker. Even the lamp glow was cheerless and inadequate; it could not penetrate the shadowy corners. "I don't mind rain," intoned EB wearily, "but when it gets to the stage where you have to send forth a dove to see if the waters are receding, it's ridiculous."

Once during the month of October he and I indulged in a palliative: an interval of hearty laughter while we turned the pages of a valuable album of original Max Beerbohm cartoons, once the property of K's sister Elizabeth. It had turned up among K's treasures and was destined for Roger. It was not in good condition but EB hoped that a craft-minded librarian or bookbinder could restore it. One Beerbohm caricature was our favorite; perhaps it didn't actually appear in that collection but if not, it made no difference because we knew it by heart. An unkind spoof on the relationship between Queen Victoria and her recalcitrant son, the Prince of Wales, it depicts the middle-aged prince standing face to the wall in a corner, small-boy fashion with hands clasped behind him, while Queen Victoria, the epitome of all aggrieved parents, sits nearby. Beerbohm's drawing tool cut deep; the caricature is a masterpiece of satire executed in a few deft strokes. It scarcely requires the accompanying caption: "The rare, the rather awful visits of Albert Edward, Prince of Wales, to Windsor Castle."

"When I was a youngster," recalled EB, "almost every child had a grandmother or a great-aunt who resembled Queen Victoria. How grandmothers have changed since World War I!"

On another day, a crisp frosty one that managed to remember autumn while hinting of winter, he seemed disposed to reminisce about his youthful travels across the country in the Model T. The saga is well documented in the *Letters* and in the small book *Farewell to Model T*, but that morning he brought his memory to bear on other facets of the itinerary: how alien the land looked to an Easterner; how odd the cadence of the midwestern voice; how he and his companion Howard Cushman fretted about the large and small exigencies of making their exhilarating way to the West Coast.

"Didn't your parents worry awfully?" I asked. "Young people didn't venture so far from home as a common thing in those days."

"I wrote to them fairly regularly and figured that was all that mattered." The phone rang; he answered quickly and came back, his train of thought undisturbed. "I got paid back, though, for my casual attitude. I didn't begin to realize what they had been through until it was my own turn with Joel. He was nearly always on water instead of on land but that didn't make it any easier. There was many a night that K and I scarcely bothered to go to bed; we knew there'd be no sleep for us. What a lot of wasted time! Wish I had it back again. Joel was the most reliable of sailors and always came through all right, and just think of the writing I might have done in those hours if only I could have put my mind to it."

October 18 had not been scheduled for a workday; Russ and Ernest therefore had appropriated the car for a two-day trip to New Hampshire on errands connected with the new homestead. Unexpectedly, however, EB had a spate of letters to be sent out and phoned to say so. We had moved to temporary quarters, the summer home of friends who lived in New Jersey, and I was sorry to have to ask him to provide transportation, but it didn't seem to disturb him in the least; and Jones and Susy, extra passengers, were highly pleased. It meant two unanticipated rides for them. Susy, ensconced on the back seat, leaned forward and breathed gently in my ear but Jones sat aloof and uncaring on the front seat between his master and me and would not condescend to be patted.

"The *Essays* made the *Times* best-seller list," proclaimed EB grimly, en route. "It's number thirteen. There used to be only ten books on the list but they enlarged it to thirteen to include me on the bottom." (When I looked it up, I discovered that the list had been enlarged to fifteen and he was therefore two places above the bottom. By November 27 the book had climbed to eleventh place.)

An elderly lady, well known in our little town of Brooklin, where she had lived all her life, had died and her funeral was to be held that afternoon. Her Naskeag Point home was not far from our present temporary quarters, and EB was reminded of her as he turned down the Point road at noon. "Two fine persons are being buried today," he remarked soberly, "Bessie Smith and Bing Crosby."

·ᴈ THIRTEEN ɞ··

Three fifth-graders from the Paul P. Gates School in Acton, Massachusetts, had been carrying on a regular fan-mail exchange with K and EB for several years. A group of original thinkers, they didn't stop at routine praise for *Charlotte's Web*, *Stuart Little*, or *The Trumpet of the Swan*. Recognizing K's interest in horticulture, they regularly sent crocus bulbs to be planted at the Whites'. K always returned a grateful acknowledgment and went to extra trouble to include kernels of home/ farm news. After her death came a letter of condolence, followed by still another gift of bulbs. The thoughtfulness of the girls who sent them pleased EB immensely and he replied personally with a description of the spot where the crocuses would be planted, and the remark that he would be reminded of Maura Harrigan, Jennifer Doran, and Midori Evans when the blossoms appeared. We predicted that the three, with their love for growing things, for reading, and for kind gestures, would grow up to be exemplary citizens and fine wives and mothers.

Leo Dolenski and his wife came to North Brooklin on October twenty-second to remove the 550 books that had formed the starred list on which K had expended so much labor for so many years. The empty shelves shook EB to his foundations even though he had been anxious for the exodus; he phoned on Sunday to ask for a postponement of the Monday work session to Tuesday.

As the month wore on, he exhibited recurring signs of sorrow and fatigue. One of his new fears was that he might have an allergy to leaf mold, of which there was a lot around as the result of a prolonged rainy period. He spoke of wanting to get away from home (a most unlikely desire for such a fervid home lover as he) but confessed he hadn't the courage to indulge his wanderlust alone. "And I can't get anybody to go along because I'm too fussy. Nobody suits me. A lot of them drive too fast, some of them tailgate, most of them are nonstop talkers." He needed someone who was relaxed, a competent driver with a cheerful personality who could travel for hours without speaking. Most important, it had to be someone who was in no hurry to return home. "But anybody who might fill all the qualifications is on some sort of schedule these days or has a family to hurry back to." I thought briefly of Kathy Hall and of nurse Linda Lincoln, and indulged a profitless few minutes hating the innocent offspring of one and the innocent husbands of both; but actually, had they been free, there was no certainty that EB would have accepted a female companion, even an unencumbered one. The subject was not raised again except perhaps in EB's own daydreams; it belonged to the department of wishful thinking.

Hallowe'en came and went, with K's loss making no appreciable difference in neighborhood visitations to the White homestead. EB and Edith laid in the usual lavish provisions, and if the young trick-or-treaters noted the absence of the elderly lady on her walker who had always shared in their reception previously, they gave no sign of it. They were profusely complimented on their costumes and beguiled with

Isabel Russell

some light repartee by their host before being plied with apples, doughnuts, cookies, and candy to round out the visit.

The end of the week found EB laid low with a backache, but still able, from his command post on the hall sofa upstairs, to scratch off short notes for me to pad out into what he termed "acceptable letters." The sofa wore a flower-patterned slipcover with a deep ruffle; Jones disappeared under it most of the time, reappearing when footsteps approached. On one reappearance he poked only the top of himself out and managed to achieve a ludicrous effect with his head framed like a fashionable nineteenth-century lady in a flounce bonnet. Had EB been confined to the spot several days it is probable that Jones would have stayed too—unfed, unaired, suffering but loyal, giving his all in the service and protection of his master.

"I'm sick and tired of promotion requests," the backache sufferer complained, tossing a slim manuscript to the floor and narrowly missing Jones's head with the envelope he flung after it. "Return this one if you want to bother. It's time I stopped being so polite, sending back all the stuff at my own expense. If I heaved a few into the trash basket maybe word would get around that I'm an irascible old fellow and had better be avoided lest I light a fire with their precious gems." I sympathized with his complaint but could not help feeling sorry for the poet, so I retrieved manuscript and envelope and murmured a few soothing phrases on the return letter. When it came to the matter of glib remarks on dust jackets, recommending the writer to the reader, EB treated the great and the rank amateur with the same hauteur. Race, creed, friendship, or political persuasion made no difference, at least during my term of residence. "Let them flourish without my help; nobody helped me," he pointed out when several requests arrived in one mail.

November offered no surcease in the way of correspondence. "Don't they have anything else to do but write a writer?" demanded the writer one morning, dumping out a jammed mailbag on the floor of his study. Jones and Susy had appropriated the loveseat there and were stretched out so companionably, paw to paw, that there wasn't room for more than a sheet of newspaper between them.

"Do you mind hauling in the last piece? It's in the kitchen." EB sat down with his chin on his hand, surveying the mass of mail with a jaundiced eye. I had worked for weeks on the junk-mail situation to little avail. A polite letter had gone to each advertiser and each promoter of a worthy cause stating the fact of K's death and requesting that her name be removed from the mailing list. Out of fifty-three such requests, we received one acknowledgment. It contained a promise to remove the address and a caution that it would take many months to accomplish the deed. We were not, naturally, seeking acknowledgments. All we sought was a cessation of junk mail addressed to the deceased.

The item I was requested to bring from the kitchen was the ultimate in wasted paper and postage, it seemed to us. The Literary Guild, celebrating its golden anniversary, had mailed an ornate placard to its contributors. A book of EB's once having been an alternate selection, his name was on the roster of authors listed on the giant card. What appalled us was not the way the Guild chose to celebrate a fiftieth milestone—that was innocuous enough. The incredible part of it was the size of the celebratory document. It was larger than a fireplace screen; I couldn't lift the package and was obliged to drag it into the study. It took much tearing, slitting, yanking, and a bit of cussing to release the memorial from its stubborn sheath. Once released, of what value was it? Where could it be displayed without proving to be an object for the unwary to trip over? "Everybody take a good look at this so you can tell future generations about it," said the honored author, toting the huge sheet of cardboard from kitchen to barn, to show his staff. "You won't get a second chance because it's about to be consigned to the dump. I wish people would stop sending me things. All things. Any things. Things."

Gradually, after K's death, EB began to develop a complex about the telephone. At first it was pushed far back on the closet shelf, and the connecting door from closet to living room was kept closed so he wouldn't have to look at the offending instrument when he was reclining in his favorite chair. For a short time span, as he became reconciled to the phone's frequent summons, it reposed on a small table in the living room, but more and more often it was to be found on the floor under the table, well out of sight. Its last resting place was the lowest bookshelf under the windows. Having pursued it everywhere else, I hadn't noticed this newest locale and a lot of ringing went on one November morning before I could trace the sound to the set. It had rung incessantly with requests that had to be handled by EB himself, and on a day when he was trying to correlate instructions for reaching North Brooklin from a starting base of Framingham, Massachusetts. After the third interruption, he flung the sheet on my desk with a query attached: "Do these sound all right to you? I haven't driven into Maine from Mass. for many years."

He was again departing from custom: he had granted an interview about K's *New Yorker* career to a Simmons College graduate student. Linda Davis would begin her trip at Framingham late on a Thursday, spend the night at the Blue Hill Inn, and secure her interview on Friday. I was his best critic, "direction-givingwise," having been born with a total incapacity for understanding maps or finding route numbers. If I could follow his road report, anybody could. Peering at the sheet from Linda's inexperienced viewpoint, I found myself well lost between Bucksport and Blue Hill, and I also sighed over his failure to indicate on which side of the road his house was located. We reached a compromise eventually, sending to Linda a map that was twice as involved as he deemed necessary, and half the length I knew was essential.

Asked a few days later how the interview had gone, EB awarded high grades to Linda for personality, efficiency, and background research, but flunked her on fashion. "She must have applied too much grease to her boots or else it was a brand that should be taken off the market. It filled the living room with such a smell of oil I was afraid I'd pass out." Subsequently came the traditional thank-you note from Linda. By that time the memory of the offending boot grease had faded somewhat, and EB could read with amusement that she would be happy to squire him on the Grand Tour of Boston sometime—which encompassed, in her mind, the Wayside Inn and Harvard Square.

He was giving his sharpest attention to modern language usage that morning and in a note to his typist, who must have been elsewhere when he was ready to sound off, his tone was caustic: "Why does a hospital have to be known as a facility? Why is a history course listed as a discipline? Vagueness, pretentiousness, distortion; our mother tongue is ailing all over."

He had been invited to dinner the previous evening, with four other guests, at Amen Farm. The pièce de résistance, he informed us, was a delicious coq au vin; the wine a connoisseur's delight, and it was "just like having dinner at Buckingham Palace except the queen wasn't there."

As November wore on, I steered the conversation one morn-

ing to the matter of scheduling an appointment with the replacement secretary. "If you wait too long I'll be leaving and
you won't even have been introduced to her," I reminded him.

"Do I need to be introduced? Can't she just come in and
begin to type? If she did and if I were careful not to look
straight at her, I might not notice that I had a different secretary."

"If you will please just face up to the change you'll find
yourself being pleasantly surprised, Mr. White. Wait till you
meet her; truly, no employer was ever so fortunate. She's efficient, attractive, speaks in cultured tones, has a quiet, easy
presence—"

He interrupted. "Stop it, Isabel; you make her sound like a
paragon of all the virtues. Nobody could live up to all that, and
when she fails, I'll be all the more in trouble."

"—and has a fascinating store of anecdotes about Burma,
Rangoon, and other interesting foreign places," I went on as
though he hadn't spoken, "to say nothing of a nice diplomatic
manner. She'll always be unobtrusive. There'll be no feeling of
disturbance when she's in the house."

He sighed. "All right, all right. I suppose you mean she isn't
going to rave about causes and injustices the way you and K
once did? And she won't weep if I bring in a dead bird or Susy
gets a thorn in her paw? At least that will be a great relief."

After a bit more banter on the subject of secretaries in
general and the paragon of perfection he was about to acquire,
he turned the tables on me neatly.

"Make an appointment for next week; write her the sort of
communication she would expect to receive from a fidgety old
gentleman who is hanging breathless on the hour of her arrival.
It must be letter-perfect, no erasures, centered exactly on the
page, so she'll know we don't tolerate slipshod work around

here. Come on Jones, come on Susy; let's get the mail."

There was time to spare that day so I utilized a few minutes of it on revenge. "Dear Lorraine," I typed in sloppy fashion on a sheet of paper bearing a *New Yorker* magazine letterhead and no date.

"Andy White has finally, after much proding on my part, come around to seting a date for meting you. It will be next Wednesday unless he finds sumthing more important to do then. He's a hard taskmaster and acept no typing flaws, no tardyness, no chitchat with the help in the kitschen. Espeshully no maudlin conversation with the dogs. Dress neetly and be alert at all times. The pay is indiferent but the prestige is nice. Luv, Isabel."

A few words were crossed out and there was a small rip at the bottom of the page. I placed it on top of the finished letters on his desk; on the bottom of the stack was another missive to Lorraine, a proper one, couched in dignified terms and typed in my best style. I was out of the house and away before he found time to sift through that day's efforts, but on Friday morning the fake letter lay on my typewriter with a pink slip attached: "I mislaid the other thing to Lorraine somewhere. Shall I send this one? Luv."

When she arrived on November 21 to meet her prospective employer, Lorraine had plenty of time to cover all questions about her work while we awaited the summons from EB. He had been mobbed that morning by neighbors with books to be autographed, as well as by someone who was a friend of a friend and who was accompanied by a photographer from *Women's Wear Daily*. *WWD* planned a segment titled "Maine Life" for the December 23 issue of one of its offshoot publications, and was full of confidence that it could secure photos and an interview with Maine's shyest author, to be used as the lead story in the feature. I would have said its chances were less than fifty-fifty, so much less that they approached zero, but the friend of a friend won through—a persuasive gal indeed.

Photographer Harry Benson got two remarkable studies of the man and his dog. Not Jones by any means; Jones never once had consented to keep an appointment with a camera. Not even the sneakiest practitioner of the art could sneak up on him unaware, and no amount of coaxing from his beloved master could persuade him out of hiding for a picture. His sensitive antennae began to quiver when the car of a camera owner was midway between Blue Hill and North Brooklin, and at that point he retired to subterranean levels known only to himself, and did not emerge until the enemy had been long gone from the premises. The two pictures of EB and Susy were striking likenesses of both. EB seemed about to break forth in spirited protest against, for instance, some outrage perpetrated by man on his environment, and Susy obviously had her eye on a saucy bird or an argumentative squirrel. The accompanying story was equally good, a neat linguistic etching of the author and his surroundings. Its only flaw was a minor one that doubtless went unnoticed by ninety percent of its readers. However, it loomed large on EB's list of what was not permitted—a spelling error in Katharine's name, a mistake that affronted and grieved the virtuoso whenever and wherever it occurred. He had been known to point out the misspelling, with some asperity, to heads of corporations, an esteemed *New York Times* columnist, and a governor of a state.

Those who knew EB best averred that he always was more interested in acclaim for Katharine than he was in fame for himself, and he proved the belief in 1978 when he began assembling her *New Yorker* garden columns into a book. He never truly got accustomed to his own laurels, anyway; for a man whose works had been so highly praised, he was incredibly modest. The day I laid Colman McCarthy's encomium (written shortly after EB received the National Medal for Literature) on his desk, he skimmed through it and then stated of the artistic closing paragraph: "Nobody should get that much praise while he's still alive. It goes to a man's head and makes him obnoxious to his associates."

One of the last neat phrases of his own, of which I was so enamored, was spoken offhandedly on November 23: "Publishers move in a mysterious way their blunders to perform." It was "last" only in the sense that it related to my waning days with him. After my departure it must be assumed that he continued to create similar phrases as tirelessly as ever; indeed, they showed up now and then in his letters received at our new residence, but it could never be the same as hearing them spoken. For instance, on the twenty-third Jones had been raising his voice in a session of inordinate length. His master ordered gently and affectionately, "All right, Jones, subside, relax—" then loudly, with scarcely a pause for a comma, "and shut up!"

When Jones had retired, sulking, we worked on some newly labeled folders for EB's files. Having become enamored of the file-folder system used at the law firm of Hale and Hamlin, with which he became well acquainted when executing K's will, he had secured a set of the folders and was ready to revamp an antiquated method. He had an odd mental block on filing, though, and that was not about to be changed or improved. Instead of placing material in a given folder in an order that brought the most recent material to the front, he reversed the procedure. Older sheets came first in each folder; current items were relegated to the back. Poor Lorraine; it was going to take some getting used to. "It's just like repeating the alphabet backward," I protested in a futile attempt to get things properly oriented.

"No problem, I was pretty good at that, too, when I was a lad in knee britches," was all the satisfaction I got.

November 26 was my final day. It was also, I told myself, likely to be the last time I would see EB, given my dislike of travel, and the increasing infirmities the passing years might bring to him. I pounded the typewriter keys in a fine frenzy of late application to duty and then was rewarded with a cutting and pasting assignment for "Newsbreaks." EB handed over paste and scissors with the satisfied air of a person who has contrived to get an obstreperous creature (two-pawed or four-pawed) out of his hair for an hour or two. It was an appropriate task for that last morning: much to laugh at, and nothing that required particular concentration.

There was one phone call to be made to the *New Yorker*'s efficient and friendly Harriet Walden in connection with a permission request from a publisher in Sweden; then, as the hands of the clock worked their way steadily toward noon and there was no sound to indicate that EB was anywhere in the house, I began to have high hopes that I would be able to slip out quietly without repeating the emotional good-byes we already had said on Labor Day. But good fortune did not attend the parting. A few minutes before the clock struck the hour, EB appeared with my paycheck.

"It's time to quit now, Isabel. Leave something for Lorraine to do in case I don't have a chance to prepare anything over the Thanksgiving holiday." I accepted the check, said "Thank you," and handed over the "Newsbreak" sequence. Then I just sat there, somewhat obviously waiting for his exit.

"Aren't you going to cover the typewriter?"

Meekly, I covered it. It was not a very cold day so my outer wrap consisted only of a light sweater. He picked it up from the chair and held it for me. "Don't say anything now, please," I cautioned him, "I must not go through the kitchen crying."

"All right. I won't even say 'Happy landings, happy days!' as I'd planned to." He hugged me until I worried that my ribs would crack; then I went weeping, just as I had feared, through the kitchen and out the back door, having managed no more than a wave to the rest of the staff.

·⫣ FOURTEEN ⫢·

Our 1977 Christmas in New Hampshire held out little promise that EB would be forgotten in 1978; there was to be a continuing reminder of him every week of the fifty-two: he had, unnecessarily but generously, renewed the *New Yorker* subscription K had always given to us. The handwritten gift card wished us "happy reading in the world's most unpredictable magazine." He hoped we were well settled in our new home and ready for the holidays. His Christmas card ended with a predictable reference to his health; he'd had an attack of bronchitis for two weeks but was pulling out of it. Finally came a basket of Florida fruit with a poignant enclosure: "We all miss you. Love, Andy White." The day the basket arrived I decided it was going to be impossible to banish him from my thoughts, and gave up trying.

There were many inescapable reminders. His name surfaced in likely and unlikely spots in 1978. Reviews of the *Essays* proliferated; they, at least, were to be expected; reviewers still hadn't run out of superlatives. What was unexpected was a quotation in *Town & Country.* Poke around long enough and you could find EB speaking about almost anything under the sun, and *T & C* had dug out a sentence they used to conclude their treatise, a remark about a man finding it easier to be loyal to his club than to his planet. Elsewhere in print Norman Cousins was discussing the recuperative, healing power of laughter as compared with the similar power of medicine. He cited a siege in a hospital where he managed to hasten his own recovery by reading from the world's best humorists, EBW prominent among them.

Letters exchanged between New Hampshire and North Brooklin during the winter included one in which EB referred back to the article in *Women's Wear Daily* and complained that two persons had suffered a lot that day when the photos were taken, himself and Disappearing Jones.

There was a phone call, initiated by me in April when we read the announcement of the Pulitzer citation EB had received. The call was timed to coalesce with the evening happy hour and it worked like a charm. He admitted to being at ease in the living room with glass in hand; I sat on a high stool at our kitchen counter holding a similar glass, and we talked at length on almost every topic except the award. Of that he would remark only, "Somebody had a guilty conscience. 'Poor old man,' they said, 'better do a little something for him before he dies.' Anyway, I'm overloaded with honors. I don't need them. What I need is the tooth I lost on the train when I came back from Florida, and my reading glasses." The reading glasses, because they were so often mislaid, should have been attached to a conservative-looking ribbon or cord worn around his neck, but none of us had been able to induce him to use one.

He spoke of the trip to Sarasota with Roger, Carol, and John Henry. His hosts in the city, Greta and Parker Banzhaf (old friends of both Whites) had made him royally welcome, he emphasized, but travel simply was not his forte. "I'm not my own man when it's someone else's house. I hired a car and did a lot of flopping around in Sarasota traffic."

It was doubtful that anything would change his mind, ever, about the miseries of travel, which often exhausted him to the illness stage. Home was the only place to be; why should a man ever turn his back on its comforts? It brought to mind an occasion when K and I were trying to persuade him to go somewhere (New York, probably) to accept an important award in person. I kept a record of his exact words that day because they were so typical:

"I couldn't possibly—you know I couldn't, K. I'm just not the man for auditoriums and people. And applause terrifies me. What do you do? Just stand there with your wrists hanging out? If only I were a woman, at least I could curtsey."

One good episode, I learned from the phone conversation, had come out of the Florida trip. On the return journey, after visiting a good friend, Doctor Wearn, in South Carolina, EB had then stopped over in New York, reserved a small apartment in the Algonquin, and "had the time of my life. I called everybody up and people came to see *me.*"

A letter in late spring and another in summer requested information on material he needed for the new book of K's garden pieces, *Onward and Upward in the Garden.* The May letter, in addition to the questions it posed, stated that he was involved once again with the material he was donating to Cornell University and that Kathy Hall and Joan Winterkorn, of the Cornell Library Rare Books Department, would be visiting him for a stay of a few days.

Replying promptly to his questions, I prefaced that segment of my letter with a personal observation: "It sometimes seems to me that you are utterly and completely and continually surrounded by women. I wonder that you manage to rise above it. It's a fortunate circumstance that so many of them are young and personable. I hope all went well with Kathy and Joan's visit. You did not, of course, keep a carbon copy of your letter to me (unless Lorraine has some harsher way of dealing with you than I had). Assuming you didn't, because she hasn't, I'll give you a digest of your question with each answer. . . ."

It was disappointing to discover in August 1978 that EB was beginning to shy away again from social occasions. His beloved granddaughter Martha White, of whom he was proud as well as fond, was married that month at the tiny Naskeag Point Chapel in Brooklin, but he did not attend. He spent the weekend instead at Blue Hill Hospital, having signed in the Saturday morning of the wedding.

In November retired *New Yorker* staffer Hawley Truax died, and the obituaries brought forth a reminder of K, who had cautioned me always to use her personal stationery in letters written to Hawley or to his wife Althea. The magazine letterhead was used for everybody else connected with *The New Yorker* but not for Hawley. "He would think I was being wasteful to use it for personal correspondence," explained K. "He is a frugal man in the best sense of that word. Not parsimonious, you understand—just old-fashioned New England frugal, even though he has no connection with this region."

In a preholiday phone conversation EB informed us he was planning to celebrate Thanksgiving with Roger and Carol in New York. "Steve is going to drive me to the city in my car and then leave me to my own devices. I have a dozen schemes for getting back home, all of them implausible and weird." So implausible and weird indeed did the whole venture sound that we were not surprised to hear it had been canceled along the way. The travelers got only as far as Augusta, Maine, when

Isabel Russell

suddenly the enormity of what he was about to do overcame
EB and he asked his grandson to turn around and drive him
home again.

An interesting book published that fall was Roger Sales'
Fairy Tales and After with the subtitle, *From Snow White to
E. B. White.* Its general content was pleasing to many readers;
in our household what mattered most were the highly compli-
mentary references to EB and his works, with the emphasis on
Charlotte's Web.

December featured Charlotte's creator all over the place.
The Christian Science Monitor picked up and reprinted a letter
EB had written to *The Ellsworth American.* Composed with
the expected light touch, it flayed such modern additions to the
English language as "ongoing," "input," and "feedback." How
innocent were such offenses as compared to those that have
become routine in the 1980s! Are there enough critical phrases
left with which to condemn them, even for such a genius as
he? In *The New Yorker* on December 11, 1978, in an article
that listed ways and means of gifting a child at Christmas, EB's
books and his recording of *The Trumpet* were lauded. In *Time*
magazine's Christmas issue Wilfrid Sheed's *The Good Word
and Other Words* was reviewed, and the so-called "milkman
quote" surfaced again. It had been used by Sheed when he
reviewed the *Letters* and many EB admirers treasured the
implication that his throwaway scraps to deliverymen equaled
in wit the carefully contrived, more permanent gems of many
of his professional contemporaries.

When Norman Rockwell died late in 1978 an obituary in a
New Hampshire paper informed us of a fact that was not
mentioned in the larger dailies: a painting of John Sargeant
(sic) and the Indians was left unfinished on an easel in Rockwell's studio. Despite the misspelling of "Sergeant" we were

convinced the unfinished painting was a representation of K's illustrious ancestor, and EB confirmed the conviction when I spoke to him about it by phone.

"I had seen a couple of obits of Rockwell but neither of them mentioned a final painting. I suppose he knew all about John Sergeant because of his residence being Stockbridge but I'm surprised that he was trying to get John on canvas. I wonder what will happen to the unfinished picture? Maybe I'd better let Yale know about it, because they have all the Sergeant papers in their library. K was so proud of ancestor John. Most of his contemporaries were pretty stuffy about the Indians but John saw them as human beings. . . ."

A note on EB's Christmas card tidied up the loose ends. He had written to the Norman Rockwell estate asking what they were going to do with "John Sergeant and his Indian" and a letter came back from the director of the Old Corner House, Stockbridge, saying that Rockwell had decided to give the painting to them to add to their collection of some two hundred of his works.

In February 1979 *The Christian Science Monitor* featured a valentine theme on its "Home Forum" page. E. B. White and Robert Browning shared the space, each represented by a romantic letter to his love. Browning's epistle, written in 1845, was the epitome of grace, the famous first letter addressed to his "dear Miss Barrett." EB's, composed 109 years later, was probably the three- or four-hundredth note he had penned to his wife. The *Monitor* presumably quoted it from the *Letters* but alas for accuracy, the town name of Brooklin and the personal name of Katharine were misspelled. For EBW afficionados, it was a limp sort of honorific.

The March 10, 1979, *New York Times* offered artistic photos of sunrise and sunset—the sunrise over Brooklyn, taken from the vantage point of Governor's Island; the sunset bathing Manhattan in a romantic pattern of light and shade. Rhapsodizing about the dawn and dusk charm of its city, the *Times* introduced the pictures with a quote from EB's *Here Is New York*. They condensed parts of two sentences into one, but failed to indicate the break and omission with the traditional ellipsis points. This inept condensation sent me back to the book to read the pristine words in their entirety. A lot of their crispness had been lost when a sharp-toothed editor bit into them.

An April letter from EB, typed by himself, had two items of consequence to reveal. He had procured a ride to New York (courtesy of a kind person he met while dining at the Blue Hill Inn), but had no sooner checked in at the Algonquin when he fell ill with a cold, which was succeeded by minor heart problems. So he made a swift and inglorious retreat to Maine instead of proceeding to Florida as he had planned. But he was proud to relate that Bryn Mawr Library had mounted an exhibit of K's books, photos, and letters, with a grand opening on April 4. According to the report he received from stepdaughter Nancy Stableford, it was a most pleasant and auspicious occasion.

Doubtless the display, which was to continue until September, was written up in numerous dailies and weeklies on the east coast. The account I read in the May 13 edition of *The Philadelphia Inquirer* was my only source of information. *Inquirer* staff writer Art Carey must have spent many hours in the rare book room; his descriptions and conclusions suggest that he had more than a cursory knowledge of the careers of both Whites. I was familiar with most of the material he quoted, but one EB interoffice memo to K was new to me and delightful: "... And thanks for unforgettable nights I never can replace."

Kathy Hall's bibliography *(E. B. White: A Bibliographic Catalogue of Printed Materials in the Department of Rare Books, Cornell University Library)* listing 2,190 items written by EB, was the subject of Herbert Mitgang's "Book Ends" column in the June 24 *New York Times Book Review*. The one item that caught EB's attention was the unfortunate giveaway of the anniversary he was striving so hard to keep secret, his eightieth birthday. We knew he was hiding out somewhere in Vermont by July 23, so it was safe to assume that he had crossed the border by early dawn of the eleventh.

A gift copy of *Onward and Upward in the Garden* arrived in mid-July and exceeded all my expectations. Farrar, Straus and Giroux had done Katharine—and by extension EB— proud in the design of the volume. Typography, illustrations, arrangement, jacket design—everything combined to under- line and complement and compliment the text. EB's introduc- tion, all thirteen polished pages of it, was as sparkling and witty as any phrases he had fashioned in his more prolific periods. The inscription was generous beyond anything I deserved: "Isabel—Here it is. I'm sure the author would have been eager to sign a copy for you, especially since you gave her such strong and affectionate support in all her efforts. For which I am deeply grateful. Andy White, North Brooklin, June 1979."

Subsequently I wrote to him:

"... the book was a tremendous surprise from first to last, despite the fact I previously had read all of it in the *New Yorker* pasted-up version, during the sessions when Mrs. White got out the big black notebook and embarked on fascinating discussions of what needed to be done to the work in its magazine form. I am now rereading every word, having forgotten much. How different the pieces seem, encased in hard covers and set out in orderly fashion with the strategic chapter decorations from the old catalogues! Perhaps I read too hurriedly back in North Brooklin. I know I read in fits and starts and short takes; this time around the prose flows as smoothly and gently as the cool sound of a brook along the roadside when you are taking a walk in the country.

"Naturally I had expected great things of your introduction and you exceeded all expectation; but what greatly pleasures me is the design of the whole: the Daffinger painting on the jacket, the book title at the top of each page. It . . . lives up to Mrs. White's own strict standards of professionalism; she would approve of it and take such pride in it if she could see it. It is nearly too much to be borne that she cannot. . . . How disheartening it is, too, that Buckner Hollingsworth could not have lived long enough to hold a copy in her hands while listening to a cassette and hearing her own name mentioned. There are others—Marianne Moore, Jean Stafford, Eleanor Emory, to list a few—who would have rejoiced in its publication.

"The first item I searched for was the Ogden Nash bit about Mr. Powers; I was pleased to find that memory served. His verses and the ingenious allusion to Mrs. White's 'own Mr. Powers' who had a 'perpetual case of pollinosis' were in the second article, on the flower arrangers, exactly as . . . anticipated.

"The photo of Aunt Kitty 'and black attendant' [cat] was new to me. If you subscribe to the aphorism that a picture is worth a thousand words, it was an adequate substitute for the missing chapter. I don't fully accept that philosophy; besides, I recall only too keenly the depression Mrs. White sometimes slipped into when she wanted to begin that summing-up chapter but wasn't well enough or at ease enough to collect her thoughts; but even though fate prevented the chapter from being written, you found the perfect picture to illustrate your explanation. Our own black attendant, Tuffi, was suitably impressed. 'I wish I had been alive then and could have walked in that garden,' he sighed."

Onward and Upward belonged to a specific genre; its appeal would be to readers who gardened and to readers who liked to read about the gardening efforts of others. However, to the surprise of all of us who cared about the success of the book, it seemed to appeal to a wider range of buyers and borrowers and reviewers. Jean Strouse, writing in *Newsweek,* was the first to voice the sentiment that a non-gardener would enjoy the essays; Michael Demarest echoed the belief in *Time;* Anatole Broyard in the *New York Times* and Eden Ross Lipson in the *New York Times Book Review* joined the chorus, with Lipson hinting that the book could be read in terms of a Katharine White autobiography. Smaller periodicals echoed the praise, and long after reviewers had run out of superlatives, *Onward and Upward in the Garden* continued to appear in lists under such designations as "Editors' Choice." All the while the publishers dealt generously with their product in an advertising campaign that meant it was seldom out of the public eye. In the *Times Book Review's* annotated list of the best books published in 1979, K's modest offering was placed among the forty-three titles that comprised the essays and criticism section. It was in its fifth printing and had been designated a Book-of-the-Month Club alternate selection.

EB could not help but be gratified at the reception being accorded K's book, but a January 1980 letter from him leaned more heavily on the death of terrier Jones; he emphasized how remarkable it was that such a small dog could leave such an immense hole in the house by his absence.

A late spring telephone conversation began on a dour note; he was rueful about an interview he had granted, at the instigation of Farrar, Straus and Giroux, about the garden book. "It didn't come out the way I intended," he admitted, "and I'm in a mess because of it; everybody's feeling sorry for me and trying to do things to get me out of some sort of slough of despond I'm supposed to be in. I never should have let myself be talked into it." I did my best to divert his attention to happier topics, and was successful in a small way when he changed the subject to some domestic animals at North Brooklin. "What about rabbits?" I asked him. No, he had never actually raised any but he liked them. Good! I had just devised a little nothing of a verse on the subject—would he listen? What choice did he have? He was his usual urbane but gracious self, and was kind enough to laugh and request a copy:

DISORDERLY CONDUCT

I made a messy metaphor
(A very dreary habit)
I don't know what I did it for
Except I saw a rabbit;
He hopped along a picket fence,
Right by a flower border;
I do not know what brought him hence
(I *do* know this is no defense)
I'd rather watch him, than commence
To put my ode in order.

When summer brought another brief telephone reunion EB spoke of "a short period of disorientation; I suppose it could have been a mini-stroke but probably it was just a bad case of Long Weekend Trouble, capitalized, which for me is a disease in itself. Years ago they had a better name for it—it was called melancholia."

My July 9 birthday letter to EB, encompassing much trivia set round about with nostalgia, engendered a dour reply, full of technical details about the ill-health that often beset him in hay-fever season, but it was comforting to learn in the last paragraph that Susy was well, there were two sets of goslings, and I was missed.

Early in October 1981 our family made a sentimental return journey to Brooklin, the first since our reluctant departure in 1977. Our hosts, Robert and Jacqueline Heaton, were the same generous friends whose home had been our refuge when we prepared to flit south. I had decided in advance that there was scant hope of seeing EB in person; his letters indicated that he was shrinking more and more from personal contact except, occasionally, with children and dogs. I was not disappointed when I reached him by phone to find that he had an errand to do in regard to his ailing car, and an appointment to be kept for autographing. When it became apparent that I wasn't going to push for a face-to-face encounter, his sense of relief could be picked up electronically in the few miles that separated us. He settled down amiably for a fine long chat. There was no discord; all was harmony. There was only one slight problem to disburden himself of: the long stint he had put in editing K's notes about Brendan Gill's *Here at The New Yorker* so that they could be sent to Bryn Mawr to be included with the material that formed the so-called Bryn Mawr list. Uppermost in his mind was his own *Poems and Sketches;* the ten author's copies had just arrived and he would be sending one along by mail soon. His voice sounded strong and pleasant, the timbre of it not one bit changed from the tone I remembered so well.

When the new selection reached our New Hampshire home I read some of it aloud to an appreciative audience of two (three, including the cat) and some to myself; and more often than not, the book was missing from my bedside table when I was ready for a treat at the end of the day's chores. Another family member—probably not the cat—was feasting at the banquet. The inscription was felicitous: "For Isabel. Some dusty old pieces to add to your collection. With love, Andy," and at the bottom, "See p. 92." I knew without turning the pages what was going to be found there, "Wedding Day in the Rockies." Because I had cajoled him into including it, that selection offered greater satisfaction than could have been derived even from a sequel to *Charlotte's Web.*

In November, acknowledging the gift, I tried to keep everything in context and to restrict voluminous words of praise, but the typewriter galloped along at its own speed, ignoring all stop signs, even though the substance of the letter was condensed into a list, to help harness the garrulous approach:

1/ I'm glad the book was marked "For Corona." She deserves the implied compliment-award. 2/ Most poignant of all the delightful new poems is "To My American Gardener, With Love," for obvious reasons. 3/ How splendid it is that the world now can become acquainted with the deathless line about love being an idle drudge, as well as the entire stirring sentiment of "Wedding Day in the Rockies." 4/ I loathe most sports, especially professional baseball, but Russ is an ardent fan of every athletic endeavor and especially of baseball. For opposite reasons, therefore, we took turns reading "The Seven Steps to Heaven" aloud to each other and laughing uproariously. 5/ You look **cross** in the jacket photo but Susy comes through sweet and attractive as always. My sympathy, of course, lies with the photographer. 6/ Best of everything and most valued is your kind

inscription in my copy of the book. Anybody else will be able
to buy the book but nobody else can have my own personal
inscription. . . .

My files hold no record of a Christmas card that year, but
the basket of Florida fruit would have contained a greeting. At
least one greeting card and two or three of EB's handwritten
notations from the 1970s are gone from the strongbox under
my bed. They are now in the possession of some fortunate
teenagers who were in elementary school in the early 1980s. In
the New Hampshire interval between Brooklin and Belfast
residence, I presented programs in schools of the state, programs that were part educational, part entertainment, and EB
was often mentioned. Afterward came letters of thanks, a few
of which included such impassioned pleas for "a souvenir" that
I could not refuse. A fourth-grader who referred to EB as
"Charlotte's Web's Father" undoubtedly has the 1981 Christmas card.

In 1982 EB sent a five-dollar payment for a "Newsbreak,"
and admonished in the accompanying note that I was not to
spend it all in one place. It should have been a salubrious
occasion but when Russ, Ernest, and I learned that the
high potentate of all "Newsbreaks" was marching out of the
temple after fifty-six years—because he was losing his central
vision—we were aggrieved. Was it fair that both K and
Andy should be plagued by failing sight in the latter years
of their lives?

Perhaps a long letter was incongruous, when his birthday
card went out from New Hampshire that summer, but I enclosed one anyway. A modicum of humor in almost any context
might be welcome if he were feeling morose.

". . . I chuckled over the enormous remuneration from *The New Yorker* (did they pay the same sum way back when you first began the "Newsbreaks"?) and also over the warning that I am not to spend it all in one place, but was soon done with any inclination toward laughter when I learned about your eyes. . . . One's sight matters more than one's hearing or the ability to speak, to walk—it matters immeasurably. It seems grossly unfair that any problem should come to you vision*wise*, because you have contributed so long and so largely to the enjoyment of all of us who can read easily. Did the magazine offer some special laudatory comment at the close of your years of service? What an absurd question for me to ask, just as though I thought you would answer it, when during all the years you have been hiding modestly behind your desk, refusing to acknowledge any accolades. Unlike you (and perhaps because I have had so little publicity) I rush to the nearest newsstand for extra copies when something of mine appears. And when the phone rings and someone says, 'Well, we read about you in the paper tonight—shall we save our copy?' I do not blush to answer with great practicality, 'Yes indeed. Save your own copy and collect a few from the neighbors.' Then I dash to the local copy shop and print off a few more so there surely will be enough to distribute to my Vast Reading Public. . . ."

In 1983 the health of *Charlotte's* creator was going downhill slowly but at a sufficient rate to be perceptible in the cadence of his voice on the telephone. We were ecstatic visitors to Brooklin again, snugly established in a log cabin of flexible construction and whimsical furnishing (thanks to the generosity of our friends DeWitt and Eleanor Goddard, who offered their sea-view shelter for a two-week period each of three years and would have continued to offer it had we not moved back to Maine in 1985). In 1983 there was an item, saved from some obscure source, to read on the phone. "The Chairman announced that the stores will remain open to their scheduled time. 'That's what they're scheduled to open until,' she said." EB's thoughtful rejoinder: ' "Unless they chance to change before,' she added."

Shortly before Christmas of 1983 I was reminded vividly of K and I longed for her to be alive again so that I could apologize to her for something she knew nothing about: a statement in my diary that ridiculed her for writing letters to nearly everybody on her Christmas-card list to inform them that she and Andy were not going to send greetings one year. I found myself in a similar dilemma and I solved the problem just as she did. A dreary sense of déjà vu surrounded me and the typewriter that year, and Andy himself was among the first on the list to be notified, because there was also a want-ad goof from a New Hampshire newspaper with which to regale him: "Wanted: housekeeper for a large family home, includes windows and floors." His dry retort by telephone, "The walls collapsed recently."

In February 1984 I was hard at it on my favorite subject, animals. Had he read in a newspaper or seen on TV the story of a duck who befriended a blind calf and guided it, in the manner of a seeing-eye dog, all around the barnyard? And how about the raccoon who painted pictures while sitting in a bathtub? When finished, he rinsed his paws under a faucet; his colorful productions were to be preferred over many artistic attempts by modern two-pawed painters, was my humble opinion, in which EB heartily concurred.

Scott Elledge's *E. B. White, A Biography* was published by W. W. Norton that year, and the *Times Book Review* allotted it one and a half pages in a kind and friendly assessment by Russell Lynes, a former managing editor of *Harper's Magazine*. Having followed Mr. Elledge's peregrinations through so many years, and having almost given up hope of ever seeing his manuscript published, I was pleased to read Mr. Lynes' estimate, as well as that of *Smithsonian Magazine,* to say nothing of devouring every word of the book itself.

A letter in place of a birthday card went out to EB that July. No local store offered anything that suited my exacting tastes for such a special person, so I sent a "happy birthday letter" instead, with a reference to an extraordinary circumstance in our house:

"Perhaps nobody else except you would be interested. In the center of our dining-room table sits a glass goblet filled with various types of greenery. Just before our garden flowers begin to bloom lavishly, I fill the goblet with myrtle leaves and their purple blossoms; as the blossoms begin to fade, there are yellow daisies to take their place. On July 4 we discovered a miniature white spider at the end of one of the myrtle leaves. I searched through several nature books but could find nothing about the white spider genus. None of us has ever seen one; all our spider encounters have been with the brownish-gray ones who weave dusty webs in ceiling corners. In deference to Charlotte, of course, we have never felt it was right to brush them away. This white one is fascinating. Some days it is invisible as we sit at the table for breakfast and lunch; then again, when the light is just right, it reappears. What does it eat? No, not my own *haute cuisine*—it spurns that. How does it live? I wonder if there is any way I can assist it? Today how exciting it was to see three strands of a web it had woven from one leaf high up on a stem to another leaf lower down. That means a home, doesn't it? I wonder if it catches its own flies for food. No, that would be impossible, it is so tiny. Do I recall correctly from *Charlotte's Web* that all web weavers are females? Well, anyway, because of the date of discovery we have christened 'her' Betsy Ross Russell. These questions are all rhetorical. I do not want you to bother to reply. You have brought so much joy into the world with your books you deserve the happiest of birthdays, and we hope you will receive your just desserts."

There was no response, nor did I expect any. We spent part of September in Brooklin that year but in our many journeys past the big farmhouse we did not even glance toward front yard or driveway in the hope of seeing the owner. Rumors that EB was suffering from Alzheimer's disease were rampant; in cowardly fashion we contrived to change the subject before much could be said. I wanted EB to depart this earth as graciously as he had written about it, so I closed my mind to what might be going on near Allen Cove that autumn and eased my conscience with plans for a long letter, in addition to the usual card, at Christmas.

We had begun to dislike more and more the hectic computerville pace of southern New Hampshire and were increasingly missing our Maine friends. The severe health problem was no longer endangering my sister's life; other relatives, too, were understanding about our love for the Maine coast; therefore, during our September vacation we sought and found a home in Belfast and moved into it at the end of November. There were, however, no excited Christmas messages announcing the new address. Early in December my husband suffered a paralyzing stroke, and died the following March. At that period I realized fully for the first time the anguish EB had endured over K's loss. Remorse shook me when I recalled all the silly platitudes I had offered on that occasion. Worst of all, it was too late now to try to apologize or explain. I remembered EB's birthday in 1985 as always, but for the first time I hadn't enough good cheer left in me to include a message that told of the small happenings in our new home.

Brooklin neighbors reported that life was different indeed at the farmhouse that summer of 1985. EB was bedridden; there was no writing for him nor walks to the shore nor the overseeing of his beloved barnyard dwellers.

October 1, 1985, was an average day. My friend Ernest and I were engaged in the sort of project EB himself would have enjoyed and approved: stacking wood in the basement against the storms of winter, against the possibility of a power failure. It was such a warm day for October that fog overlaid the sun and obscured some of the autumn foliage. It was too early, actually, to begin carving a jack-o'-lantern (or, lacking the essential skill with a knife, to paint a face on a pumpkin) but in the afternoon I was preparing a pumpkin because guests were coming later in the week—guests from Brooklin who would enjoy the decoration as once they had enjoyed the jack-o'-lantern, gift of E. B. White, that had adorned our own Brooklin home.

In the evening we sat down comfortably to listen to whatever small segments of local news the Bangor television channel had garnered for that day.

·ᴈ FIFTEEN ɕ··

Our telephone jangled incessantly; the mail over-flowed the box; it was as though the stars were stayed in their courses. From Vancouver, B.C., down to California and all across the country, West coast to East, and north to south, came the clippings from newspapers and magazines, each accompanied by a message of sympathy from the sender. How immensely the writer and his writings were admired. How deeply was he mourned in his passing. . . .

This is the way I choose to remember him. One July week-end, EB constructed a unique birdhouse to be donated to the arts and crafts fair held to benefit Blue Hill Memorial Hospital. Two chimneys and a narrow porch all around made his creation a standout in birdhouse architecture.

"It's going to be billed as a retirement home for birds," said North Brooklin's avian architect, leaning ever so slightly on the word "billed."

There will be a gathering
of friends and relatives
at the
Blue Hill Congregational Church
Blue Hill, Maine
on
Saturday, October 26, 1985
at 2 p.m.
in memory of
E.B. White

Everyone is welcome   *Please, no flowers*